Clayton W. Barrows
Robert H. Bosselman
Editors

Hospitality Management Education

Pre-publication
REVIEWS,
COMMENTARIES,
EVALUATIONS . . .

"**F**inally, a book about hospitality education for hospitality educators and would-be educators. Since mid-century, the education of practitioners in the hospitality field, once gained solely on the job, has relied upon institutions of higher learning. The authors have done an outstanding job presenting the field of professoring in a clear, comprehensive, and extensive fashion."

Frank Lattuca, EdD
Professor and Department Head,
Department of Hotel, Restaurant,
and Travel Administration,
University of Massachusetts
at Amherst

More pre-publication
REVIEWS, COMMENTARIES, EVALUATIONS . . .

"*Hospitality Management Education* is an excellent resource for anyone interested in hospitality management education. For the industry professional, it provides a wealth of information on hospitality management programs and thus the background and experiences of the graduates that industry is hiring. For potential hospitality management students, it provides a great source of background information to help in making a more informed selection from the various programs available. For the hospitality management educator, it provides a guide and summary reference for most of the frequently asked questions regarding this field.

This book provides the answer to many of the questions most often asked by industry professionals and students regarding how hospitality management education works. It takes the mystery out of how hospitality management education programs function and serves as an excellent resource for individuals interested in pursuing hospitality management education."

Joe Perdue, CCM, CHE
Director, Executive Masters Program,
College of Hotel Administration,
University of Nevada,
Las Vegas

The Haworth Hospitality Press
An Imprint of The Haworth Press, Inc.
New York • London

Hospitality Management Education

THE HAWORTH HOSPITALITY PRESS
Hospitality, Travel, and Tourism
K. S. Chon, PhD
Executive Editor

Marketing Your City, U.S.A.: A Guide to Developing a Strategic Tourism Marketing Plan by Ronald A. Nykiel and Elizabeth Jascolt

Hospitality Management Education by Clayton W. Barrows and Robert H. Bosselman

Legalized Casino Gaming in the United States: The Economic and Social Impact by Cathy H. C. Hsu

Consumer Behavior in Travel and Tourism by Abraham Pizam and Yoel Mansfeld

The International Hospitality Business: Management and Operations by Larry Yu

Practice of Graduate Research in Hospitality and Tourism by K. S. Chon

Hospitality Management Education

Clayton W. Barrows
Robert H. Bosselman
Editors

The Haworth Hospitality Press
An Imprint of The Haworth Press, Inc.
New York • London

Published by

The Haworth Hospitality Press, an imprint of The Haworth Press, Inc., 10 Alice Street, Binghamton, NY 13904-1580

Cover design by Jennifer M. Gaska.

Library of Congress Cataloging-in-Publication Data

Hospitality management education : Clayton W. Barrows, Robert H. Bosselman [editors].
    p.   cm.
    Includes bibliographical references and index.
    ISBN 0-7890-0441-0 (alk. paper)
    1. Hospitality industry—Management. 2. Hospitality industry—Vocational guidance. I. Barrows, Clayton W. II. Bosselman, Robert H.
TX911.3.M27H62324 1999
647.94'068—dc21   98-38132
                                                                             CIP

This book is dedicated to the memory
of Dr. Stevenson W. Fletcher III,
for everything that he did
for the field of hospitality education
during his professional career.

CONTENTS

ABOUT THE EDITORS

Clayton W. Barrows, EdD, is Associate Professor of Hotel, Restaurant, and Tourism Administration at the University of New Orleans. He has developed and taught a variety of courses at the University, including service organization management, food and beverage cost control, and club management operations. Prior to joining the university faculty, Dr. Barrows spent ten years in the hospitality business working as a manager in a variety of operations, including luxury hotels, fine-dining restaurants, and private clubs. A prolific writer, his articles have been published in such journals as *Journal of Hospitality and Tourism Research, International Journal of Hospitality Management,* and *Journal of Restaurant and Foodservice Marketing.* Dr. Barrows' current research interests include food and beverage training in private clubs and the marketing of brewpubs.

Robert H. Bosselman, PhD, is Associate Director of Graduate Studies and Research and Professor in the Department of Food and Beverage Management in the William F. Harrah College of Hotel Administration at the University of Nevada, Las Vegas. His responsibilities at the university include managing the Masters Degree Program and supervising research activities within the college. The author of over forty academic papers, Dr. Bosselman is the founding editor of *Hospitality and Tourism Educator* and a former editor of *Hospitality Research Journal.* A registered dietician, his research interests include food sanitation, food service operations, labor relations, and hospitality education.

CONTRIBUTORS

Claire Bolsing, PhD, is Associate Professor and Director, Marketing Program, James Madison University. Her areas of expertise include marketing research, database and direct marketing, and customer satisfaction.

Carl P. Borchgrevink, PhD, is Assistant Professor, School of Hospitality Business, Michigan State University. His areas of expertise include food and beverage management, service and production management, and superior/subordinate relationships.

Harsha Chacko, PhD, is Professor, School of Hotel, Restaurant, and Tourism, University of New Orleans. His areas of expertise include hotel organization development and tourism research.

George G. Fenich, PhD, is Associate Professor, School of Hotel, Restaurant, and Tourism, University of New Orleans. His areas of expertise include operations analysis, convention operations, and casino operations.

Reg Foucar-Szocki, PhD, is Marriott Professor of Hospitality and Program Director, Hospitality and Tourism Management Program, James Madison University. His areas of expertise include creativity and problem solving and experiential education.

J. S. Perry Hobson, MS, is Senior Lecturer, School of Tourism and Hospitality Management, Southern Cross University, Lismore, NSW, Australia. His areas of expertise include consumer behavior, leisure shopping and tourism, hotel development in Asia/Pacific, and youth tourism.

Michael P. Sciarini, PhD, is Associate Professor, the School of Hospitality Business, Michigan State University. His areas of expertise include human resources, career exploration and development, and lodging operations.

Alan T. Stutts, PhD, is Barron Hilton Distinguished Chair and Dean, Conrad N. Hilton College of Hotel and Restaurant Management, University of Houston. His areas of expertise include curriculum development, facilities layout and design, lodging operations, and marketing.

Preface

The field of hospitality management has now been taught at the university level in the United States for seventy-five years. During this time, it has undergone tremendous changes—from an exclusively "hands-on"-based discipline to one which is now more theoretical in nature. The field finally seems to be maturing—there are close to 200 established four-year programs in existence with several offering graduate degree programs; our graduates are actively recruited by hospitality companies; and hospitality programs have achieved a certain level of respect on campus that was at one time lacking. In addition to the changes affecting the programs themselves, many other changes are developing. Among others is the continued proliferation of academic journals that publish research produced by hospitality faculty. One journal in particular, the *Journal of Hospitality & Tourism Education*, has been chronicling educational activities and practices since 1988. The success of this journal can be attributed to educators', as well as practitioners', desire to keep up with the educational side of the industry.

This book, which is the result of ten hospitality faculty members' contributions, takes a detailed, introspective look at the field of hospitality education. While most hospitality books on the market today focus upon various operational aspects of the hospitality industry, this book focuses on the business of hospitality education—the nuts and bolts of hospitality programs, their missions, their constituents, and the outcomes of their efforts.

The editors and contributors believe that this is a particularly timely project given that the formalized study of hospitality has reached the seventy-five-year mark in this country. Many changes taking place right now are affecting the face of this discipline, both nationally and internationally. These developments and changes have yet to be chronicled in one place and we strongly believe that the time is right to do so now.

This book includes twelve chapters, each focusing on a different aspect of hospitality education. Various aspects of hospitality programs are covered in detail from program missions to faculty responsibilities. Together, these chapters will shed light on how programs operate while paying particular attention to the role of hospitality faculty. This book should prove useful to graduate students interested in entering the field of hospitality education, industry recruiters, and current faculty members, among others.

Chapter 1

Introduction to Hospitality Education

Clayton W. Barrows

INTRODUCTION

The field of hospitality education is a unique, rather close-knit academic area. Though maturing, there are still fewer than 200 four-year programs in the United States. At the undergraduate level, in particular, hospitality management education's primary concern is with the professional preparation of individuals who desire to work in one of the broad group of professions that make up the hospitality industry. The size and scope of the hospitality industry itself has always been difficult to define since few people can agree on what it encompasses (see Chapter 2). An early definition of hospitality included any and all businesses and services whose primary objective was serving people outside of a private home. For purposes of this book, we will use the accepted definition as stated by the Council on Hotel, Restaurant and Institutional Education (CHRIE), which includes food, lodging, recreation, and travel-related services.

No matter how the hospitality industry is defined, its constituents generally agree that it is a large, fragmented industry with its own unique set of challenges. These challenges require its managers and workers to be specially trained and/or educated to work effectively in such a customer-driven industry, no matter the segment. Professional preparation for managers and line-level employees alike is available from a variety of venues including government-sponsored work/training programs, trade schools, community colleges, and universities, among others. Each venue serves a specific segment of the employment market and, in some cases, acts as feeders to each other. This is particularly true in the area of higher education. The best example of feeder programs exist in states such as Massachusetts, Illinois, and Florida, where there are extensive community college systems. Many students, after completing two years of post-secondary education, will decide to continue by transferring to a four-year school (often referred to as 2+2). One way or another, students of the industry are able to find the appropriate means of professional preparation once they have determined their career objectives. And, of course, there is always on-the-job training, which can provide the necessary expertise for many jobs, including management positions.

Although it occupies its own niche, hospitality management education is, in fact, one segment of the larger hospitality industry. It could be argued that the formal preparation of industry professionals, via hospitality education programs, is the single most important segment. After all, it draws large numbers of people into the study of hospitality management and is generally committed to professionalizing the industry of which it is a part. A common misconception is that formal education programs exist to serve the industry—that is not possible, as they are already an integral part of the larger industry. Indeed, educational programs serve a variety of purposes, which will be discussed in some detail in later chapters. Certainly, one of them is to provide the industry with qualified managers.

This book is primarily about hospitality education and, specifically, four-year hospitality management programs. Such programs have many constituents. These include, first and foremost, the students who enroll out of high schools, trade and culinary schools, community colleges, and many other diverse backgrounds. Other constituents include the recruiters and employers, program advisors, graduates, administrators, and faculty members. It is for this entire group that this book is being written, although the focus will be primarily upon four-year programs and the role that faculty play—arguably the most important and interesting role of any of the constituents. Hospitality education is a world and a culture unto itself and it is the professors who find themselves involved in every aspect of it. It is the professors who provide the educational opportunities and influence the scope and direction that hospitality education has followed and continues to follow.

SIZE AND SCOPE OF THE DISCIPLINE

Four-year programs alone graduate approximately 5,000 students each year, most of whom take jobs as entry-level managers. The growth in this particular segment of hospitality education, particularly over the past twenty years, has been phenomenal. These four-year programs are a mix of large and small, public and private, old and new, and everything in between. Together, they supply much of the fresh management talent on which the rest of the industry depends. But why do students choose to spend four or more years studying hospitality management rather than simply learning by doing and working their way up through an organization? There is no single answer. Some students simply want to learn more about the industry before delving into it as a career choice. Others have pretty much decided that it is what they want to do with their lives and enroll in programs to participate in the formal learning process about the industry. Still others view a degree in hospitality management as a quicker route to the top. In short, the reasons are varied and for many, their expectations of what the education and degree will tender differ greatly from reality. This and subsequent chapters answer many of the questions about hospitality management as a career choice.

HOSPITALITY MANAGEMENT
AS A FIELD OF STUDY

So what is hospitality education? Carl Riegel (1995) has defined it as "a field of multidisciplinary study which brings the perspectives of many disciplines, especially those found in the social sciences, to bear on particular areas of application and practice in the hospitality and tourism industry" (p. 6). Simply put, it is a field devoted to preparing students, generally, for management positions in hospitality. The hospitality student benefits from the merging of several educational models, including business and the social sciences. It is my belief that a student with either a two-year or a four-year degree will derive far more educational benefits, and progress further in the industry, than the individual spending those same years working who may not have the benefit of the formal education or, ultimately, the degree. Of course, as will be emphasized later, the combination of education *and* experience is usually the best vehicle for success.

Formal hospitality education in the United States can be attained via several venues; four-year management programs, the primary subject of this book, are but one alternative. Students can also prepare for a variety of careers including line-level supervisory and back-of-the-house positions by attending culinary schools or two-year management programs. There are also numerous graduate programs, which will be discussed in Chapter 11. Further, within each of these areas, there exist many specialized segments. For instance, a student can graduate with a specialization in Baking and Pastry Arts at the Culinary Institute of America; Housekeeping Management at Cuyahoga Community College; Gaming Management at the University of Nevada–Las Vegas; and Club Management at the University of New Orleans. Students can also combine minors, concentrations, and specializations in many instances. This array of choices has only become possible in recent years, though, after years of development.

Whatever the degree or specialization, the degrees earned by students are worth what the students themselves put into earning them. That is not to underestimate the significance of a hospitality degree, though, since they have certainly become a commodity valued by industry. For many companies, and even entire industry segments, the degree has become a threshold requirement for many entry-level management positions. Many leading hospitality companies now recognize that a student who possesses a degree in hospitality management has a base of knowledge that will assist him or her in succeeding in the industry.

The formalized study of hospitality management at the post-secondary level is not as new as some might believe. Hospitality management programs have existed in colleges and universities for about seventy-five years. During this time, it has developed into a legitimate academic area of study that boasts many authorities in several different content areas. These content areas are often either classified by a subsegment of the hospitality industry (e.g., food service or lodging) or by functional area (such as accounting, marketing, or management information systems). Generally, faculty will gravitate to one or more of these areas as a result of their industry experiences, their graduate studies, or both. The expectation then is that faculty members will teach, conduct research, and interact with the industry counterparts in their specific areas. Thus a faculty member who has chosen to specialize in the food service management area might teach such courses as "Food and Beverage Cost Control" and "Commercial Food Service Systems" or "Beverage Management." They would also involve themselves in the various local and national foodservice-related associations, such as the National Restaurant Association, as well as their state restaurant associations. Finally, their research, which may or may not result in publication, would also follow suit. The emphasis on this last area seems to be increasing and as a result, the quality and quantity of hospitality-related research (see Chapter 8) continues to escalate.

Clearly, the field has reached an important stage in its development, as evidenced by the increasing number of new academic programs, increased specialization of faculty members, the increase in academic journals devoted to hospitality, and the strengthening relationship between educational institutions and industry. As further evidence that the field is continuing to mature, the association that brings hospitality educators together, CHRIE, recently celebrated its fiftieth anniversary in 1995.

Above all, hospitality education is finally getting the respect, as a field of study, that it has deserved for so long. Much of this newfound respect is due to the array of professional activities with which hospitality professors are involved, including involvement in industry trade associations, research activities, and consulting, just to name a few.

HISTORY OF HOSPITALITY EDUCATION

Hospitality education, in the literal sense, has been around since the days of the very first inns and taverns—ever since the first time the owner or operator of a small business needed to show someone else how to perform certain tasks. Later on, as the hospitality industry began to grow, the need for formal apprenticeship programs developed. Apprentice programs in the hotel and restaurant industries have been common in Western Europe for many years while certain countries, such as Switzerland and Britain, are generally credited with establishing the basic model on which many other apprenticeship programs have been based. Early apprenticeship programs often were several years in duration and required apprentices to spend a substantial portion of their time in the back of the house. This usually prepared them for subsequent careers in the back of the house. Other alternatives were available for those interested in pursuing careers in the front of the house.

Generally, the early apprenticeship programs were geared toward effectively preparing students for successful careers in hospitality. Based on the success of the European experience, early American food service apprenticeship programs were modeled after the same programs. This suited the hospitality industry perfectly at the time, as the need was primarily for people having skills-specific training (Fletcher, 1994). This skills training approach predominated for many years and, in fact, still exists. The culinary schools, as we know them today, were an outgrowth of the early apprenticeship programs and were the earliest established formal programs for careers in hospitality. They continue to perform their functions admirably, and with the increased interest in back-of-the-house careers, culinary programs are experiencing a period of sustained growth.

The oldest continuously operated culinary program in the country is the Culinary Institute of America (CIA), which was founded in 1946. What began as a program enrolling some fifty students in New Haven, Connecticut has since relocated to Hyde Park, New York and now has some 2,000 students enrolled in a variety of programs. The majority of students at CIA are enrolled in the two associate degree programs in which students can concentrate on the culinary arts or baking and pastry arts. A relatively new change in the curriculum also allows students to earn a bachelor's degree for which students develop both culinary and management skills. The CIA is just one program which started as a two-year culinary school and now offers a four-year option. There are many other programs, both community college and proprietary, which serve the same function.

Another prominent program, Johnson & Wales (J & W) University, like the CIA, expanded its offerings beyond the traditional two-year culinary degree and now offers a four-year degree with various specializations. It has even added a master's degree to its program offerings. The trend toward combining culinary learning and management is a trend that is only likely to continue as the need for managers with strong technical skills increases.

HOSPITALITY MANAGEMENT PROGRAMS

Educational programs that are geared specifically to preparing students to be managers in the hospitality industry are much newer than the formalized apprenticeship programs that prepared students for back-of-the-house careers. Hospitality management programs date back to the introduction of the first four-year program, the Hotel School at Cornell University, in 1922. The first two-year hospitality management program appeared a few years later at the City College of San Francisco (CCSF) in 1935. As with many hospitality programs, the Hotel and Restaurant Department at CCSF was started when representatives of both industry and education came together in an attempt to meet industry's needs. This particular program has a long and very interesting history, particularly during the wartime period, when its primary mission was to support the Maritime Services in training stewards. Today, the program remains in the forefront of hospitality education, preparing students for careers both in the front of the house and the back of the house. CCSF effectively combines classroom training with practical experience which students gain through their Work-Experience Program. The program continues to emphasize the food service side of the industry. Students gain additional experience helping to run the college food service operation. Upper-level courses focus more on supervisory elements of food service such as cost control and supervisory development. CCSF is a very good example of a two-year program that is highly focused and continuously achieves its mission of supplying the local industry with trained professionals who are proficient in technical skills. A sample of their course offerings from 1936 (see Exhibit 1.1) highlights the similarities between what was once taught and what continues to be taught in hospitality programs around the country.

EXHIBIT 1.1. Curriculum in Hotel and Restaurant Management, San Francisco City College, 1936

FIRST SEMESTER						
Hours	Monday	Tuesday	Wednesday	Thursday	Friday	Saturday
8:00 to 8:50	English A	Elementary Hotel Accounting	English A	Elementary Hotel Accounting	Chemistry 52A Lecture	Field Survey Work
9:00 to 10:00	Business Mathematics 51A	Elementary Hotel Accounting	Business Mathematics 51A	Elementary Hotel Accounting	Chemistry 52A Lecture	Field Survey Work
10:00 to 2:00	Elementary Food Preparation by Chef Lecture and Laboratory					Field Survey Work
2:30 to 4:20	Elementary Cookery	Engineering Drawing 52A	Elementary Cookery	Engineering Drawing 52A	Chemistry 52A Laboratory	Field Survey Work
4:30 to 5:20	Physical Education	Hygiene	Physical Education	Hygiene	Chemistry 52A Laboratory	Field Survey Work

SECOND SEMESTER						
Hours	Monday	Tuesday	Wednesday	Thursday	Friday	Saturday
8:00 to 8:50	Business Correspondence	Elementary Hotel Accounting	Business Correspondence	Elementary Hotel Accounting	Chemistry 52B Lecture	Field Survey Work
9:00 to 10:00	Business Mathematics 51B	Elementary Hotel Accounting	Business Mathematics 51B	Elementary Hotel Accounting	Chemistry 52B Lecture	Field Survey Work
10:00 to 2:00	Food Cost Accounting and Restaurant Operation Lecture and Laboratory					Field Survey Work
2:30 to 4:20	Elementary Cookery	Engineering Drawing 52B	Elementary Cookery	Engineering Drawing 52B	Chemistry 52B Laboratory	Field Survey Work
4:30 to 5:20	Physical Education	Public Health	Physical Education	Public Health	Chemistry 52B Laboratory	Field Survey Work

Note: All students are required to manage and operate a large cafeteria and dining room throughout two entire school years.

Today, in fact, two-year programs outnumber four-year programs by about four to one. While there are many differences between the missions of these types of programs, the differences are becoming smaller. Many, in fact, offer course work which is increasingly similar to that of four-year programs. As more schools establish articulation agreements with one another, the course work is becoming more similar out of necessity. One basic difference which remains is that two-year programs generally provide more "hands on" learning in which the students acquire some of the basic technical skills needed for both line and supervisory positions. These are many of the same courses that students take in the lower levels at four-year programs. For students with associate degrees to successfully transfer into four-year programs, the courses that they have already taken need to be similar enough in scope to be accepted. Although the focus of this chapter, and book, is on four-year programs, two-year programs are mentioned in several chapters because of their continued ability to help educate and train future managers. Although the mission of two-year programs may differ from that of four-year programs, they tend to be very focused in their approach to education and continue to contribute to the overall mission of hospitality education.

The history of four-year programs, as mentioned previously, began with the Cornell Hotel School in 1922. The program was initiated after a request, and subsequent support, from the American Hotel Association (AHA). Today, Cornell is still one of the most prominent programs in the world offering undergraduate and graduate degrees in hotel administration. Cornell also has several international initiatives underway including a program in France and a cooperative agreement in Australia.

Following Cornell were several schools that were started during the later 1920s through the 1930s. These programs, such as those at Purdue University, Michigan State University, and the University of Massachusetts, were all based at land grant institutions and developed out of the need to teach applied skills to college students (Kreul, 1995). Others followed during the 1940s and 1950s (Pennsylvania State University and the University of Houston). A study by Zabel (1992) found that only twelve of the 128 programs investigated were older than thirty years.

This handful of programs dominated higher education until the early 1970s when the number of four-year programs more than doubled. Most of the responding programs in Zabel's survey were identified as being between ten and twenty years old (having been established between 1970 and 1980). There were multiple reasons for this drastic increase, as discussed below.

Reasons for Growth

The fact that there are now about 175 four-year hospitality programs probably could not have been anticipated a few decades ago. The past twenty to twenty-five years have seen unprecedented growth both in higher education in general and particularly in hospitality education programs. This growth cannot be attributed to any single reason, but rather to several. One common explanation for the increase in programs was that hospitality programs were simply paralleling what was happening in the industry. The industry obviously enjoyed tremendous growth in the 1960s, 1970s, and 1980s, during which time the business environment was favorable to growth. This is also one of the primary reasons for the explosion in hospitality programs. The need for qualified managers mushroomed during this time and the industry could not produce nearly enough trained managers to serve its own needs.

As the growth continued, the industry also became more sophisticated and specialized, intensifying the need for educated/trained individuals. Predictably, hospitality companies became much more dependent on the graduates of hospitality programs. In fact, as was the case with CCSF, the University of New Orleans, and others, many programs were started as a direct result of industry's needs. Since then, the relationship between education and industry has continued to grow and strengthen.

Finally, the increasing complexities of running a business require greater academic preparation than has been necessary in the past. This factor has allowed all professional programs, including hospitality, to play a more important role, and accept more of the responsibility, in the development of future managers. Also, hospitality businesses have become increasingly specialized. Recent examples are the various programs which have added gaming specializations to better address the need for managers in the casino industry.

The industry's need for managers, industry-based financial support, and increasing complexity and specialization are some of the primary factors that have fueled the growth in hospitality education in recent years. However, these factors would have been irrelevant had not there been a steady supply of students enrolling in hospitality programs and courses. With some aberrations, more and more students are looking to major in areas which provide a certain amount of technical preparation (note the increased interest in business schools in the 1980s). Also, there are simply more students attending colleges and universities than there were ten years ago. In fact, college enrollments have generally increased during the last ten years, with the exception of 1993. Further, college enrollments are expected to increase through the year 2007 (*The Chronicle of Higher Education,* 1998).

Combine all of these factors and the growth of our programs should not come as a surprise. Whether the university enrollment growth will trickle down to hospitality programs, however, is debatable and is the subject of a later chapter in this book.

Industry Benefactors

During this same period of growth, companies began to aggressively recruit on university campuses, often hiring large percentages of entire graduating classes. This symbiotic relationship continues today, although recently some companies have begun to cut back on the campus recruiting efforts.

The relationship between some hospitality programs and individual companies goes far beyond making recruiting visits, however. Many programs are endowed by such companies. Examples include the Cecil B. Day School of Hospitality Administration at Georgia State University, the William F. Harrah College of Hotel Administration at the University of Nevada–Las Vegas and the Conrad N. Hilton College of Hotel and Restaurant Management at the University of Houston. Even where programs do not carry the names of their benefactors, they are likely to receive the support of industry through student scholarships, faculty support, and personal mentoring of students by managers. Over the years, industry has proven to be very supportive of educational efforts and the trend of direct industry support is likely to continue. This financial support has allowed programs to grow at the rate that they have.

THE PHILOSOPHY OF HOSPITALITY EDUCATION

As has been illustrated, there exist many programs—all very different from one another. While these different programs have different missions and objectives, most would agree that one of the major philosophies of hospitality education is that education alone is not enough to succeed in the hospitality industry. Rather, as more than one person has said, the quickest path to success is some combination of formal education and practical experience. As a result, most programs have been developed based upon this premise. At the undergraduate level, programs tend to be grounded with practical business applications. Further, most programs actually build an experience practicum into their graduation requirements that requires students to work an average of 800 to 1000 contact hours in a hospitality-related job. This is done to assure that, upon graduation, students have experienced the real world of hospitality.

The education/experience philosophy which is common to most programs is but one of the canons of the field. The continued growth, and subsequent increase in competition, has caused many hospitality programs to reevaluate their missions and even their reasons for existence. This seems to be a natural part of the maturation process. As hospitality education, and the greater hospitality industry, continues to develop and change, it must continually reevaluate its mission and objectives and process for achieving both.

Pavesic (1991) recently revisited the debate over whether hospitality management programs are in the business of training or educating, and in doing so makes the excellent point that both are critical in the development of successful hospitality managers.

Riegel (1990) goes so far as to suggest that the entire field is struggling for self-definition, as evidenced by the various views on accreditation standards and research, among others. Again, the process of maturing dictates that an individual, or collective group in this case, grapple with such issues. If all of these debates were simply limited to philosophical discourse among academics, their significance could be questioned. The results of these debates, however, extend far beyond the walls of academia and are likely to determine how hospitality programs are managed, the structure of curricula, and the fate of our graduates. For this reason, they warrant further examination.

So what is or should be the basic philosophies that help define and drive the field? This is a subject of great debate, first and foremost because hospitality programs award professional degrees. Lewis (1993) has suggested that, as professional degree grantors, we should be ahead of the greater hospitality industry in such areas as teaching and research. Instead, he comments, we are lagging behind the industry. For better or for worse, we will always be tied to the industry for which we prepare our students. This means that, at the very least, individual faculty members must become students of the industry to better understand it and its needs. This notwithstanding, it is questionable whether hospitality education will ever lead the industry because it has been playing catch-up with the industry for so long. This has occurred primarily because the hospitality industry is such a dynamic one and has been through many changes in its history. Educational programs are much younger—the industry was in place long before the first hospitality programs appeared. In reality, the field of hospitality is still defining itself. Also, hospitality educators are often caught between satisfying the requirements of academic institutions and meeting the needs of industry. Sometimes the processes of achieving these two objectives are consistent with one another—sometimes they conflict. Examples of these quandaries abound in later chapters.

The fact remains, hospitality programs must strive to satisfy all of their constituents. It would not be realistic to suggest that programs can satisfy all of them all of the time. Hospitality programs have spent much of their first seventy-five years of existence proving that they are the academic equals of other higher-profile disciplines on campus. These programs have not achieved the same stature as chemical engineering, and probably never will; however, our recent development and maturation has brought a certain amount of recognition and respect. Much of this has been earned through the scholarly research that the academy publishes, the student credit hours (SCHs) that programs generate, graduates in upper-level management positions, and the growing academic credentials that faculty are now earning. For these reasons, and others, the relative rank of hospitality programs on college campuses has been raised in recent years. With this increased respectability, individual programs are attempting to redefine themselves, or at least better define themselves. As a result, many programs now have tangible mission statements from which specific objectives develop.

So what does a typical mission statement of a hospitality management program look like? An example from the University of New Orleans is presented here. The School of Hotel, Restaurant and Tourism Administration, during the process of their self-study for accreditation, developed the following statement:

STATEMENT OF MISSION

The mission of the School of Hotel, Restaurant and Tourism Administration at the University of New Orleans is to develop and maintain itself continuously as an accredited academic unit of overall high quality that seeks to provide the highest possible level of academic service to the hospitality and tourism industries in the areas of teaching, research, community assistance and economic development.

This mission statement was developed in an effort to capitalize upon the unique position (the heart of a major tourism destination) that this particular program finds itself in. As with a company's mission statement, this statement identifies the program's primary reason for existence. First and foremost it focuses on its overall academic charge; second, it addresses the individual areas of responsibility including teaching, research, and responsibility to the outside community. In short, it suits the program at UNO and is probably quite different from the type of statement that would be developed by another program.

Riegel (1990) argues that the entire hospitality discipline must reach some kind of consensus regarding a "commonly held philosophy of purposes" (p. 18). While one cannot argue with the logic of having a singular mission, the fact is that every program is quite likely to, or should have, a unique mission. Missions are affected by many factors including, but not limited to: location (urban versus rural), size, the academic unit in which the program is housed (home economics versus business), the extent of involvement with the local hospitality industry, age of the program, and level of learning (graduate, undergraduate, or both) as well as many others. To take the argument one step further, vocational education programs will clearly have vastly different missions than will comprehensive hospitality programs at major research universities.

Pauze (1993) also suggests that the time has come for hospitality programs to reexamine their missions. At the same time, he concedes that different institutions will likely have different mission statements. He offers a generic statement for purposes of discussion which reads in part, "the hospitality management programs activities are directed to interested students, hospitality organizations, and other communities of interest" (p. 62). He repeatedly cites the need for reexamination in an effort to better utilize the resources available to programs and to better position themselves.

Much of the debate surrounding programmatic mission statements focuses upon the teaching element. Debates about programmatic missions aside, we must realize that no matter how much we are able to teach students in a scant four years, our graduates will still have to acquire a great deal of knowledge on the job. Can we as educators really be expected to turn out twenty-one-year-old experts in human relations, accounting, and finance? Human relations, in particular, is one area where skills are developed through experience. In this case, classroom exercises may be used to help students identify their management values and, to a certain extent, model behaviors, but certainly not to hone these all-too-important skills.

All programs operate under a tremendous number of constraints, financial and otherwise. Institutions dictate how many hospitality courses our students are allowed to take. The total number of credit hours that students must earn for graduation is full of general education and college requirements (business, human ecology, or other). In some cases, hospitality students take as little as one-fourth of their total credits in the hospitality area. This is the equivalent of one full year of instruction in hospitality, when compared to the typical four years required to complete a degree.

Perhaps educators will never fully resolve the ongoing debate regarding whether we should be training or educating students. Nor are educators likely to ever agree on exactly what knowledge should be imparted to our students. Such debates are healthy, however, and are a natural part of the development and maturation of the discipline.

In summary, the mission statement must reflect why the program exists—and this may be different for its many constituents. Ideally, though, the mission statement, and resulting activities, will be consistent with the objectives of the university and other academic units, accommodate the students, and meet the needs of the industry. This becomes increasingly difficult as the business environment changes as quickly as it has in recent years. Some of the recent changes that are affecting hospitality education are discussed below.

HOSPITALITY EDUCATION DURING CHANGING TIMES

As this chapter has indicated, many changes are taking place at all levels of hospitality education, prompting the need for a project such as this which takes a closer look at the inner workings of hospitality education and the environment in which it operates. The discipline is perhaps proving to be even more dynamic than some hospitality education pioneers would ever have imagined. Some dramatic changes have occurred just during the current decade.

First and foremost, the growth of the discipline has slowed significantly. Some programs have ceased to exist (Oregon State University), while others have undergone, or are pending, organizational changes though mergers with other academic units (Georgia State University, Pennsylvania State University). Still others have had to downsize for a variety of reasons. Many of these changes were due to the drop in student enrollments in the early part of the 1990s. A workshop at the 1996 annual meeting of CHRIE was titled "Hospitality Program Survival" and focused on ways to strengthen a program's position within the university. While this trend seems to be reversing itself, programs are still dealing with the consequences of smaller enrollments. Programs are retrenching and offering even more options to students by way of specializations and concentrations.

Second, the majority of programs are having to become much more self-reliant as a result of massive budget cutting at the state level. Since most programs are part of larger state university systems, few have gone unaffected. As a result, programs are looking more to external sources of funding rather than relying on state appropriations. In some cases, hospitality programs are forming closer alliances with local and national hospitality companies, as mentioned earlier in the chapter.

Finally, as the industry continues to change, we must reflect on how these changes affect what we are teaching our students as well as where we are putting our research efforts. Programs must continue to develop new standards and reevaluate existing ones. Further, it becomes paramount to increase and improve industry relations and solicit feedback. This has become more difficult because the number of companies that actively recruit on campuses has decreased. Still, faculty must make an even greater effort to invite managers into the classroom and, in return, spend significant time with them at their companies. This theme is further explored in Chapter 3.

This discipline exists because of the greater hospitality industry but it is important for academics and managers alike to understand that it will take more of a collaborative effort for both parties to excel at what they do. This text will hopefully increase both parties' understanding of the business of hospitality education as well as the need for increased cooperation between both groups.

OVERVIEW OF THE TEXT

The remainder of this text covers a wide variety of topics, all relating to the business of hospitality education. These chapters cover many of the issues discussed above, in much greater detail. Chapter 2 focuses on the industry side by discussing the various segments of the hospitality industry as well as the career opportunities for graduates of hospitality management programs. The chapter also focuses on what makes the hospitality industry different from other industries and why a special curriculum is even needed for educating our students and preparing them for the workplace. Different career opportunities are reviewed and recommendations are made for developing strategic career plans.

Chapter 3 examines the importance of establishing links between educational programs and industry—for the benefit of industry, students, professors, and their programs. One key element of this relationship is experiential learning in the hospitality environment. Experiential programs, such as internships, have been the foundation of many other professional disciplines as well as many successful programs within hospitality. They serve multiple purposes, not the least of which is to give the current student a "real life" experience in the workplace before committing to a particular career. This chapter also looks at the various interactions that occur within the triad of student, faculty, and industry. The various professional associations, which provide another crucial link with industry, are reviewed. Finally, it also looks at one of the ways in which industry, and graduates for that matter, can stay involved with programs through serving on advisory boards.

Chapter 4 reviews the various means by which higher education, and specifically hospitality education, maintains quality standards. External and internal means of assuring quality are discussed with an emphasis upon accreditation—something relatively new to hospitality education programs.

In Chapter 5 the book begins to focus on the role of the hospitality professor, beginning with the sequence of activities required to enter the world of academia. The importance of proper educational preparation and degree choice are discussed. The mechanics of the job search, the importance of networking, and the choosing (or being chosen) of a program are then reviewed. Finally, the chapter reveals what new assistant professors (the academic equivalent of entry-level) can expect to encounter during their first five years on the job.

Chapter 6 covers the roles that teaching, research, and service all play in the professional lives of professors (each of these areas also has a single chapter devoted to it). This chapter goes a long way in refuting the myth that teaching is the be-all and end-all of what professors do. Tenure and the tenure process are also examined in detail.

Chapter 7 takes a closer look at curriculum and instruction issues including helping new teachers develop a teaching philosophy and establish a teaching strategy. It then offers various recommendations for preparing for the classroom, utilizing different teaching styles, and the use of testing. Finally, the concept of the teaching portfolio is discussed with implications for professional enhancement.

Research in hospitality is the focus of Chapter 8. The role and importance of research is often misunderstood by both academicians and industry practitioners. The chapter begins by emphasizing the importance of research, its impact on the industry, and the different types of research that might be conducted, including applied versus pure research. The merits of qualitative versus quantitative research methods are then explored. This chapter concludes by presenting a model of the hospitality research process.

Chapter 9 defines the service element requirement in hospitality programs. Service refers to professors' involvement outside of the classroom and office. Service is often the least understood of a professor's primary responsibilities. This chapter clearly distinguishes between internal and external service requirements and gives numerous examples of each in explaining the various levels of service—from university governance to association and industry service.

Chapter 10 presents an international perspective on hospitality education programs. Recently, many American programs have come under fire for not providing enough international scope. This chapter presents several different curriculum models from three different countries and explains the reasons behind, and the ramifications of, the different models.

The proliferation of graduate programs is the subject of Chapter 11. Graduate programs in hospitality are just coming of age and tend to serve several different functions from preparing managers to preparing aspiring faculty members. These various purposes are discussed, as are some of the programmatic and curriculum-related issues.

Finally, Chapter 12 summarizes many of the changes that are currently taking place, both internally and externally. Changes that are discussed include the increasing emphasis upon research, and greater interaction with industry and international cooperatives, among others. This chapter essentially posits that hospitality education is experiencing a transitional period in its development.

Together, these chapters should give the reader a better understanding of the business of hospitality education: how it developed, how it functions, and where it is going.

REFERENCES

Chronicle of Higher Education Almanac (1998). Projections of College Enrollments, Chronicle of Higher Education Web Page. http://www.chronicle.com

Fletcher, S.W. (1994). Hospitality education. In *Hospitality Management: An Introduction to the Industry*, Seventh Edition. Editor: Robert Brymer. Dubuque, IA: Kendall/Hunt Publishing Co.

Kreul, L. (1995). Hospitality management education: The U.S. and Purdue University experience. Paper delivered at the annual conference of the Australia and New Zealand Academy of Management, Townsville, Australia (November).

Lewis, R.C. (1993). Hospitality management education: Here today, gone tomorrow. *Hospitality Research Journal, 17*, 273-283.

Pauze, E.F. (1993). Time for a new mission in hospitality education. *Hospitality and Tourism Educator, 5*, 61-62.

Pavesic, D.V. (1991). Programmatic issues in undergraduate hospitality education. *Hospitality and Tourism Educator, 3*, 38, 39, 49-51.

Riegel, C.D. (1990). Purpose, perspective and definition: Toward an encompassing view of HRI education. *Hospitality and Tourism Educator, 3*, 18, 19, 28, 30-32.

Riegel, C. (1995). An introduction to career opportunities in hospitality and tourism. In *A Guide to College Programs in Hospitality and Tourism*. New York: John Wiley and Sons, Inc.

Zabel, D. (1992). Undergraduate and graduate programs in hospitality: A typology. *Hospitality and Tourism Educator, 5*, 31-36.

Chapter 2

Hospitality As an Occupation

Alan T. Stutts

The field of hospitality is unique for many reasons. This chapter describes how large and varied the industry really is, and briefly describes some of the more prominent segments. Finally, it discusses some of the characteristics of successful managers and stresses how formal education can contribute to a successful career.

WHAT MAKES HOSPITALITY DIFFERENT?

The hospitality and tourism industry includes multiple segments, all interrelated yet discrete, including lodging, food service, contract services, gaming services, private clubs, meeting planning, theme parks, suppliers, and hospitality education, among others. The single factor common to each of these segments is dependence upon the successful provision of service as a means of generating revenue for the bottom line. It is difficult to imagine a multi-billion-dollar industry that produces a commodity that cannot even be seen—service to people—but that is an accurate description of today's hospitality industry. The very essence of the hospitality industry is people interacting. Thus, it is difficult for the hospitality industry to follow the lead of many businesses and become automated, eliminating the human element wherever possible. True personal service cannot be mechanized or automated. Some technologies are being instituted to speed up routine tasks, but the human element is the determining element of the hospitality business (Lattin, 1995).

Those considering a career in the hospitality industry must first consider the very core of the industry. The hospitality industry is different from other industries, especially those that produce tangible products. Hospitality means people dealing with people. This results in a less standardized product and a less controlled environment. Whereas managers of manufacturing operations can stop the assembly line, or deal with product defects at a later time, the entire hospitality industry is in a constant state of making and delivering products. Products are produced and consumed at virtually the same time, allowing little margin for error. Thus stress for a manager and for the manager's staff are inherent in the process of a personal service industry such as hospitality (McCleary and Weaver, 1991). Success in the hospitality industry requires a high level of commitment, no matter which segment or career path an individual may pursue.

OPPORTUNITIES FOR GRADUATES

The opportunities for graduates of hospitality programs are significant. Some of the more common career paths that graduates choose are discussed below.

Lodging

The lodging business in the United States consists of approximately 3.4 million rooms and generates nearly $80 billion in revenue ($11.3 billion in profits). By the turn of the century, the U.S. lodging business is expected to surpass 3.6 million rooms, $100 billion in revenues, and $21 billion in profits (Ader and LeFleur, 1997).

The lodging industry has experienced a long and checkered history. The past three decades, in particular, have done much to shape the industry as it appears today. The early 1970s saw a boom in the expansion of the lodging business. The interstate highway system neared completion, opening new interchange markets along major routes across the country. The beltway system of interstate bypass roads around major urban centers created scores of new suburban markets. Easy capital provided the fuel for this development. Aggressive franchise sales activity by the major brands also fueled growth as hotel companies could expand their market presence with little capital investment by selling franchises.

The surge in the supply of hotels led to the invention of market segmentation, whereby one hotel company would have several brands aimed at several different customer niches. The advent of segmentation marked the maturation of the lodging business into its present form. This segmentation was especially pronounced in the lower-price portions of the industry as budget and economy chains attempted to draw more and more minute distinctions between brands. An increasingly savvy hotel customer began to fine-tune his or her purchasing behavior by distinguishing among the different brands on pricing and amenities and services offered.

With the political and economic turmoil of the mid-1970s, the lodging business suffered. The oil embargo of 1974 and the ensuing energy crisis crippled the travel industry with rationing, gas short-ages, and higher prices. Demand in 1975 fell below 1974 levels as a direct result of the energy crisis. As gas began to flow again, travel picked up and hotel demand began to grow in 1976.

In the 1980s, a period of construction began, which was labeled the "go-go eighties." Beginning in 1981, changes in the tax law dramatically increased the attractiveness of hotels as an investment. Accelerated depreciation allowed hotels to operate at a paper loss, providing substantial tax shelters against other sources of income. Unfortunately, many hotels were built based on their ability to generate paper losses for their investors, rather than their ability to attract customers. Adding fuel to the fire was the additional avail-ability of capital created by the deregulation of the savings and loan industry. Traditionally a source of financing single-family homes, these institutions were now free to make significant levels of com-mercial loan.

Another significant change in the structure of the lodging indus-try that developed in the 1980s was the separation of hotel owner-ship from management. Hotel companies realized that the hotel business was really a combination of two business, real estate and lodging. Each aspect of the industry had different characteristics, making it attractive for different reasons. The hotel business is a high-margin operating business with a significant level of operating leverage. The industry is characterized by high-fixed and relatively low-variable costs. It requires a lot of money to open the doors of a hotel, but once these fixed costs are covered, a larger and larger portion of each incremental dollar in revenue falls to the bottom line. On the other hand, the real estate business is characterized by high levels of depreciation and interest expense. Hotel companies began selling ownership of the existing hotels to, and developing new projects with, investment groups who sought the benefits of real estate ownership, but who had no interest or expertise in hotel operations. In return, the hotel companies kept long-term management contracts, giving them operational control over the properties for a stipulated management fee. The arrangement could include either the right to use a brand name along with the management services, or just management services, with a brand provided by a third-party franchiser.

The Tax Reform Act of 1986 was a significant event in the history of the U.S. lodging industry. Depreciation schedules were increased from eighteen years to thirty-one and a half years, the investment tax credit was repealed, and earned income could no longer be sheltered by passive investment losses. The rug essentially was pulled out from under the vast majority of hotel deals that had been made in the 1980s.

Although the reform was catastrophic, the effects were not immediately apparent. A national recession hit in the early 1990s and demand growth faltered. This was compounded dramatically by the Persian Gulf War of 1990-1991, which further curtailed travel. In 1989 room demand was 4.9 percent higher than in the previous year. In 1990, the year-over-year demand growth slipped to 1.6 percent. By 1991, demand actually fell by 1.6 percent. The dramatic supply growth of the late 1980s compounded the problem and occupancy rates fell from 64.3 percent in 1989 to 61.8 percent in 1991, a level not seen since the very early 1970s. The triple whammy of recession, war, and unnaturally high supply growth put the industry into its worst tailspin since the Great Depression. It would not be until 1994 that the lodging industry would be able to generate year-over-year percentage increases in average daily rate that exceeded inflation.

The economic conditions of the early 1990s virtually shut off all funding for the industry. Lenders stopped lending and investors stopped investing. Supply growth came to a halt. Even as the industry returned to profitability in 1993, the drought of capital continued, setting the stage for the current growth. In 1996, room demand increased 2.3 percent over 1995 levels, while supply increased by 2.8 percent. This was the first year supply growth had surpassed demand growth since 1991.

The distribution of hotel construction has been uneven throughout the United States during the post-1991 recovery. Divergent supply/demand dynamics among the various regions cause differences in region-by-region and market-by-market analyses. Much of the recent spate of development has been concentrated in the central part of the United States. Texas, California, and Florida are the top three states, ranked by the number of projects. One out of every three hotel projects in the 110 top metropolitan statistical areas (MSAs) are currently located in one of these three states. Over 20,000 rooms are currently in the development/ construction pipe line in each of these three states.

The states of Arizona, Illinois, Ohio, Georgia, North Carolina, Washington, Tennessee, and New Jersey cumulatively have between 7,000 and 20,000 rooms in the construction pipeline. Combined, these states account for 30 percent of the total number of rooms under construction. Typically, casino projects are not included in construction data compiled by such firms as F. W. Dodge. However, if they were, Nevada would rank among the top states for new projects.

It is clear that the future of the lodging industry is bright and that career opportunities exist for people with the proper mix of experience and formal education. Table 2.1 illustrates an example of a career path that is typical of many lodging organizations.

Food Service

Sales in the food service industry exceeded $313 billion in 1996, according to the National Restaurant Association. These sales accounted for over 4 percent of the U.S. gross domestic product. The U.S. food service industry continues to be dominated by small businesses and operates through some 773,000 locations employing

TABLE 2.1. Career Path in the Lodging Industry with Position and Years to Achieve Position

15 years	General Manager	
10 years	Director of Operations	
5 years	Rooms Division Manager	Food and Beverage Manager
	Front Office Manager	Assistant Food and Beverage Manager
4 years	Assistant Front Office Manager	Outlet Manager
1 year	Guest Services Manager	Assistant Outlet Manager
	Management Trainee	Management Trainee

Source: "An Introduction to Career Opportunities in Hospitality and Tourism," Carl D. Riegel, *A Guide to College Programs in Hospitality and Tourism,* John Wiley & Sons, Inc., New York, 1995.

some nine million persons. Employment in food service businesses is projected to increase to nearly twelve million persons by the year 2005.

The customers of U.S. food service businesses include nearly one-half of all adults on a typical day. The National Restaurant Association reported that nearly 44 percent of the U.S. consumer's food dollar goes to meals and snacks away from home. This has risen nearly 25 percent from 1955 (National Restaurant Association, 1996).

Different classifications can be used to describe the principal segments of the food service industry. Most often economic objectives are the basis for classification. The terms commercial, institutional, and military are most often used for economic classification. Commercial food service exists to make a profit on the sale of food and/or beverage products. The primary objective of institutional food service is to minimize expenses. Military food service's main objective is to stay within a congressionally appropriated budget.

In 1996, the commercial food service group accounted for nearly $281 billion of the total $313 billion in sales. Quick service continues to lead the commercial food service classification with nearly 48 percent of total food service industry sales. Sales at full-service restaurants exceeded $100 billion dollars in 1996, 32 percent of total food service industry sales.

Table 2.2 is illustrative of the career path in a typical chain restaurant or multiunit restaurant company.

TABLE 2.2. Career Path in the Restaurant Industry with Position and Years to Achieve Position

10 years	Regional Manager
7 years	District Manager
3 years	Manager
2 years	Assistant Manager
1 year	Shift Manager
Graduation	Management Trainee

Source: "An Introduction to Career Opportunities in Hospitality and Tourism," Carl D. Riegel, *A Guide to College Programs in Hospitality and Tourism*, John Wiley & Sons, Inc., New York, 1995.

Private Clubs

There are more than 10,000 clubs in the United States. Having been around since the seventeenth and eighteenth centuries, clubs have a tremendous history. The Royal and Ancient Golf Club of St. Andrews, Scotland, founded in 1758 and said to be the birthplace of golf, is the forerunner of the modern country club. Today's city clubs are similarly related to the English social club, where members met over drinks and dinner in local taverns. The Mermaid Club, founded by Sir Walter Raleigh and attended by Marlowe and Shakespeare, met at London's Mermaid Tavern (Chon and Sparrowe, 1995).

Clubs are typically referred to as either equity or proprietary clubs. The equity club, the oldest and most common, is not for profit. It is typically owned and organized by its members for their own enjoyment. The proprietary club is owned by an individual or company, and operates for profit. Individuals purchase a membership from the club's owner or owners.

Further classification might include country clubs, city clubs, military clubs, and yacht clubs. In recent years, the growth of member-owned clubs has subsided but proprietary clubs continue to open. Together, clubs represent one of the most overlooked career options for graduates of hospitality programs.

Gaming

Casino gaming remains one of the fastest-growing and largest segments of the hospitality industry in the United States. Americans typically wager approximately $297.3 billion on all forms of legal wagering, which includes casino, lottery, paramutuel, and charitable.

The growth in the gaming industry is being driven by supply- and demand-side forces simultaneously. Governments need new revenue and methods of job creation. The deteriorating fiscal condition of many states is one of the driving forces of gaming proliferation. Gaming has become an accepted economic stimulus for local, state, and federal governments. The gaming industry has proven that, if properly implemented, it can provide an effective program to create jobs and generate additional tax revenues.

The declining marginal cost of wagering is helping drive industry growth. As casino gaming has spread into new markets over the past few years, the average win per position experienced by the operators in a new market far exceeds that of the traditional markets.

Acceptance of casino entertainment among Americans remains high. According to the Harrah's Survey of U.S. Casino Entertainment, more than 51 percent of the adults in the United States found casino entertainment acceptable for anyone, and another 35 percent considered it acceptable for others, but not for themselves. In addition, a 1993 CNBC-Gallup poll showed that over two-thirds of Americans approve of some type of legalized gaming (Ader, 1995).

It is estimated that by the end of the decade, a casino will exist within a 200-mile radius of 95 percent of all American households.

The large companies with significant capital and human resources will be in the best position to benefit from worldwide growth of casino gaming.

Meetings and Events

The growth of the meetings and events industry has been significant in the past thirty years or so. Today, meetings, conventions, and expositions are serious business, generating about $60 billion annually in the United States. As the saying goes, everybody is a member of an association and associations like to meet. The growth has been due in large part to a combination of meeting planners associations, air transportation, lodging, convention centers, convention bureaus, conference centers, and meeting technology.

During the past twenty-five years or so there has been tremendous growth in the number of convention centers. Space, accessibility, and storage facilities have made convention centers a one-stop arena for meetings, conventions, and expositions. These facilities now require a staff that not only books space, but provides a variety of services to customers including setup/tear down, exhibit design, security, food and beverage, and so on.

The convention and visitor bureaus encourage groups to hold meetings, conventions, and expositions in a city, assist groups with meeting preparations, offer services during their events, and encourage tourists to visit and enjoy the historical, cultural, and recreational opportunities that a city might have to offer.

Conference centers are another result of the growth in the meetings business. They may be found at airports, aboard cruise ships, and owned by private corporations for their exclusive use. The revolutions in technology in recent years have driven conference centers into video technology, teleconferencing, and computer applications.

The role of the meeting planner began to evolve in the late 1970s. A meeting planner organizes the details that make the meeting, convention, or exposition operate smoothly. Meeting planning entails a variety of tasks including site selection, reservations (meeting space, equipment, lodging, meals, transportation), attendee registration, attendee information and materials, program planning, exhibit layout and setup, floor plans, security, transportation, and evaluation. Meeting planners may work directly with hotels, associations, or corporations, or they can work as independent contractors hiring their services to hotels, associations, or corporations.

Career opportunities exist in managerial roles with convention centers, convention and visitor bureaus, conference centers, associations, and in meeting planning from an association or corporate perspective.

Theme Parks

When theme parks are mentioned the name Disney comes to mind. However, there are others including Six Flags, Busch Gardens, Knotts Berry Farm, Wet n' Wild, Universal Studios, and Sea World. A quick examination of a theme park shows a very complex food and beverage operation and often a similar lodging operation. Graduates from hospitality management degree programs are well prepared to direct the hotel and restaurant operations of these entertainment businesses.

Resorts

A resort provides special recreation and entertainment to its guests. Personalized service is the hallmark of a resort. Such names as La Costa, Pebble Beach, The Boulders, Broadmoor, Greenbrier, The Breakers, The Cloister, Pinehurst, and Club Med are the among the trademark names in the resort industry.

Resorts are often one-property businesses though some, while being quite large and complex, are really small businesses that have been held by one family for multiple generations. Typically one may not start out in the management of a resort, but in one of the multitude of supervisory or other positions. After a period of service and demonstrated commitment to the resort one may find his or her way into management.

Managed Services

In the hospitality industry there are many companies whose business is the operation and management of services and facilities for others. For example, in the lodging segment of the industry it is common to find hotel management companies that operate hotels for the owners under one or many different names. The same holds true in the areas of food service and facilities management.

With respect to the food service segment of the hospitality industry one will find multibillion-dollar corporations such as ARAMARK, Delaware North, Sodexho Marriott Services, and the Wood Company, which operate in the food service segments focusing on employee/corporate food service (and in some cases, additional services), health care food service, school feeding, and educational food service, among others. This is an already vast and still-growing segment of the hospitality industry. As corporations, universities, and similar organizations continue to look to outside companies to help them operate their food service (and related services) this segment can only continue to grow.

Often the demand for entry-level managers has exceeded the supply and those with an educational background in hotel, restaurant, and hospitality management and related experience are sought after.

Allied Industries

As the hospitality industry has exploded globally to become the second largest industry on the planet, so has the demand for products, systems, and services for this industry. Those with an educational background in hotel, restaurant, and hospitality management with related experience in the management of one or more segments of the industry may find lucrative opportunities in corporations whose principal business is to sell products that meet the industries' needs such as Sysco and Kraft Alliant, who purvey food products to the industry, or Computrition or C-Bord, who are the purveyors of food/beverage computer systems, and companies such as Pannel, Kerr, Forster (PKF), who assist the industry in researching complex financial or product development decisions.

Education

Over the last two decades, hospitality management education programs have blossomed. As the hospitality industry has expanded, the supply of qualified human resources in the supervisory and managerial ranks has not kept pace. Thus, the demand for more and

better-qualified supervisors and managers has given rise to a multitude of postsecondary education programs providing two-year,
four-year, and postgraduate education. Interestingly enough, as a
shortage of talented supervisors and managers gave rise to more
hotel, restaurant, and hospitality management educational programs,
it also accentuated the shortage of talented educators to populate
such programs. There is regularly an abundance of opportunities in
two-year, four-year, and graduate degree programs for talented educators. Typically such programs are looking for persons who have
attained successful managerial experience in multiple segments of
the industry prior to their matriculation into education.

In recent years another aspect of education has emerged that may
open an entirely new opportunity for those interested in teaching. In
high schools across the United States electives are being offered to
juniors and seniors that give them the chance to study the operating
units of hotels and restaurants, first in a classroom and then hands-
on. These high schools for hospitality, as they are known in Texas,
have opened up another career path for those interested in education. With the right combination of professional experience and
education, the education field provides yet another career option for
graduates of hospitality management programs.

CONCLUSION

The future of the hospitality industry is bright. The hospitality
industry is the largest or second largest industry on the planet depending upon how one counts the dollars, with no end in sight to its
growth. By the year 2005 it will generate a projected gross output of
$5.5 trillion and employ over 150 million persons globally.

Historically, the legends in the business of hotels, restaurants,
clubs, etc. with names such as Hilton, Marriott, Stouffer, Carlson,
Disney, Kroc, and others learned by doing, and over the years
experience has come to be a credential that is highly valued by
employers in the hospitality industry. However, as the complexity
of the industry has increased and the competition become more
fierce, so has the need for new ideas and ways of thinking about
doing business. Thus, education has become more highly valued.
Graduates will always need the proper balance of education and

experience to advance their careers. It is clear that successful managers in the future must be well grounded in management associated with team building, strategic planning, profit improvement, quality improvement, and innovation.

In addition, they must be able to cost effectively and customer effectively integrate technology into an industry that has been driven by an extensive use of human capital. Advances in property management systems, telecommunications, robotics, interactive training, call accounting, security, video conferencing, and virtual reality all pose challenges and opportunities for the coming generations of managers of hotel, restaurant, and hospitality businesses.

The manager of the future must clearly see that the ethics of a decision and the ethics of the workplace are determinants of the long-term success of the enterprise just as sure as cost effectiveness and customer satisfaction are determinants of success. Once an ethical environment is established, it becomes easier to deal with difficult decisions. An understanding of the legality of alternative courses of action will facilitate ethical decisions by managers and other personnel.

As the global composition of the available supply of human resources changes, the successful hotel, restaurant, and hospitality business must be successful in integrating older workers, physically and mentally challenged workers, and culturally diverse workers into their operations.

The successful completion of an undergraduate degree program in hospitality management that is respected in the industry will be a prerequisite for entry, and continuing education to postgraduate degrees will be strongly recommended for advancement. A critical examination of hospitality management education is in the offing, an examination that will focus on curriculum (relevancy, industry partnership), faculty (academic and experiential balance), facilities (ability to apply traditional classroom lecture/discussion), and industry partnerships. Thus it will behoove the educational consumer to carefully evaluate the myriad of educational programs that are, and will be, introduced into the marketplace.

While education and continuing education are essential, the successful manager in the hospitality industry will always be evaluating and reevaluating personal career objectives and updating the status and opportunities within those companies that seemingly can facilitate those objectives. In addition, the successful manager will always be networking and valuing professional development. Networking takes place at state, local, national, and international professional association conferences and meetings; professional development takes place at seminars and conferences, and by reading and reviewing the trade journals that are reflective of one's career objectives (Exhibit 2.1). Scholarly journals are listed in Exhibit 2.2. Industry associations also provide a means of continuing one's education and maintaining important contacts (Exhibit 2.3). These are discussed in further detail in Chapter 3. In summary, the important role that hospitality management programs play in the greater hospitality industry is increasing.

In conclusion, the successful manager is always ready to articulate career accomplishments in detail or as a summary, and understands those questions that should be asked in order to correctly evaluate a potential career opportunity that is presented, whether that individual is involved in the supply side of hospitality or working in an educational capacity. The next chapter further explores the links between the hospitality industry and hospitality education programs.

EXHIBIT 2.1. Industry Trade Journals

Travel Weekly
Lodging Hospitality
Lodging Magazine
Lodging Outlook
Association Meetings
Club Management
International Journal of Gaming and Wagering Business
Hotel and Motel Management
Hotel Business
Meetings and Conventions
Nation's Restaurant News
Restaurant Business
Restaurant Hospitality
Restaurant and Institutions
Restaurants USA
Successful Meetings
Tour and Travel News
Travel Agent

EXHIBIT 2.2. Scholarly Journals

Annals of Tourism Research
International Journal of Hospitality Management
Journal of Applied Recreation Research
Journal of Hospitality and Leisure Marketing
Journal of Hospitality & Tourism Research
Journal of Leisure Research
Journal of Restaurant and Food Service Marketing
Journal of Travel and Tourism Marketing
Journal of Travel Research
Tourism Management
Cornell Hotel and Restaurant Administration Quarterly
FIU Hospitality Review
Journal of Hospitality and Tourism Education
International Journal of Contemporary Hospitality Management
Journal of College and University Food Service
Journal of Gambling Studies

EXHIBIT 2.3. Professional Associations

American Bed and Breakfast Association
American Culinary Federation
American Dietetic Association
American Hotel and Motel Association
American Society for Hospital Food Service Administrators
American Society of Association Executives
American Society of Travel Agents
Club Managers Association of America
Council of Hotel, Restaurant and Institutional Education
Foodservice Consultants Society International
Hospitality Sales and Marketing Association International
International Association for Exposition Management
International Association of Amusement Parks and Attractions
International Association of Fairs and Expositions
International Association of Hospitality Accountants
International Hotel and Restaurant Association
Meeting Planners International
National Association of Catering Executives
National Executive Housekeepers Association
National Restaurant Association
National Tour Association
Professional Convention Management Association
Society for Foodservice Management

REFERENCES

Ader, J.N. (Ed.). (1995). *Global Gaming Almanac*, New York: Smith Barney.

Ader, J.N. and LeFleur, R.A. (Eds.) (1997). *U.S. Lodging Almanac*, New York: Bear Stearns.

Chon, K.S. and Sparrowe, R.T. (1995). *Welcome to Hospitality—An Introduction*, Cincinnati, OH: South-Western Publishing Company.

Lattin, G.W. (1995). *The Lodging and Food Service Industry*, Third Edition. East Lansing, MI: Educational Institute of the American Hotel and Motel Association.

McCleary, K.W. and Weaver, P. (1995). Realities of a Career in the Hospitality Industry. In *Hospitality management,* Brymer, R.A. (ed.). Dubuque, IA: Kendall/Hunt, pp. 68-77.

National Restaurant Association and Deloitte and Touche. (1996). *Restaurant Industry Operations Report,* Washington, DC: NRA.

Riegel, C.D. (1995). An Introduction to Career Opportunities in Hospitality and Tourism. In *A Guide to College Programs in Hospitality and Tourism*, CHRIE (Ed.), New York: John Wiley and Sons, Inc.

Chapter 3

Linking Hospitality Management Programs to Industry

Reg Foucar-Szocki
Claire Bolsing

INTRODUCTION

One of the unique characteristics of hospitality management education is its professional orientation. Like business schools (of which many hospitality programs arc a part), hospitality programs tend to stress practical skill development. For this reason, hospitality programs develop and capitalize upon associations with professionals in the hospitality industry as a means of enhancing student learning and their educational programs in general. One example of such an arrangement is the development of student internships. Internships have now become a vital part of the total student learning experience. A second method of developing and maintaining industry connections is through involvement with various industry associations. Association involvement is important for both faculty and students in hospitality management programs. A third means of developing more significant ties to industry is through the use of advisory councils. This chapter explores all of these dimensions of typical hospitality management programs—all of which tend to set them apart from mainstream academic disciplines and even other professional fields. Experiential learning (internships), professional organizations available for the hospitality educator, and advisory councils are all discussed, and recommendations are made for maximizing the effectiveness of each.

EXPERIENTIAL LEARNING

Internship/experiential learning is used throughout this chapter to mean all forms of internships, externships, co-ops, work-study programs, experiential learning, field experiences, and structured work experiences. The authors believe that whatever it is called, the goal is still the same—to provide the student with a meaningful learning experience that will assist the hospitality student in his or her professional development in the hospitality industry.

As one begins a career as a hospitality educator, it is not unusual for the "new kid on the block" to become the internship coordinator. This section of the chapter provides working definitions of the key players involved in internships, the purpose and scope of these activities, and strategies to help one's students attain success. It includes a discussion of the specific responsibilities for the faculty, the sponsoring organization, and the student in internships.

Internship Terminology

- The *sponsor* is the key contact person at the work site. This individual may be the intern's direct supervisor or a member of the human resource staff.
- The *cooperating organization* is the business where the intern is working.
- The *intern* is the hospitality student.
- The *faculty supervisor* is the educator/coordinator on site at the university or college.
- *Learning activities* are assignments or projects that enhance learning on the job. Each faculty supervisor, academic institution, and sponsoring organization select which one of these is most appropriate for the internship experience. At some institutions a formal fifty-page report is required, while at other institutions a weekly log of activities suffices.

Purpose of Internships/Experiential Learning

The purpose of an internship or experiential learning experience is to enable college students to gain valuable work experience within the hospitality industry. This experience should be designed to complement the course work taken so that the student's background of education and experience is enhanced. Experiential learning is an educational plan that integrates classroom study with practical work experience. It is intended to contribute meaningfully to the overall preparation of the student by providing an opportunity for the practical application of skills and concepts learned in the classroom. It is much more than a job; an internship is an opportunity that offers every student an individualized educational experience through the study of a structured employment situation.

The Scope of Experiential Learning

The perfect internship has not been created, nor are all models created equal. There are tremendous differences from program to program. At some schools, students receive academic credit ranging from one to fifteen credits for their internship experience, while at others no academic credit is provided. At some institutions students are required to be paid, while at others they are not. The expectation of hours worked ranges from four per week at one institution to over fifty at others. What is known is that good internships evolve using a total quality management (TQM) related model of continuous improvement. Ultimately, it is the faculty supervisor's role to determine the scope and parameter of the internship.

Objectives of an Internship Program

One of the key goals of experiential learning is to provide students with practical experience in a professional and/or business setting. Experiential learning assignments vary in terms of direction, duration, and requirements; yet there exists enough uniformity to suggest a standard structure for them. The following list of objectives are classified by the specific skills they are meant to enhance.

Conceptual Knowledge

- To increase the student's knowledge and understanding of the organization and operation of a food service business or unit.
- To develop the student's skills in given areas of production and/or service.

- To increase the student's appreciation of the opportunities and advantages of the hospitality industry.
- To continue to develop the student's interest in, and understanding of, the hospitality industry.
- To gain knowledge of the tourism, leisure, and hospitality industries.

Management Skills

- To increase the student's tolerance for, and understanding of, people.
- To increase the student's understanding and tolerance for some of the disadvantages and problems of the industry.
- To develop a mature sense of responsibility.
- To demonstrate the student's ability to use the knowledge of management theory as learned in college courses to analyze the practice of management as observed in the hospitality industry.
- To introduce the student to systems operation, personnel, public relations, and quality standards in the operation.
- To understand the importance of human relations in the operation and increasing ability to work effectively with staff.
- To see and evaluate students as a potential manager.

Communication Skills

- To demonstrate the student's ability to write a professional report that presents all essential information in a style that is appropriate for a prospective manager in the hospitality industry.
- To demonstrate the student's ability to relate information in an organized and concise manner using speaking skills that are appropriate for a prospective manager in the hospitality industry.

Career Development Skills

- To provide the student with job search skills.
- To provide recruiters evidence of a student's knowledge of, and commitment to, the hospitality industry.

- To better prepare themselves for their chosen careers while enhancing their employment potential.

Application of Work Environment Skills

- To provide the student with meaningful work experience.
- To supplement academic subject matter with practical experience so those classroom presentations of theories, principles, and techniques are more meaningful and realistic.
- To apply classroom knowledge to "real world" situations.
- To ensure that students completing the program will have had well-balanced practical background equivalent to the theoretical knowledge learned.
- To be able to work under considerable pressure with a minimum of difficulty.
- To be able to work independently with a minimum of supervision.
- To apply principles and theory related to the hospitality management industry in a meaningful work situation.

Program Needs Assessment Skills

- To provide a constant interaction between the academic institution and the sponsoring organization.
- To provide a company with a competitive edge in recruiting the highest quality students in a particular program.
- To strengthen the program's recruitment program.
- To provide academic institutions with mutual opportunities to evaluate students in terms of their understanding of the industry and the relevance of the curriculum to industry needs.
- To provide internship staff with opportunities to evaluate the effectiveness of their programs in terms of student involvement.
- To set mutually satisfactory and feasible goals with the sponsoring operation's supervisors.

Once the objectives of the experiential learning experience are developed, it is much easier to look for potential sponsoring organizations. These objectives should be part of the ongoing assessment of the hospitality program. As always, these objectives should be viewed as a work in progress.

Accountabilities

As stated in the beginning of the chapter, there are three major players in the experience—the student, the sponsor, and the faculty supervisor. Collectively, all three players need to work together and communicate to ensure a positive learning experience. What follows is a detailed list of responsibilities for the student, the faculty supervisor, and the sponsor. These may be modified depending upon the particular circumstance.

The student's responsibility during the internship is to follow all policies and procedures of the sponsoring organizations. The following is a checklist for the faculty and the student:

- Confidentiality
- Dress code
- Health records
- Injury/preemployment physical
- Medical insurance
- Smoking
- Tardiness
- Termination of assignment
- Transportation
- Use of drugs or alcohol
- Vacations and holidays
- Warning procedures

In general, housing, transportation, and living expenses during the internship arc the responsibility of the intern. There are always exceptions to this rule—so students may want to ask the sponsor during the interview. Students should discuss any special needs that they may have, especially the need to be away from work certain days or times. Advance requests are more easily accommodated than last-minute ones. Communication is the key.

Guidelines for Serving As a Faculty Supervisor

The faculty supervisor is expected to be a resource to the student. Listening and giving advice are valuable activities. Also, taking control and giving very specific assignments and feedback are important to the overall experience. The ideal faculty supervisor is a professional friend to the student, someone who is there to encourage, reinforce, and counsel the student, while making sure the student accepts responsibility for his or her actions.

It is rewarding to serve as a faculty supervisor in a learner-controlled experience. While the student is discovering what the hospitality industry is all about, the supervisor gets a chance to experience different aspects as well.

The faculty supervisor will:

- Aid the sponsoring organization in seeking to bring students and employers together.
- Assist the student in actively seeking a position.
- Monitor student progress with sponsors via telephone and personal visits when necessary. At the end of the work period, an evaluation will be requested from the employer regarding each student.
- Integrate student background with the intern position in order to provide an experience relative to the student's career interests.
- Provide information concerning the program and applications to prospective cooperating organizations.
- Evaluate all aspects of the program: the department's role, the organization's contribution, and the student's performance.

Sponsor Responsibilities

The sponsor is the key contact person during the experience. Responsibilities are many, but it is important to realize that the experiential learning program is just one small piece of the sponsor's job responsibilities. The following list presents various responsibilities that are up to the faculty supervisor to coordinate with the sponsor to provide the best possible experience for the student. The sponsoring organization should, to the best of its ability, try to:

- On a weekly, if not daily, basis provide various forms of feedback on student performance, progress, and areas of concern.
- Provide, at the end of the term, an evaluation of the student's progress and overall performance.

- Specify employment time periods in advance and confirm in writing a starting date and ending date that must be within five days of the student's actual employment dates. A format for this document may be found in the general affiliation agreement, which is a written contract between university, intern, and sponsor.
- Permit an internship/work experience faculty sponsor to visit the sponsoring organization periodically for the purpose of reviewing the program with the appropriate officials, and speaking with students presently at the facility.
- Whenever possible, and applicable, invite students to attend departmental meetings and/or training sessions.
- Where applicable, assist students in finding suitable and reasonable housing.
- In the event a student is not performing in accordance with the accepted standards, and has been given all necessary chances, the sponsoring organization is under no obligation to continue employment.
- Expose students to a productive work environment while providing on-the-job training in a variety of hospitality areas. In addition, an orientation to management responsibilities is an important component of the program.
- Seek a balance between work and training so that the student can accomplish the assigned job and at the same time benefit from the knowledge and experience of resident professionals.
- Provide time for several conferences between the student and the cooperating organization's supervisor.
- Prepare other employees to accept the student's participation and encourage their cooperation and support of the intern.
- Provide training for the experiential learner in specific job skills.
- Treat the intern as any regular employee whether the intern is paid or volunteer.
- Complete and return the midterm and final evaluation forms concerning the student's performance to the faculty supervisor.
- Contact the faculty supervisor immediately if questions or positive or negative thoughts occur during the course of the program.

It is clear that a successful internship program can and should benefit all of the participating parties but that it cannot be successful without clear communication and everyone doing their part. It is however, just one means of bringing students, employers, and hospitality programs together.

PROFESSIONAL AFFILIATIONS

One of the many benefits of being a hospitality educator is the true willingness of colleagues to share what they know. As you look at what professional organizations to join, this sharing of resources may be an important criterion in your selection. This section provides an overview of four prominent associations: the Council on Hotel, Restaurant and Institutional Education (CHRIE), the National Restaurant Association (NRA), the American Hotel & Motel Association (AH&MA), and the Club Managers Association of America (CMAA). There are many others, but these are the four associations of which many educators are members.

As a new faculty member, there is a professional organization which is a must-join—the Council on Hotel, Restaurant and Institutional Education. CHRIE was founded in 1946 as a nonprofit association for schools, colleges, and universities offering programs in hotel and restaurant management, food service management, and culinary arts.

In recent years, CHRIE's focus has expanded and its mission statement has evolved, making the organization a marketplace facilitating exchanges of information, ideas, research, products, and services related to education, training, and resource development for the hospitality and tourism industry (food, lodging, recreation, and travel services). The annual conference held in the summer along with CHRIE publications, *The Journal of Hospitality & Tourism Education, The Journal of Hospitality & Tourism Research,* and *Hosteur* make this the best value for any hospitality educator. To make the CHRIE connection and join, contact the CHRIE office in Washington, DC.

Another organization to consider joining is the National Restaurant Association. The mission of the NRA is to protect, educate, and promote the food service industry. For more than seventy-five years, the NRA has been the leading resource for the food service community. Since its founding, it has promoted, educated, and protected the food service industry—currently the employer of 9.4 million employees. The association provides members with a wide range of education, research, communication, convention, and government affairs services.

Membership in the NRA is for the dedicated professional who wants to keep current with vital industry developments. Membership links your business with more than 30,000 members across the globe, representing over 175,000 food service outlets. The association's membership includes a variety of businesses, professionals, and the academic community associated with food service and hospitality.

The Educational Foundation of the National Restaurant Association, a nonprofit organization based in Chicago, is the primary source of education, training, and professional development for the food service industry. The foundation is dedicated to enhancing the professionalism of the food service industry through education and training. It works to develop and promote all segments of the industry including institutions, associations, colleges and universities, independent operators, and international customers.

The Educational Foundation offers more than 100 educational products and services consisting of textbooks, student manuals, instructor guides, manager and employee training programs, videotapes, examinations, seminars, and certification programs. The foundation also organizes and conducts a wide array of training seminars designed to keep food service operators educated on current topics and trends occurring in the food service industry.

On the lodging side, there is the American Hotel & Motel Association. AH&MA is the voice of the $72 billion U.S. lodging industry. With headquarters in Washington, DC, AH&MA offers communication, governmental affairs, marketing, hospitality operations, educational, convention, risk management, technology, information, and member relations services for hotels, motels, and lodging facilities throughout the world.

AH&MA offers its 11,000+ members guidance in developing programs and activities of value in such areas as guest and employee communications, information processing and related technology, international travel, external and internal marketing, quality assurance programs, industry research, safety and fire protection, and so on.

The association is dedicated to providing members and the media with up-to-date information, industry trends, and association news via the World Wide Web. Today, this network ties AH&MA's Washington office with the fifty-one member state associations that make up the AH&MA Federation. Eventually, this technology will link AH&MA with every member property, enhancing service to them.

The Educational Institute (EI) is the hospitality industry's first source for organizational development and training. Founded over forty-four years ago as a producer of educational materials for home study and hotel school classrooms, the institute has grown to become a strategy-based company proactively leading hospitality operations through today's changing business environment.

Relying on comprehensive research, input from a vast network of top advisors from industry and academia, and the latest learning technologies, EI helps hospitality companies and individual properties improve operational efficiency and employee skills development. The institute is committed to eliminating learning barriers, be they language or cultural, in order to deliver resources that motivate people to perform.

EI also takes a leadership role in bridging the gap between what students learn in the classroom and the skills and knowledge needed for career success. In fact, the institute is the primary source of hospitality curricula in more than 1,200 academic institutions worldwide.

There are many professional organizations that specialize in one field within the hospitality industry. One such specialty organization is the Club Managers Association of America. CMAA is the professional association for managers of private membership clubs. It has more than 5,000 members who manage more than 3,000 country, city, athletic, faculty, yacht, corporate, and military clubs. The objectives of the association are to promote and advance friendly relations between and among persons connected with the management of clubs and other associations of similar character, to encourage the education and advancement of its members, and to assist club officers and members, through their managers, to secure the utmost in efficient and successful operations.

The association's Club Foundation supports the advancement of the club management profession. The foundation sponsors research, funds education programs, provides internships for faculty, provides financial assistance to educational institutions, and awards scholarships to outstanding students interested in this profession. CMAA's budget is $4.5 million and the staff numbers twenty-eight. There are fifty chapters, both in the United States and abroad.

There are dozens of professional organizations to join. Be selective. Talk with senior faculty in your program and see what they think. The World Wide Web home address for each organization is listed below. Most sites have over twenty pages of material. Many also have special membership classifications for hospitality faculty, often at a reduced rate. In short, associations provide an effective way of networking with industry professionals as well as other faculty members. In addition, these professional organizations provide a great avenue for potential advisory council members, which is the last section of this chapter.

CHRIE	http://www.chrie.org
NRA	http://www.restaurant.org
AH&MA	http://www.ahma.com
CMAA	http://www.clubnet.com

INDUSTRY/ACADEMIC COOPERATION: THE USE OF ADVISORY COUNCILS

This final section discusses the roles and objectives of industry advisory boards, which many hospitality programs have. Such boards can serve a variety of functions—this section provides some additional ideas for maximizing their effectiveness.

A Strategic Rationale for Cooperation

In an increasingly competitive job environment, hospitality educators must prepare students to know and meet the particular needs of their future employers. Consider the fact that employers in travel and tourism, hotel, and restaurant businesses are the ultimate consumers of the skills and cognitive abilities that educators impart to students. As business organizations have learned the importance of customer-focused strategies in their pursuit of competitive advantages, hospitality programs are also under increasing pressure from various sources to become more customer-focused in their curricula and instructional methods.

How might hospitality educators learn more about their customers' needs? First, educators must welcome the practitioners as stakeholders and contributors to the educational process. In return, recruiters and industry representatives must be willing to interact with educators. Cooperation and trust are key administrative values when empowerment and involvement are educational goals. Too few faculty members have experience as managers, let alone leaders. Successful faculty members in many four-year colleges and research universities must establish a substantial record in research and publication. Tenure and promotion more often depend on satisfying one's professional colleagues in a particular highly specialized subject area than on responding to the challenges faced by hospitality, restaurant, and tourism business communities. In contrast, industry usually is best equipped to train employees for enterprise-specific needs. A partnership between academe and industry, with both groups reviewing and contributing to programs that enhance theory, practice, and learning, will bring the strengths of both groups to bear on improved student education. The glue for this collaborative effort will be the value each group places on the other group's expertise.

Second, programs that choose to may invite practitioners to participate in the planning and implementation of a relevant educational experience for future employees. Being a guest speaker in a class on travel services is admirable, but these stints do not let a business executive advise and influence educators in the planning of the course curriculum. Real collaboration requires formal procedures for putting educators and practitioners together on an ongoing basis to create a partnership for improving management education.

Last, efforts to learn about the hospitality industry as a customer using partnering processes will bring educators and customers together who may have different motives or reasons for entering a partnership. Rather than ignoring or criticizing these differences, partnerships can thrive on the diversity of such a group. Hospitality managers and leaders emerge from places other than business schools. Graduates from the liberal arts, law, and the sciences frequently choose the hospitality field and succeed in leadership positions. These practitioners can highlight skills from their degree programs, which are needed by all hospitality employees. Educators are likely to find that creativity, judgment, interpersonal or social-psychological skills, vision, and ethics are as essential to the student learning process as strong analytical and rational decision-making skills. Practitioners must also balance their goal to find new recruits for their own businesses with a more holistic view of collaboration. The "employment agency" mentality currently dominates most corporate/academic school relationships. This short-term, bottom-line perspective does not encourage the industry participants in a partnering process to empathize and appreciate what the academics wish to accomplish. Colleges and universities require students to have a balanced prebusiness foundation of arts and sciences combined with practical work experience that prepares them for responsible citizenship and personally and socially rewarding lives and careers. Practitioners who contribute to academic processes often do so because they have a personal need to make a difference in the learning experiences of future graduates and/or they wish to find more and better future employees.

ONE MODEL OF COOPERATION— THE ADVISORY COUNCIL

A collaboration model seeks to develop an environment in which student-centered and experiential learning is valued and in which students, faculty members, and practitioners jointly engage in the design of educational improvements. One example for consideration is the use of a hospitality advisory council for cooperative involvement. The remainder of this chapter reviews the issues related to putting a hospitality advisory council in action. As we highlight each issue, we will use italics to show how one university defines the scope and tasks of an advisory council.

Purpose of an Advisory Council

The following is a description of an advisory council that is in place at James Madison University:

> *The purpose of the Hospitality and Tourism Management Council is to enhance collaboration between the Hospitality and Tourism Management Program (HTM) and the business community. The Council will provide advice, insight, and vision to the faculty and students of the HTM Program. Specifically, the Council will engage in strategic planning and curriculum development.*

An advisory council consists of stakeholders who are willing and able to assume leadership roles in the development of complete educational experiences for students in hospitality programs. Members of an advisory council must be able to think strategically when planning complete educational experiences. An effective advisory council will explore a variety of ways in which hospitality management and leadership potential are presently being identified and developed and will entertain an array of new possibilities. Quick fixes for developing program problems or cursory analyses of industry trends and opportunities should not be the focus of an advisory council. A strong commitment to establishing and extending linkages among schools, industry, government, and nonprofit organizations should become a priority.

In defining the council's purpose, the faculty and director of the hospitality program establish the framework and direction of this body. Some councils exist in name only, while some provide a single-dimensional focus, such as fund-raising or internships, and still others are more inclusive, as suggested by the italicized paragraph above. In determining what is best for each program, several factors must be considered—size of program, number of faculty, degree type (certificate, associate, bachelor's, or graduate), support within the unit the hospitality program is housed in, and short- and long-term needs of the program, to name a few.

Objectives for an Advisory Council

Once there is a clear purpose for the advisory council, specific objectives need to be established. One way of looking at these objectives is to view them as destinations. There are many ways of getting to the same location: some will travel by car on expressways, while others may take the scenic roads, and still others may ride a bike there. The important point is that you can determine when you reach your destination. Objectives should be specific enough for you to assess the overall effectiveness of your advisory council.

Council members familiar with this industry will:

1. *Provide advice and counsel to the HTM Director, faculty, and students to assist the program in relating its curriculum to the changing needs of business and society.*

   We, as faculty, pride ourselves in staying current by reading the latest books or attending conferences, but this is not enough. Hospitality professionals working in the trenches day in and day out provide tremendous insight into the necessary elements of an HTM curriculum. Their voice is critical in keeping a program current.

   All hospitality programs should have a mission statement as well as a list of program objectives. The advisory council is the guide by the side, participating in program assessment.

2. *Provide advice and assistance to the HTM Director and faculty on matters related to professional faculty development.*

   Faculty are pulled in many different directions. Skills developed early in academic careers may not be upgraded, and industry innovations may not be studied and incorporated into curricula on a timely basis. The advisory council provides the mirror for faculty to critically look at themselves. More important, council members can encourage hospitality faculty to visit sites, use industry technology, and attend workshops and seminars to upgrade skills.

3. *Support programs that focus on the hospitality industry, such as career and internship fairs, recruiters in residence, hospitality and tourism speaker panels, and hospitality and tourism educational experiences.*

There are many ways the advisory council can help the hospitality program. Some are listed in point 4. The goal is to develop partnerships in which total quality improvement of the hospitality program is the main objective. Historically, if an instructor says something in class, students may react with a nod of the head or some other sign of approval, but when a person from the business world says the same thing, students are far more attentive.

4. *Assist the college, university, and student development centers at the university to create internships and employment opportunities for students.*

   In many schools, the hospitality and tourism management major is not fully understood. Administrators and staff know our students get jobs, but this objective tries to move the council beyond hospitality management to the larger world of business.

5. *Engage in other activities proposed and approved by the Council.*

   All council members have passion for some aspect of education. It is up to the program director and the faculty to find out what that passion is.

Creating an Advisory Council—Selection of Members

The Council will consist of a mix of senior-level executives and recent alumni recommended by members of the Council or Dean of the College of Business and appointed by the Hospitality and Tourism Management Director. Membership is based on exceptional stature in the hospitality industry and/or commitment to the university. Council members, not to exceed twenty-five in number, will be appointed to serve three-year terms with the opportunity for renewal.

The Hospitality and Tourism Management Director will serve as an ex-officio member of the Council and other faculty or administrators of the College of Business and the university community may be appointed to serve in ex-officio capacities to the Council and its committees. Unless there are extenuat-

ing circumstances, no more than one Council member should represent the same organization.

Now that the purpose and objectives for the advisory council are established, it is time to identify and invite potential members to join. This section explores membership selection strategies, establishes the ideal council size and looks at minimum expectations of each council member. The only guarantee with an advisory council of working professionals in the hospitality field is that there will never be 100 percent attendance at a meeting. This guarantee is not limited to hospitality councils, but to all advisory councils, regardless of discipline. Even when a member confirms attendance, business may dictate that the member stay at work rather than come to the meeting. It is important not to construe these absences as disinterest. Rather, initiate a procedure to call or fax regarding absence (or a partial absence). It is frustrating when the calls and faxes come in the morning of the meeting.

Also, it is helpful to not assume there is one best set of individuals to serve on an advisory council. The following paragraphs offer some suggestions for choosing representatives.

Managerial Experience

Given the importance of a strategic orientation to council deliberations, practitioners with upper-level management experience are critical to the success of an advisory council. Representatives who have gained experience in various hospitality areas bring a much richer perspective to discussions centering on needed industry and life skills for hospitality graduates. Senior executives are also less parochial, seeing beyond the need of basic functional skills for specific jobs. Upper-level managers will show sensitivity to the difference of acquiring personal and career growth skills versus specific job skills, while middle-level managers or corporate recruiters will focus almost entirely on the latter.

However, some representation at functional levels is also desirable. Colleges and universities are recognizing the growing importance of specific occupational skills, notably in the areas of information technology and technical expertise. Graduates who choose to acquire conceptual and practical skills in these functions will find that certain areas of the hospitality business will welcome the depth rather than breadth of their training. Advisory councils with practitioners spanning both upper and middle levels of management can take a balanced, short- and long-term view of curriculum development.

More important, managers at all levels must appreciate and participate in discussions involving cross-training of employees. Cross-functional teams greatly increase shared insights and learning, as well as reduce the time involved to initiate and implement change in the workplace. The industry has recognized the merits of cross-training and its importance to competitive excellence. Advisory council members, who encourage similar cross-functional learning at the undergraduate or graduate school level, are recognizing that the more instruction and experience with team building in school, the faster graduates will acclimate to the real world.

Representation Across the Hospitality Industry

A broad definition of the hospitality industry requires broad representation in an academic advisory council. Inclusion of travel and tourism, lodging, restaurant, managed services, special events, and meeting services executives are important to ensure comprehensive coverage of the industry. Various types of hospitality organizations should be included. For-profit businesses, which will hire the majority of the hospitality graduates, should hold many of the council seats. But there are a number of other hospitality institutions, directly or indirectly involved in education, that can contribute to the training of tomorrow's business leaders. National educational associations, such as CHRIE help faculty explain the role of hospitality in today's society and encourage the development of professional hospitality skills. State-sponsored hospitality associations, for example, the New York Restaurant Association and the New York Hotel Association, are eager to participate in the education of future restaurateurs and hoteliers. Local chambers of commerce and business development councils may contribute representatives to advisory councils, given the number of hospitality businesses directly helped by these groups. Trade associations usually will have education and training departments, which may also provide enthusiastic participants to an advisory council.

Multiple Stakeholders

Advisory councils flourish in an environment in which students, faculty members, staff, and practitioners jointly engage in learning, discussions, and strategic change. Thus, advisory members should be selected from all of these walks of life. All stakeholders are encouraged to recommend improvements to the hospitality program. Students are viewed and treated as adults who make informed judgments and choices. Academic change agents, both faculty and staff, should be selected who reflect broadly based academic and extracurricular talents, values, and achievements. As already noted, practitioners must shed parochial or company-specific values and perspectives to embrace shared academic vision and goals for curriculum and/or research development.

A council of multiple stakeholders eliminates the we/they perspective that characterizes so many academic organizational structures. In its place, there is a flat, collegial structure where decisions that affect the academic community typically grow out of a process that thoroughly involves its members.

To summarize, when selecting members to serve on a council, the goal should be to assemble a group with diverse representation but operating with a common vision—to assist academic institutions in delivering the highest quality of educational experience. The following is a summary of the types of hospitality practitioners you might want to include.

Internship Coordinators and Mentors

Most hospitality programs require some type of experiential learning—whether it is an internship, a special project, or a tour of a facility. This is a great way to find potential council members. Ask the interns if they worked with a dynamic manager or department head who was a mentor and seemed interested in the educational process.

Local Business Leaders

As stated earlier, a college town always has multiple hospitality operations, no matter how small the community is. Why not look to some of the local managers to join the advisory council? Inviting a potential council member to a class for a guest lecture is a great way to start. For introductions, there is an obvious need to find out the guest speaker's background, educational preparation, and career path. In addition, based on the presentation, reaction to questions, or student response, you will know if there is a match between the practitioner and the academic community. However, it is important not to make the sole judgment for inviting the manager to join on the basis of a presentation and student feedback. At times it may be appropriate to look beyond classroom popularity and focus on the local practitioner's enthusiasm, dedication, and ability to contribute to the overall hospitality learning experience.

Positive relationships between the local business community and the college are important. There are additional benefits of having local hospitality leaders on the advisory council, such as potential internship sites, tours of local facilities, use of equipment, part-time student jobs, and consulting work for the program.

Alumni

One of the biggest thrills for recent alumni is to come back to campus to share what it is like in the real world. Their energy, message, and ability to relate their current work experience to existing class work are essential to a dynamic council. Recent alumni (fewer than three years since graduation) have less flexible work schedules, but they do have passion.

Parents of Hospitality Students

Once the question is asked, "Who has a parent working in the hospitality field?" a potential list of council members is generated. These individuals have a natural tie to the program, are very concerned about the quality of the curriculum, and have multiple reasons to come back to campus.

It is important to rotate people on and off the council. New ideas and perspectives are cornerstones of successful strategic advisory councils. Also, if the same group stays in place, members begin to play the same roles and this leads to a "business as usual" approach.

Defining Expectations of Council Members

Setting expectations clearly states the level of involvement needed from council participants. You can avoid major disappointments with the realized productivity of an advisory council by articulating your needs and member roles before asking individuals to join the group. Again, the level of involvement is determined by the size of your hospitality program, the type of curricula in place, the enthusiasm of your student body, and the activities of various college and/or university supporting groups (career services, alumni relations, development, etc.).

As a minimum, Council members shall be expected to:

1. *Attend Council meetings. Members missing two meetings in succession will be asked to resign from the Council, unless excused in advance.*

   As stated earlier, situations occur where a council member was planning on being in attendance, but a work emergency occurred. Common courtesy of calling prior to the meeting is an excused absence. This rule should be discussed and voted on by every council member. If all members agree this is the way to handle attendance, the hospitality faculty is not the heavy, but the members themselves.

2. *Provide internship opportunities for students within their firms, and/or linkages to opportunities in other firms.*

   Not all organizations can supply internship sites, but all council members should be able to refer students to firms and other organizations open to student experiential learning opportunities. In addition, part-time and summer jobs should be made available, if appropriate.

3. *Host one faculty and/or student visit per year at their companies during their term as council members.*

   The best way to see the potential connections of a council member is to see the member at work. This opportunity to share perspectives and see possible connections is a great way to develop rapport.

4. *Visit JMU personally, and/or provide another from the firm who will be a guest presenter in HTM 100, the Executive Lecture Series.*

The goal here is a win-win. It means exposure for the council member's company and a chance for the guest speaker to influence the thinking of future professionals.

5. *Assist with the development efforts to support the HTM Program.*

There are many gifts beyond dollar support. Providing a guest lecture by the executive chef or allowing a student team to borrow an item for a class presentation or event are some of the many examples of this "giving to the program."

6. *Aid in mentoring relations with students in the hospitality and tourism program.*

The council member is an excellent sounding board for a hospitality student. The member has the insight of what it takes to be successful in our industry. This sharing with the student begins to develop a mentoring relationship.

Committees

Committees will be created or dissolved as determined by the Hospitality and Tourism Management Director and Council. Committees can be established in the following areas:

- *Curriculum development*
- *Faculty development*
- *Student development and placement*
- *Long-range planning*
- *Resource development*

Breaking advisory council work into committees is one way to move forward on a number of different program fronts. Each industry representative will gravitate toward a particular topic, often based on organizational resources but also because of personal interests. Using topical groups is a great way to get council members involved, rather than allowing them to listen passively to presentations on council meeting days. The only caveat for using committee formats is to make sure there is substantive work to do in each assigned topic area.

"Corporate Culture" Mind-Sets

Even the most dedicated advisory council member from an industry setting will have some difficulty orienting himself or herself to the way work is done in academic contexts. Corporate culture, with its emphasis on quick response for building a competitive advantage, is different from the pace of decision-making in academia. Academics develop curricula and schedules sometimes a year prior to actual teaching. Some of these courses are offered in multiple sections, with many different instructors covering the course sections. Incorporating new hospitality course material identified in advisory council deliberations will take time. Faculty must arrive at a consensus on teaching content and sometimes delivery techniques. Approval for new courses must go through curriculum and instruction review processes, student handbooks must be rewritten, and so on. Funding for academic initiatives covers the same slow, winding path taken by curriculum review. Practitioners may chafe at these bureaucratic timetables and procedures. Program directors and advisory council faculty will find themselves spending time educating practitioners on the ways of academe. Be prepared to help industry representatives function in a strange environment! Their ultimate contributions are worth the effort.

Strategies for Successful Meetings

> *The Council will meet three times each year with at least one meeting in the fall and one in the spring. The HTM Director will coordinate Council activities and advise and assist the Council as needed.*

Oftentimes, it is the little events leading up to a council session and the interactions that do or do not occur during the meeting that determine the success or failure of an advisory council get-together. We have taken our own experiences (both the successes and the failures) and developed a checklist of procedures for running a successful meeting. We have not included a time frame for each step, because the size of the program, availability of resources, and so on really determine the amount of time that must be allotted to each activity. Our parting advice—always build in more time than you think it will take. Faculty never seem to have large chunks of uninterrupted time for thinking and doing.

*Develop a Timetable for Industry Involvement
for the Entire Academic Year*

Provide at least sixty days notice prior to a council meeting. If possible, establish set times for the meetings and distribute these dates for the next year. For example, the last Friday in October and the last Friday in March might be regularly scheduled council sessions. This way the council members have it on their schedules well in advance.

*Link Advisory Council Work
to Recruiting Schedules, if Possible*

It is cost-effective to try to link advisory council meetings with ongoing events such as career fairs, internship fairs, or other regularly scheduled events. It is more difficult to justify two trips in a semester to a school than doing it all at the same time.

*Develop a Timetable of Events
for Twenty-Four to Thirty-Six Hours*

There is no ideal amount of time for a council meeting. The agenda dictates the amount of time necessary. We have found meetings on Fridays work out best. At times we have a social event late on Thursday afternoon for the council, encouraging certain members to talk to Thursday afternoon classes, and then having the formal meeting on Friday. We have also had some success with meetings on Friday, with a final wrap on Saturday morning followed by some type of social event—a football or basketball game.

Student Sessions

Student interaction both formally and informally is well received. At JMU, we brought the advisory council to a class where students had prepared for some questions dealing with the use of the Internet. Web sites were pulled up in class and referred to during the discussions. Both students and industry executives enthusiastically joined the discussion. Or, you might consider attending a class and using small group sessions to discuss a program topic, combining practitioners and students in each small group. Practitioners all agree that the student sessions are some of the most preferred agenda sessions.

Strategic Sessions

Advisory council members are successful businesspeople who are normally in charge and do not like to be talked at. The importance of this fact to the success of a council cannot be emphasized enough. Be sure to have substantive strategic reviews and discussions planned where practitioners can make a contribution.

Awards Sessions

Recognition of council members, as well as student and faculty success, is paramount. All the better if council members' organizations are sponsors of a particular student award. Industry representatives appreciate seeing their company's efforts recognized and linked to a particular student's success.

Photo Sessions

A picture tells a thousand words. Companies who sponsor student awards like to see their efforts detailed in a program or school newsletter. Many council members appreciate a picture to take back to their organizations to show the level of involvement they have with program events.

Update of University Events

Plan on having a session early in the meeting that reviews major changes in the program or college. A significant shift in mission or goals, organizational structures, or resources creates contextual changes, which may influence council decision making. Think broadly as you review university changes; restructuring within career services or student advising centers may necessitate changes in the way council members' organizations interact with your university. They will appreciate these updates.

Technology Demonstrations

As the use of information technology becomes even more prevalent in hospitality programs, you may want to include student demonstrations of how they use technology to solve problems or improve operations. Or, consider having one of the council members whose organization donates technology—software or hardware—demonstrate its application in an advisory council session. Seeing technology in use, followed by a discussion of how to use applications in the curriculum, may spark other practitioners to donate items to your hospitality programs.

Break-Out Sessions

If you are using committees to involve council members in a number of strategic issues, you may want to have break-out sessions as one way to bring council participants up to speed on developments in topics outside of their area of expertise. Leaders of each strategic area can chair the sessions.

Reserve Rooms for Meetings, Receptions, Meals, Classes, and Break-Out Sessions

Be sure to review the kinds of sessions you will have during the meeting. Planned sessions and expected number of participants influence the kind of room setup you will want. Council sessions always work best when participants are seated in a way that maximizes free-flow discussions. Chair placement, whether at a large conference table or in U-shaped work-table formats, encourages discussion. If you are planning a long advisory council meeting, vary your session settings. Participants will welcome the variability and change of scenery.

Develop a Hotel Strategy

Reserve a block of rooms for council participants who must travel a great distance to the meeting. Some organizations expect their employees to use specific hotels for business travel. When we are getting a head count for the council meeting, we send out a confirmation form (to be faxed back to us), listing where a block of rooms is being held, other hotels in the area with their phone numbers, and a response form for whether a student ambassador will be needed as a driver. These measures insure quick confirmation and a minimum of last-minute arrangement changes.

Communicate with Your Members

Use mailings. As previously mentioned, keep council participants informed of meeting dates, agendas, and any prior work you expect council members to do in preparation for the meeting.

Electronic Distribution Lists

This communication vehicle is becoming quite popular as more organizations assign electronic mail addresses to their employees. If you have committees, each one might use a distribution list to keep committee members informed of needed work and information.

Proceedings and Other Documents

Develop proceedings for the council meeting, which includes a table of contents, day schedule at a glance, and a listing of all council members. This document should be bound and as professional looking as possible. Include samples of university publications, particularly if hospitality activities are highlighted. Include campus maps, notepaper and pen, and other items needed throughout the day. This packet is easy to send out to potential council members or to members who missed the meeting.

Remember the Tangibles

Tangibles might include:

- Parking
- Welcome signs
- Welcome gift

- Orient new council members
- Campus tours
- University/program literature and videos

CONCLUSION

The goal of this chapter is to encourage hospitality educators to look beyond their academic communities to the wealth of interest and assistance in creating valuable links to industry. These links can be established in a variety of ways including student internships, association membership, and the use of advisory councils. Industry practitioners are often eager to assist in any way possible. In short, the stronger ties that can be established with the hospitality industry, the more effectively certain objectives can be achieved.

Chapter 4

Quality and Its Assurance in Hospitality Education

George G. Fenich

INTRODUCTION

Higher education, like most businesses and organizations today, is increasingly concerned about the quality of its goods and services. There is increased competition for a shrinking pool of students and those students (customers) are becoming more sophisticated and demanding. While some organizations make products that are largely tangible, higher education's product is largely intangible. As a result, assurance of quality can be more difficult than in traditional manufacturing industries. Further, unlike tangible goods, the higher education product cannot be returned if the customer is dissatisfied. The money-back guarantee is virtually unheard of. The process of total quality management (TQM) must be a goal of higher education, if higher education is to survive in the twenty-first century.

But, to understand this objective, quality, the term must be defined and discussed. *Webster's* dictionary defines quality as not only the basic character or characteristic that makes something good or bad, commendable or reprehensible, but also the degree of excellence a thing possesses, or superiority. Webster's goes on to define quality control or assurance as a system for maintaining desired standards in a product. These two definitions comprise the most simplistic basis for achieving quality assurance in any organization, including higher education. As will be seen later, the concepts of basic character and maintaining standards is at the heart of the accreditation process. Obviously an organization must define itself, as through a mission statement and then set goals and objectives that will support that mission before it can hope to measure its outcome against the stated goals. This is quality assurance. There are distinct parallels between higher education and the business community in their collective concern for quality assurance.

"Quality is everybody's job, part of our job requirements. You cannot create quality without a quality culture in your organization. Change in culture starts from a change in leadership culture and continues only with continuous measurement and feedback" (Lickson, Kauppinen, and Ogg, 1994, p. 7). This quote applies equally to businesses and to hospitality management programs. Luckily, the concept of total quality management (TQM) has become widespread during the 1990s and, even if it is slow to adopt business concepts, the academy is embracing TQM.

The global quality assurance movement is increasing business's capacity to survive increased competition. So too, it will be with higher education. In both, customer expectations have been raised. What were heretofore considered high standards are now barely acceptable to ever more demanding customers. "Quality process management is fast becoming an organizational survival skill" (Lickson, Kauppinen, and Ogg, 1994, p. 7). Total quality management is a system of delineating, measuring, and periodically comparing objectives and outcomes, with the goal of improving organizational work processes, products, and services. The purpose is to deliver perceived quality and value to the customer.

ISSUES OF QUALITY IN HIGHER EDUCATION

The quest for quality in hospitality management programs cannot be separated from the broader issues of quality within the overall organization. Thus, this section begins with a review of organizational theory and structure in the academy. This is followed by a more focused discourse on quality in hospitality management programs that includes a colloquy about the relationship of programmatic, human, physical, financial, and learning resources to achievement of quality. The section concludes with a review of the need for accountability of hospitality management programs to all constituencies.

Quality and Structure of Higher Education

As was mentioned in the introduction, the quest for quality is not undertaken in a vacuum, but is inherently dependent on the organization. How an organization defines itself, what it ascertains to be its product mix, and the expectations it creates in its customers will all work together to set the parameters for quality. For example, Ritz Carlton and Red Roof Inns are both lodging companies whose core product is a comfortable night's sleep for travelers away from home. Yet the quality of their products, both tangible and intangible, is very different. The absolute level of quality is vastly superior at the Ritz Carlton. But, is that to say that Red Roof Inns cannot achieve quality? Of course they can! They can achieve quality because they define their product differently than Ritz Carlton and create an expectation in the customer that is different, that does not include as much in the way of service and amenities. But how do these two companies, and others, differentiate themselves?

The basis for differentiation, and the first thing an organization or company must do, is to define itself. This is done by creating a mission, what the company is about and what it hopes to achieve. But, in order to have guests and employees who understand the company mission, it must be shared with them. This is accomplished through the mission statement, which is usually disseminated in written form, but can be shared through various media including audio, as in a president's speech, or visually through advertising on television. After the mission statement is developed, organizational goals and objectives are created which, if met, allow the organization to accomplish its mission. In higher education, a mission statement is almost always found in the university catalog, which allows consumers to understand what that particular institution is all about. The institution may have a mission to be an international center of the highest level of learning in the world such as Harvard University, or to be a world-class medical research institution such as Johns Hopkins. On the other hand, the institution may be a community college whose mission is to serve the needs of the local populace in providing both degree granting and continuing education. Because these institutions have defined themselves differently, their measures of quality will also be different, yet all can potentially provide excellent quality.

Still another important concept in understanding quality assurance is the structure of academic institutions. Colleges and universities tend to be very tall organizations with multiple layers of bureaucracy. In the case of a large university, the structure will include different divisions under which may lie specific colleges, which in turn contain various schools and/or departments. The structural issue concerns the interrelationship between these units. More specifically, the mission of each unit or segment must be compatible, or there will be conflict and quality will suffer. Further, the relationship of each mission to the other is sequential; the mission of the department must be compatible with and help to achieve the mission of the college, while the mission of the college must work with the mission of the institution.

It is particularly important for potential hospitality educators to understand this relationship between academic units because it will affect hospitality management's ability to achieve quality. It will also affect programmatic offerings, the qualifications of faculty, and so on. For example, there has been a trend in recent years for hospitality management programs to move into colleges of business. Given the mission of a college of business, will hospitality management programs be able to offer many, if any, culinary classes? Is learning how to cook compatible with the typical mission of a college of business? Conversely, many hospitality management programs are housed in colleges of home economics. Will the latter programs be able to offer classes in such things as casino gaming and still help to achieve the mission of the college of home economics? On a more personal level, will the individual instructor with a degree in business fit in and help to achieve the mission of a hospitality management unit housed in a nutrition setting where clinical certification is needed? Obviously, the qualifications of an individual instructor need to support the mission of the program, which helps to achieve the goals and objectives of the higher-level units in the institution. Given that this book is directed toward hotel, restaurant, and tourism programs, I will discuss the individual program.

Quality of Hospitality Management Programs

The relative level of quality in a hospitality management program is directly related to resources. Programs with more resources such as an expansive curriculum, greater numbers of faculty, a higher level of physical amenities, more money, or better learning resources should achieve a higher level of absolute quality. Their goals should be high and their standards very rigorous. It is critical for faculty, particularly those new to the ranks of academe, to understand the resources available in their hospitality management program and the effect on achievement of quality.

Programmatic Resources

One of the aspects of the hospitality management unit that affects quality is the organization and structure of the unit itself; its curriculum, its prestige, the number of student organizations, and its governance structure. The relative complexity of the hospitality management unit will have a major impact on the absolute level of quality it expects to achieve as well as the ease or difficulty in achieving relative quality. For example, a hospitality management unit that exists as a stand-alone college, has over thirty faculty, offers degrees through the doctorate, and offers upward of fifty courses per semester will probably have a higher absolute level of quality than a unit with one instructor and five courses. Further, while the first unit is much more complex and the overall effort to achieve quality may be greater, neither the large nor the small is necessarily positioned to achieve their goals of quality.

Concerns about curriculum include many areas, all of which must be considered in trying to maintain quality assurance; the most obvious aspects are the courses themselves. Quality assurance must consider the complete mix of courses. One also needs to be concerned with the skills and competencies each course is expected to develop in the student. The most obvious quality assurance measure is the comprehensive final examination. Still another aspect of the courses themselves is whether each course is required or elective. While maintaining quality is important in all courses, it might be more important to achieve high quality in the required courses since (1) greater numbers of students take them than elective courses and

(2) required courses are often the foundation for upper-level or elective courses. Compounding the difficulty in maintaining quality in required courses can be: (1) since all students must take them some will be less interested and less prepared, such as the student who is interested in food and beverage being required to take a lodging operations course, and (2) since many required courses are taught at lower levels or earlier in a student's course of study, newer, less experienced professors may be assigned to teach these classes. On the other hand, elective courses are important because (1) it is through these courses that students gain the specialized knowledge they need to be successful in their careers, (2) an appropriate (to the mission of the program) number of electives are required by many accrediting groups, and (3) electives may be the means by which students develop linkages with specialized aspects of the industry, which will enhance career opportunities.

Another aspect of curriculum that affects quality is the sequencing of courses. This was alluded to earlier with regard to required courses being the foundation for more advanced courses. But, are the courses offered in a cycle that allows students to progress through the curriculum in a timely fashion? Are they offered so as to not conflict with one another? Are some courses listed in the catalog almost never offered? Obviously, the answers to these questions will affect the quality of the program.

Still another basic aspect of curriculum is the availability of majors and minors. In some programs, everyone is simply a hospitality management major and takes the same classes without regard for their unique interests. I am even aware of one program in which the hospitality management majors were forbidden from referring to themselves as such and were required to use the name of the college in defining their course of study, in this case home economics. Often, this offering of a single major with no minors occurs in new and/or small programs with limited resources and where the students may take a plethora of courses outside of hospitality management in such areas as liberal arts, business, mathematics, language, etc. On the other hand are programs where virtually the entire course of study consists of hospitality management courses. The latter may have the potential to achieve a higher absolute level of quality, but attaining it may be more difficult because of the complexity of the offerings. The opposite could also be true since, in the case of the latter, the program has control over all the courses, while in the former, control rests outside the hospitality management program.

An important issue that comes up repeatedly in accreditation reviews is the mix of theoretical versus applied courses contained in the curriculum. Again, there is no absolute balance of the two, but rather the mix depends upon the mission of the program. If the goal is to train chefs, as in the case of the well-known Culinary Institute of America, then having of majority of courses that include hands-on experience would be appropriate. The reverse would be true of a more research-oriented program such as that found at Virginia Polytechnic Institute where lab courses, especially at the master's and doctoral levels, might be inappropriate. However, there are other programmatic issues that will affect quality.

One of those aspects is the prestige or status of the hospitality management unit. Those with higher levels of prestige might be expected to have a higher level of aggregate quality, while the reverse might be true of the others. The concept of prestige will also vary among constituencies. For instance, companies that hire graduates of hospitality programs will have a set of standards that might be based on how long the hospitality management unit has been in existence (e.g., Cornell), where graduates find employment, or whether the employer graduated from that institution. The level of prestige garnered by the hospitality management unit is also a function of how highly it is regarded by other units within the institution. In spite of its prestige in the industry, a program that commands national respect might not command the same level of respect from its peers within the university. On the other hand, the School of HRT at the University of New Orleans is well respected within the college of business where it is housed and has prestige in the university, but is not as highly regarded by national employers since most graduates choose not to relocate outside the New Orleans area. Still another element of prestige is how faculty at other hospitality management programs view the unit under review. This assessment may be based on the number of publications by faculty in the unit under review, their involvement in regional and national associations (such as CHRIE), or even how well graduates of a two-year program do when they transfer to a four-year program. Once again we see a factor, prestige, that is instrumental in setting the stage for the absolute and relative levels of quality expected of a hospitality management unit and, once again, the standard will vary from unit to unit and among those constituencies setting those standards.

The quality of the programmatic areas of the hospitality management unit will also be affected by the governance structure utilized. Are there clear and well-defined channels of communication that facilitate changes to the program offerings or does change take so long that no one bothers to attempt it, or by the time the change is implemented, the initial reason for it no longer exists?

The lines of authority also must be clear if quality is to be assured. For example, do the faculty and/or students have input into offerings or is that the sole purview of a dogmatic director? The hospitality management unit must also have reasonable autonomy in course offerings to maintain quality. In some cases, even elective courses must be approved by units outside of hospitality management that have their own best interest at heart. Still another function of governance is the assignment of faculty to classes. If it is done based on faculty skill and knowledge, it will enhance programmatic quality. If the newest faculty gets the biggest, lowest level, or worst time for classes, it will cause an erosion of quality. There must be balance. The discussion of faculty takes us into another area of the hospitality management unit that will affect quality: human resources.

Human Resources

Although many people may think that the human resources in a hospitality management unit consists solely of the faculty, this is not the case. Other human resources include the various support staff. Without adequate numbers and skill in each of these human resources areas, program quality will suffer.

Arguably, faculty are the most important of the human resources. It is the faculty who teach the courses, guide the program, deal with students, and interface with industry. But what are some of the factors that affect the quality of hospitality management unit faculty? On the broad level, the answer includes preparation for teaching or research assignments and is based on academic preparation, industry work experience, and professional development or self-improvement. The latter is often accomplished through faculty internships and attendance at conferences or workshops. Other things that will affect faculty quality in the unit include teacher-to-student ratios. Very high ratios will hamper interaction and thus reduce quality. That is not to say that hospitality management programs with low faculty/student ratios always do better. For example, some hospitality management programs have a single instructor, albeit with a small number of students, but the problem is that the single instructor must teach *all* of the hospitality management classes, including those outside his or her area of expertise.

Another factor highly related to student ratios is course load, or the number of course sections a professor must teach each semester or quarter. This will vary based on a number of factors. Looking at course load itself, faculty dealing with doctoral-level work may only teach one course, faculty teaching at the bachelors level typically teach three or four, and instructors at community colleges often teach upward of six classes per semester. This course load may be reduced if a faculty member teaches one or more laboratory courses, such as a food preparation class, which take more than the typical three contact hours per week. As a result, three lab courses might be the equivalent of four nonlab courses or a lab course might carry four credits compared to the typical three credits for a lecture course. Research activity or administrative work may result in a reduced course load. It should be clear that lower course loads allow a faculty member to devote more time to the remaining courses, or allow more time to interface with students, thus enhancing program quality. Good course delivery takes time to prepare, as does outcome assessment in the form of evaluating student work.

Another human resources issue that is particularly problematic in hospitality management, is salary. It is difficult to attract and keep good quality faculty if salaries are below par, but again, par differs between programs. A program housed in a standalone school or a college of business may be able to offer higher salaries than units located in home economics or nutrition departments, regardless of the background of the faculty. It goes without saying that there is a positive correlation between salary and quality of employee. Further clouding the salary issue is the fact that, based on the prestige of the hospitality management unit, it may or may not offer pay scales that are on par with other departments within the institution. Unfortunately, hospitality management units sometimes offer proportionally lower salaries, thus attracting potentially less qualified faculty.

One of the most important factors in program quality is the quality and quantity of laboratory support staff. If faculty using a lab can focus their efforts on delivery of the course work with a lab technician available to be sure the lab is stocked and functional, quality will be enhanced. Clerical or secretarial staff is also important. Any faculty member who has worked in a department that was without a secretary or administrative assistant, even for a short period, will attest to the difficulty of keeping the unit running. Even making copies of tests can take considerable time and will take time away from more important issues such as class preparation or research. While not the case in all hospitality management units, some benefit from help from teaching assistants (TAs), research assistants (RAs), and student work/study employees. These latter types of resources can often enhance program quality while being very cost effective. However, programs can try to be *too* cost effective, as by having TAs teach classes on their own.

While less important than the former, maintenance support staff can affect program quality. This is particularly true in food production labs, where sanitation and equipment maintenance is of prime importance. But there are other areas, such as computer labs, that require maintenance. Even office space and classroom quality diminish if not properly cleaned and maintained.

Physical Resources

While the core product of higher education, knowledge, is intangible, the tangible elements play a major role in program quality. Just think for a minute about what might attract the typical freshman to a particular hospitality management unit. Is it the quality of instruction? The quality of the research? The quality of the skills and knowledge they will acquire? No! It is the physical setting, what the place looks like, how new versus run-down it is. In looking specifically at hospitality management programs as compared to institutions, there are several physical factors that affect quality. First are the classrooms, which vary from high-quality facilities with integrated instructional media, comfortable chairs, and even distance learning capabilities, to cement boxes with not much more than a chalkboard (and probably no chalk), and chairs that are less comfortable than bleacher seats. Many students are even more concerned about the laboratories, especially those devoted to food production. Are they new, modern, replicas of state-of-the-art commercial kitchens? Or are they full of antiquated institutional food production equipment that some restaurant discarded? Some food labs even use home kitchen products that are little like those found in restaurants and institutional kitchens. Further, some hospitality management programs that teach food courses do not even have a food laboratory. Other labs such as computer facilities are equally important to program quality and may be even harder to keep up to date. There are alternatives to an in-house food lab. These can include contracting for use of a commercial kitchen off site, using the kitchen of a nearby restaurant during slow periods, or having students work in on-campus food production facilities. In any case, the quality of equipment has to be assured.

Another physical issue is that of faculty offices. To maintain high standards, they must provide for faculty needs within the context of the mission of the program and institution. Generally that would mean having a private office with appropriate equipment such as a telephone and computer, with privacy for counseling students. The level of appointments along with size will also enhance quality, or at least the feeling of quality in the mind of the instructor. Sharing offices does not enhance quality and may motivate a faculty member to spend time away from the program and its students. A well organized and stocked hospitality management program office will also enhance the effectiveness of the unit. Allied to, but not exactly the same as, physical resources are learning resources.

Learning Resources

Labs are both a physical resource and a learning resource. A hospitality management unit has to rely on internal and external learning resources, with both their availability and modernness influencing quality. Probably the first learning resource that comes to mind is the library, which can be located in the hospitality management unit, as part of a central university library, or both. The critical issues include the quantity, quality, and currency of hospitality-related materials as well as appropriateness, that is, is the conceptual rigor of holdings in tune with the needs of the hospitality management students; the hours of operation and availability for student use; the location of the library and its proximity to the hospitality management unit, that is, is the main library on a campus other than that of the hospitality management unit; and accessibility to members of the campus community with disabilities.

Still another, and critically important, learning resource today is the computer. Every hospitality management program must have access to computing resources as a minimum standard. This might include: programs specific to hospitality such as Top of the House, a CAD program for the design course; access to the Internet for both students and faculty; and word processing, spreadsheet, statistics, graphics, and database programs. The hardware must also be of sufficient quality and quantity to keep pace with the rapidly changing environment. Of course, all of these physical resources cannot be acquired and maintained without money.

Financial Resources

Financial resources that relate to hospitality management programs include operating funds along with capital investment. Also, the short- and long-term financial health of all the units in the institution above the hospitality management unit will have a significant bearing on the ability of the hospitality management unit to maintain and/or enhance quality. One of the primary elements that all accrediting groups assess is the financial stability of the entire organization. At issue in hospitality programs is, often, the question of whether such programs get a fair share of the financial resources. This relates to the status of the program, its prestige, governance structure, etc. New faculty would do well to delve into the financial status of a program before accepting a position. The type of institution, whether public or private, will have a bearing on the availability of financial resources. The former tend to be more stable over the long term, but face increasing budgetary constraints, while the latter tend to be more entrepreneurial, with greater opportunity for program development while also being riskier, financially.

The financial resources available to a hospitality management unit do not come solely from the institution. Some programs have been very successful in obtaining outside funding to support program initiatives. For example, many programs have endowed chairs such as those supported by Coca Cola, Hilton, Harrah's, Darden Foods, etc., where funds, often over a million dollars, have been earmarked for the ongoing support of a senior faculty position, with a commensurate enhancement in program quality. Still another resource that can enhance quality is the solicitation of donations from groups such as alumni, industry, or charitable organizations and which are either restricted or unrestricted funds. Lastly, some hospitality management programs such as those at Pennsylvania State or Purdue University do well in garnering competitive research grants that not only underwrite a specific project, but contribute to overhead and expenses in the hospitality management unit. Outside funding can be an excellent way to enhance the quality, prestige, and status of a hospitality management unit.

Summary of Quality in the Hospitality Management Program

As can be seen, numerous interrelated issues affect quality in a hospitality management unit, and the ultimate measures of quality may vary. Today, the primary basis for judging quality and its assurance rests largely on the mission of the hospitality management unit. This allows for programs that are vastly different in nature or characteristics to each achieve quality in their own way. The achievement of quality is dependent to a large degree upon the resources that the hospitality management unit can bring to bear. These resources can be categorized as: programmatic resources, human resources, physical resources, learning resources, and financial resources. But it is not the mere existence of these resources that assure quality. Rather, there must be an implementation strategy for regular and periodic assessment of how well the hospitality management unit is achieving its stated goals and objectives.

The hospitality management unit is accountable to many constituencies as it assesses its achievement of goals, objectives, and quality. It does not do it in a vacuum (or at least it should not). In a global sense, the hospitality management unit must be accountable to the society of which it is a part for providing adequate, appropriate, and superior-quality education that meets the wants and needs of society. If it cannot do that, it should not exist. The hospitality management unit is also accountable to its core customer, the students, for providing them with high quality education in a timely fashion (eight years to acquire a bachelor's degree is not timely), and the buyers of its product, the hospitality and tourism industry. The other major set of stakeholders to whom the unit is accountable are its employees, for providing a positive and stimulating work environment that affords a decent standard of living. But, even if the hospitality management program and its faculty understand the elements that affect quality, how can it be sure it is achieving quality? How can it measure its progress? How can it assure quality to its various constituencies? The answer is through quality assessment, and subsequent enhancement. Discussion of the means and methods that can be employed by hospitality management units in doing this are the focus of the next section of the chapter.

EXTERNAL MEANS AND METHODS OF ASSURING QUALITY

There are numerous ways that a hospitality management unit can seek to measure and enhance quality. Discussion will follow a management theory approach by breaking them into two general categories. The first are external, which are means for assuring quality undertaken by groups outside the direct control of the unit. This can include such things as accreditation, external reviews, certifications, and industry boards. The second is internal, which are activities undertaken by groups within the direct control of the unit. This might include reviews by administrators, by peers, and by (or of) students. Once again, the goal is quality assessment and enhancement as delineated by the mission of the hospitality management unit.

Accreditation

"Accreditation [is] defined as a voluntary process in which recognition is granted to educational programs which meet or exceed established standards of educational quality. One of the inherent problems in the application of the accreditation process lies in the identification of educational quality, an elusive and subjective concept" (Tanke, 1986, p. 50). There are two kinds, or levels, of accreditation. The first is institutional accreditation, which historically involved the U.S. Department of Education and the Council on Post Secondary Accreditation (COPA). This level of accreditation was driven by the need to assure the public in the United States that, if an institution was accredited, it had some acceptable, albeit minimum, level of educational quality. The U.S. government was involved because it underwrites student grants along with loans and wanted to be assured it was getting what it paid for. A number of regional bodies were developed to undertake institutional accreditation and include such groups as: the New England Association of Colleges and Schools (the oldest of the regional accrediting groups), the Southern Association of Colleges and Schools (SACS), and so on. Accreditation by the regional groups assured an institution that it could obtain federal support and that its credits would be transferable among all the regionally accredited institutions. Faculty perusing employment advertising will also see that most positions require that degrees come from accredited institutions.

The other type of accreditation is programmatic. Here, the individual discipline or program of study within an institution is reviewed by a body composed of experts in that area. This may be thought of as a means of self-regulation. The medical field is thought to be one of the first to organize its own specialized accrediting body before the turn of the twentieth century and was followed, shortly thereafter, by the formation of the Association of American Law Schools in 1900. Representatives from seventeen schools of business met in 1916 to form the American Association of Collegiate School of Business (AACSB) with the express purpose being the promotion and improvement of business higher education in North America (Tanke, 1986).

Accrediting Bodies in Hospitality

The field of hospitality management has more than one accrediting body. The oldest one is the American Dietetics Association (ADA), which reviews programs in nutrition and dietetics. The

American Culinary Federation (ACF) accredits vocational and two-year food service programs, while the National Recreation and Parks Association (NRPA) accredits tourism programs. Two newer bodies were formed since the late 1980s, both of which are allied with the Council of Hotel, Restaurant, and Institutional Education (CHRIE). They include the Accreditation Commission for Programs in Hospitality Administration (ACPHA), which assesses baccalaureate programs, and the Commission on Accreditation of Hospitality Management (CAHM), which recently began reviewing two-year programs in hospitality and tourism. All of these accrediting bodies seek to assess and enhance the quality of specialized programmatic offerings in their field or discipline. But there are some bodies that strive to enhance quality through certification.

ACPHA Accreditation

The Accreditation Commission for Programs in Hospitality Administration (ACPHA) is the body that accredits baccalaureate hospitality management programs. It was established in 1988 because of concerns about educational quality and accountability. It set, as its charge, the establishment of a process of accreditation, standards that would be applicable to all hospitality management programs, and an organizational structure that embraced the widest possible range of educational constituencies. Rather than attempting to accomplish everything at once, the commission decided to limit its scope, initially, to the review and endorsement of four-year programs in hospitality management. Since its inception, the responsibility for reviewing two-year programs has been deferred to CAHM, an offshoot of ACPHA. Plans to accredit graduate programs remain on hiatus. Both commissions are allied with CHRIE but the linkage is in the area of finance and administration while the commissions remain totally autonomous in reaching accreditation decisions.

The overall objectives in accreditation of hospitality programs are to: "(1) provide public assurance that programs in hospitality administration are of acceptable quality, (2) provide guidance to programs in the continued improvement of their educational offerings and related activities, and (3) promote educational and ethical standards of professional education and enhance the public understanding of the hospitality field" (CHRIE, 1989, p. 5). Thus, the two primary goals of ACPHA are hospitality management unit assessment and enhancement: to review programs, determine their strengths and weaknesses, and to make recommendations regarding how to bolster the weaknesses. A secondary objective is to confer accredited status on programs that have met or surpassed the minimum standards set by ACPHA. To date, approximately forty hospitality management units have achieved ACPHA-accredited status. The group includes well-known programs such as those of Purdue University, Pennsylvania State University, and the University of Massachusetts along with some lesser-known colleagues such as Mercyhurst College, the University of North Texas, and Widener University.

ACPHA has developed a set of thirteen standards that relate to (1) course offerings or knowledge base, (2) faculty, and (3) support resources. These standards are a tremendous step forward for the field of hospitality management education in that this is the first time that a universal set of guidelines, or benchmarks, that applies nationwide has been developed and can be used to assure quality. They are delineated in the *Handbook of Accreditation* (CHRIE, 1989) and can be used by hospitality management units, regardless of whether they plan to pursue accredited status. The application of these standards by ACPHA is not a "one size fits all" or "cookie cutter" approach whereby all hospitality management programs who achieve accredited status would look the same; rather, programs are mission driven. The evaluation by ACPHA is based on how well the program is achieving its stated mission, goals, and objectives and whether plans are in place for continuous improvement.

ACPHA Process. The path to achieving accredited status is lengthy. It begins when the hospitality management unit applies to ACPHA for consideration. Some minimum thresholds are required of the hospitality management unit in terms of the number of graduating classes they have processed, number of faculty, financial stability of the host institution, and autonomy in decision making. Assuming the thresholds are surpassed, the unit then begins a self-study in which a year-long assessment, or internal review, is undertaken by the hospitality management unit, to assess its strengths and weaknesses, provide supporting documentation, and establish plans for continuous improvement. The self-study culminates in a lengthy report which is forwarded to the commission. At that point, a date for a site visit along with the makeup of the site visit team is negotiated between the hospitality management unit and the commission. Team members are forwarded the self-study report for extensive review prior to arrival for the site visit. The team typically consists of no less than three members, and upward of double that number for large and/or complex programs. The visit lasts three days and the objective of the team is to ascertain the accuracy of the self-study report and not to do their own form of mini self-study. The team is responsible for producing a report on its findings which is shared, verbally, with the hospitality management unit before the team departure, and subsequently in written form.

The remainder of the ACPHA accrediting process is rather bu-reaucratic. The hospitality management unit can respond to the team report and add any documentation that clarifies its position. Then, prior to a commission meeting, two commissioners are charged with reviewing all the documentation including the self-study, the team report, the hospitality management unit response to the team report, and the team's recommendation regarding accred-ited status. They then summarize the reports for presentation to the commission for action. ACPHA can take three different actions with regard to accredited status of the hospitality management unit. It can (1) grant accredited status for a period of up to seven years, (2) deny accredited status, in which case the unit must wait at least one year before reapplying, or (3) it can defer making a decision. The hospitality management unit cannot appeal the final decision of the commission. Hospitality management units that are granted ac-credited status must produce an annual report that delineates any changes in the program that might affect accredited status and also assesses how well they are achieving their stated goals of self-improvement. In some cases, the hospitality management unit may be required to produce more lengthy interim reports, or even to have a follow-up site visit.

The ACPHA accrediting process has had mixed reactions from the hospitality management education community. On the positive side, it has made a significant impact in improving the quality of hospitality management programs, regardless of whether the unit has achieved accredited status or not. This is particularly true of newer and/or smaller programs who may not have the internal expertise to accomplish a broad-based review. ACPHA and its process has also encouraged programs to undertake extensive self-assessment that would not have otherwise occurred and the ACPHA self-study report, along with team reports, have allowed many hospitality management units to garner additional resources from their respective institutions. The other positive aspect has been increased prestige among many of the accredited programs.

ACPHA accreditation has also seen some less than stellar results. Many of the large and better-known programs have shunned AC-PHA until they could determine who was "admitted to the club" and, once they saw that other than the best-known programs achieved accredited status, declined to be involved. Further, the desire among programs to become accredited has not been as great as expected, which is evidenced by the fact that only about forty of the over 175 four-year programs in hospitality management have been accredited. (Note: very few have been denied accredited status.) Only the future will tell if ACPHA accreditation is a permanent part of the quality assurance initiatives among hospitality management units.

Certification

Whereas accreditation reviews institutions and programs, certification deals with individuals. Those organizations involved in nationwide certification usually require some delineated course of study to be completed by the individual, but it does not always have to be from a particular institution. In some cases, the program or institution must be approved by the same group that is certifying the individual. The certifying body then administers one or more examinations to assess the skills and abilities of the applicant before issuing a certificate. Sometimes, the certifying body requires commensurate industry experience before an individual is eligible for certification. The ADA and ACF both accredit and do certifications. One of the better-known certifying groups is the Educational Institute of the American Hotel & Motel Association, which administers course work and subsequent testing to confer the title Certified Hotel Administrator (CHA), Certified Financial Administrator (CFA), and so on. Other groups such as the Club Managers Association of America and Meeting Planners International (MPI) also administer certifications based upon strict standards.

Not all certifications are national. In fact, many hospitality management units offer certificate programs outside of their traditional education offerings, which are designed to be short and/or intensive training in a specific area of hospitality management. These certificates do attest to some level of expertise or quality on the part of the individual who gets certified, but will vary from as little as a few hours of instruction to quite extensive programs of work experience and education. The old adage holds true in these instances that the certificate is "only as good as the paper it is written on" or, in other words, the quality and reputation of the program offering the certificate. However, at any level, certifications and accreditation all seek to ascertain that the institution, program, or individual that is approved has met some relatively universal standard of quality. Obviously, the latter certificate programs tend to be done on a local, rather than national level. There are two other methods of undertaking local-level review by external groups: outside peer review and industry boards.

Outside Peer Review

Accreditation is one type of quality assessment that uses reviewers from outside the hospitality management unit. But this is not the only review that uses those resources. Many hospitality management units, either of their own volition, or as required by the institution, make use of peers from outside the unit, and often outside the institution, to do an assessment of the hospitality management unit. One or more individuals knowledgeable in hospitality management programs are brought to campus for a multiday site visit. They undertake an assessment of all aspects of the hospitality management unit, including all those types of resources discussed earlier. The reviewers will write a report of their findings and, sometimes, do an exit interview to give a preliminary idea of the findings, prior to departing campus. Less often, one or more reviewers are engaged to assess the hospitality management unit without a site visit, using solely written means. This method of quality assurance is less effective and is most often used when the focus of review is rather narrow, say the syllabi and course sequencing for a new program of study. In either case, the adequacy of the assessment and the validity of the results are totally dependent upon (1) having accurate and factual information available to the reviewers and (2) using reviewers who are knowledgeable and unbiased. I am aware of more than one situation in which an outside reviewer was brought in to validate the predetermined decision to terminate the program director. This is, obviously, not the best use of outside reviewers. While faculty from other hospitality management programs can undertake outside reviews, so too can industry practitioners.

Outside Review by Industry

Although outside reviewers from other hospitality management programs may be very adept at assessing the hospitality management unit's quality in terms of program offerings and so on, they may be less qualified to help with outcome assessments. These types of assessment usually focus on the skills, knowledge, and abilities imparted to students in the program, particularly in terms of what makes them better able to handle jobs in the field of hospitality management. So, it is not surprising the practitioners from industry may be called upon to undertake these types of assessments.

There are a number of means and methods of utilizing practitioners for outside reviews. One way is to have employers complete some type of research instrument that assesses their satisfaction with graduates of the hospitality management unit. Are the graduates well prepared for their positions? Do they have the requisite skills, knowledge, and abilities to be successful? The research strategy for this form of quality assurance can range from an informal discussion with the hospitality management unit director over lunch to a very formal, highly quantitative survey that lists those core competencies and then scores them on a scale, ultimately resulting in some form of statistical analysis of many graduates. This might be considered a post hoc approach to quality assurance, that is, an assessment after the fact and without the opportunity to enhance the abilities of those already graduated. A similar approach can be used to assess current students' skills and abilities if employers, during formal internships, are asked to assess their interns and report back to the hospitality management unit.

Another approach to using outside industry reviewers is to have them help in designing the curriculum, or in making modification to an existing course of study. In this case, an industry board made up of local practitioners might be empowered to quantify those skills and abilities that are necessary for graduates of a hospitality management program and to generate a list of topical areas that should be part of a curriculum and to set standards that can be measured. This is usually followed by program faculty developing the course work that will satisfy the standards developed by the industry board. On the one hand, this approach can have positive impacts because it involves industry up front in indicating what they want to see in a graduate and it makes industry a stronger stake holder in the academic process. On the other hand, this approach assumes that industry really knows what it wants in a graduate and that industry can project what it will need in, say, six to eight years, which is the period of time it takes a hospitality management unit to develop courses and for a graduate to work though years of study.

Although it is less frequent, industry reviewers may be used to assess the faculty and assess the physical facilities. For the latter, one or more members of industry may be asked to assess the adequacy of the facilities, particularly labs and their equipment as it relates to what is currently the norm in the field. This can provide an important type of quality feedback that may allow the program to garner additional resources from either the institution or industry itself. Hotel front office mangers may be used to assess the quality of front office computer software and hardware. Also, practitioners are used to assess the quality of faculty, either already employed or during interviews of potential candidates. This is usually undertaken when the skills, knowledge, and abilities of the new faculty are in a highly technical area that may be beyond the scope of existing faculty of the unit. For example, if a hospitality management unit has one chef instructor and has the need for a replacement, none of the existing faculty may be capable of determining a potential chef's abilities. The same might hold true if the hospitality management unit had its own computer lab and needed to hire a technician.

Summary of External Means and Methods of Assuring Quality

A number of ways of using people outside the hospitality management unit for assessing quality have been discussed. The most widely used approach is that of accreditation, and to a lesser degree certification. These can occur on a national, regional, or local basis. Less frequently used are outside peer reviews, with faculty from other hospitality management programs being the most common. Less common, but valuable nonetheless, are outside reviewers from industry who can assess areas such as curriculum, student outcomes, faculty skills, and physical amenities. Discussion now turns to internal means and methods of assuring quality.

INTERNAL MEANS AND METHODS OF ASSURING QUALITY

While the foregoing means of assuring quality utilize people from outside the hospitality management unit, discussion in this section focuses on using people inside the unit including administrators, peers, and students.

The most often used means of assessing quality is done by administrators, which can include deans, directors, chairs, and associates of one type or another. These assessment activities can be broken out into three different types. One type is a review of written material that relates to the hospitality management unit. The most common review of written material is an assessment of syllabi to ensure that the objectives of a course are clear, that required readings are listed, and that the means of determining a course grade are provided. In fewer cases, administrators may review written tests, especially if more than one instructor teaches sections of the same class. Less common, but one of the latest assessments to come along, is that of course portfolios where an administrator, or a panel, reviews all the materials an instructor uses to deliver a class including syllabi, required and optional readings, tests, assignments, names of outside speakers, destinations of field trips, and so on. The latter is quite comprehensive and provides assessment of the breadth and depth of a course as well as the amount of work a teacher puts into the course. These course portfolios are being used in some programs as one of the bases for promotion, tenure, and merit increases.

The course portfolio is also categorized as an assessment of faculty by the administrator. This quality initiative can also include review of an instructor's grades, student evaluations, peer reviews, and personal observation. In any case, it is a one-on-one interaction between the administrator and the individual faculty member. However, administrators are not the only individuals who may do quality assessments of instructors.

Peers, or other instructors in the hospitality management unit, may be called upon to evaluate one of their own. This process can be either formal or informal. In the first case, an institution may require that other instructors, and sometimes the director, periodically visit the classroom, observe the activities, and then complete a written commentary and assessment. Classroom peer review can also include the assessment of student comments or feedback about the class or instructor. Sometimes, an institution-wide research instrument is part of the peer review process which allows for statistical analysis across the unit and the institution. Peer review can be directed at an instructor's research output or service contribution. Peer review in the hospitality management unit can also be informal, such as an instructor requesting that a peer sit in on a class and provide feedback, or to review the draft of a paper being considered for publication.

It should be noted that peer reviews can also involve hospitality management faculty from outside the unit. This is most often done when a faculty candidate is asked to provide references, a form of quality assurance. It is also used in some tenure and promotion decisions when a packet of material, usually research output, is sent for outside peer review. This is often done because existing faculty within the unit do not have expertise in that area of research and to help eliminate personal bias (positive or negative) that is bound to exist among peers within the unit.

Internal Evaluation by and of Students

Students are the core customers of higher education and many of the quality assurance initiatives are oriented toward them. If a hospitality management program is to be successful and maintain quality, it must assess its students at numerous points during their course of study and on numerous dimensions.

Undoubtedly the most common and best-known form of quality assurance directed at students is the class evaluation. Virtually every institution requires periodic formal assessments of classes by students. Often, this process utilizes standardized, closed-ended questions that are statistically analyzed comparing the individual class and instructor to department, college, and even university norms. It is not unusual that results which deviate significantly from the norm are highlighted and can become the focus of review by administrators, especially during tenure and promotion reviews. The use of student classroom evaluations as a means of quality assurance is not without debate.

On the one hand, proponents of student evaluations claim that this provides one of the only mechanisms for students to voice their opinions of the courses and the instructors teaching them. Further, the longevity of new faculty may rest, largely, on the results of student evaluations. Very poor evaluations can lead to the dismissal of probationary faculty. On the other hand, it is argued that student evaluations are nothing more than popularity contests with instructors who make the classes easy and give high grades to ensure good student evaluations. Still another concern was stated by an instructor from a northeastern college who said, after receiving a poor evaluation, "What the heck do nineteen-year-olds know about what is good in a class anyway?"

Research regarding student evaluations (Knutson, Schmidgall, and Sciarini, 1995; Knutson, Schmidgall, and Sciarini, 1996) revealed some interesting insights into student evaluations. On the one hand they found that students, parents, administrators, and elected officials were becoming more interested in faculty accountability and the quality of teaching but that little had been reported about the procedures used to evaluate faculty and classes in hospitality management units. Their second study found that "faculty teaching evaluations are not seen as being particularly valuable to either the department or to the college" (Knutson, Schmidgall, and Sciarini, 1996, p. 27). They also found that in four-year programs they were more likely to:

1. Evaluate faculty every term or every course
2. Have the evaluation reviewed by the dean
3. Use the findings more heavily in decisions about merit pay, promotions, and tenure
4. See value in the evaluation procedure

In two-year programs they were more likely to:

5. Use written forms created by the head of the department
6. Assign more weight to teaching in the overall evaluation
7. Get the results to the faculty more quickly

Formalized, written student evaluations are the most widely used, but certainly not the only means of acquiring student feedback and quality assurance. There is a second method that, like the first, employs surveys of students. This is often done to supplement the information garnered about classes and instructors in university-sanctioned student evaluations and goes further by assessing "quality of life" issues. These program surveys may query the student about the environment of the hospitality management program, whether it is friendly, whether the faculty and director are open to approach and discussion, whether the library hours are adequate, and so forth. These surveys can lead to adaptation of the organizational culture in the hospitality management unit to better meet the wants and needs of the current generation of students. After all, what was acceptable and commonplace twenty years ago no longer meets minimum standards.

Still another use of the survey method of quality assessment is to direct the instrument toward alumni. The rationale is that, having been employed in the field for a period of time gives the alumni a more realistic and practical concept of how well the hospitality management program prepared them for career success. These instruments may include both open- and closed-ended questions and sometimes have the secondary purpose of being marketing and promotional pieces for the hospitality management unit. In a similar fashion, surveys can be directed toward those businesses that employ graduates of the hospitality management unit. In this case, the employer is asked to evaluate the adequacy of preparation for those students and to suggest modifications to the course of study.

Still another means of assessing students is through exit interviews. These are often undertaken immediately prior to graduation in the hope that the interviewee (1) has experienced virtually the entire program and (2) since grades are no longer an issue will be more candid in expressing likes and dislikes about the hospitality management program. These exit interviews may done with individual students or in groups, by the program head or by faculty, and may make use of incentives for students participation, such as free pizza.

When done with many individuals at the same time and in an open-ended format, they essentially become focus groups. However, focus groups can be utilized with students who have yet to graduate as well. The advantage of the focus group format is that individual students are more likely to express their views in a group, rather than individual, format. The risk, or down side, is that the discussion of the focus group may be swayed, or direction changed, by one or two strong-minded and vociferous participants. Therefore, it is imperative that the focus group facilitator keep the group on track without unduly influencing their discussion. Of course, focus groups could be used with alumni or with industry practitioners as well, but I am not aware of any hospitality management units doing this, to date.

While the foregoing are all examples of structured and somewhat formalized means of providing feedback and quality assessment, there are two less structured means. One is to have an advisory board made up solely of students. The purpose of such a board is to provide feedback to the hospitality management unit on a variety of issues that affect student life and quality. Either the director or a group of faculty representatives may meet periodically with the student board. It is important that these types of student boards do not see themselves as nothing more than complaint mechanisms for the other students. Rather, they should take a quality circles approach that delves into any area that affects students and could include obtaining more scholarships, organizing industry speakers, mediating in student disputes, and so on.

An alterative to the student board is to have student representatives sit on various hospitality management unit committees to provide a student view in assuring quality. For example, some hospitality management units have one or more student representatives on grade appeal committees that also include faculty members. Others may have students regularly attend faculty meetings, sit on the library committee, and even involve students in the tenure and promotion process. The objective is to balance the faculty's view of quality assurance with a student viewpoint; after all, the student is the core customer.

Summary of Internal Means and Methods of Assuring Quality

This section discussed a number of initiatives that are used to assess and assure quality using resources internal to the hospitality management unit. These approaches can be undertaken by the program head or other administrators, by peers in the hospitality management unit, and by students. The approaches range from very formal student evaluations to interviews and focus groups. Feedback from current students, alumni, and employers can also be used to assess and enhance program quality.

CONCLUSION

This chapter took an in-depth look at those elements of a hospitality management program that affect quality and the methods employed to assure quality. Quality is an elusive standard and varies from unit to unit in hospitality management. The adage that "beauty is in the eyes of the beholder" can be translated to "quality is in the eyes of the hospitality management unit." Quality standards are not absolute, but rather depend upon the mission, goals, and objectives of the hospitality management unit within the broader context of the institution. Assurance of quality can be achieved though numerous means and mechanisms. However, success in achieving quality, or quality assurance, is not simply a matter of producing scales to be used in gauging success. Rather, quality assurance involves a mix of measuring outcomes as related to objectives, while overlaying on the assessment process the resources that can be brought to bear.

The concepts shared in this chapter are important to new and experienced hospitality management faculty alike. It is important that any faculty member understand the multitude of factors that affect quality and realize that some of them are beyond the control of an individual faculty member. On the other hand, many elements that affect quality are within their control, including continuous faculty development, professional preparation, and the need for individual faculty to have their own means and methods of assuring quality.

REFERENCES

Deming, W.E. (1989). *Out of the crisis.* Cambridge, MA: Massachusetts Institute of Technology.

CHRIE (1989). Handbook of Accreditation. Washington, DC: CHRIE.

Juran, J.M. (1989). *Juran on leadership quality.* New York: The Free Press.

Knutson, B., R.S. Schmidgall, and M. Sciarini (1995). "Faculty teaching evaluations in CHRIE member schools." *Hospitality and Tourism Educator,* 7(4):5-8.

Knutson, B., R.S. Schmidgall, and M. Sciarini (1996). "Teaching evaluations in CHRIE member schools: perceptions of the faculty." *Hospitality and Tourism Educator,* 8: 27-32.

Lickson, J.E., T. J. Kauppinen, and A.J. Ogg (1994). "Quality management: The multidimensional leadership challenge." *Hospitality and Tourism Educator,* 6:7-11.

Pall, G.A. (1987). *Quality process management.* Englewood Cliffs, NJ: Prentice-Hall.

Tanke, M.L. (1986). "Accreditation: Implications for hospitality management education." *FIU Hospitality Review,* 4:48-54.

Chapter 5

Professional Preparation

Carl P. Borchgrevink
Michael P. Sciarini

This chapter is the first of several which deal more specifically with the individual faculty member, as opposed to entire hospitality programs. Instead, this chapter focuses specifically on the preparation that is necessary to launch a successful career as a hospitality educator. The issues raised include strategic career planning, educational preparation, hospitality work experience, networking personally and electronically, the job search, choosing and targeting hospitality programs, the academic selection process, anticipatory socialization, organizational entry, and the first five years on the job.

STRATEGIC CAREER PLANNING

Establishing a starting point for your academic preparation is essential. This will provide clarity and focus, and help direct your efforts and allow you to maximize your future potential. The intent is to assist you in using your time effectively and efficiently. The fundamental issue to face in planning your future career is yourself. Who are you; what do you know about yourself; what have you accomplished; where have you failed? In other words, do a self-assessment. A self-assessment can be most helpful and well worth the time invested. It will reveal your strengths, weaknesses, interests, and values, and allow you to direct your attention where it will benefit you the most. This self-assessment is similar to a SWOT (Strength/Weakness and Opportunities/Threats) analysis. Typically such analyses are performed by businesses. The approach can, however, be transferred with success to the individual level. SWOT is an acronym for the internal strengths and weaknesses of a business, and the environmental opportunities and threats the business faces. At this point we will primarily deal with strengths and weaknesses, and associated interests and values. The environmental conditions, such as the job market and other job seekers, will be addressed throughout later sections of the chapter.

Strengths and Weaknesses

According to Sciarini (1996) one of the best ways to start analyzing your strengths is to create a list of your accomplishments; things you are proud of having achieved or obtained. Such a list is helpful in many parts of the career planning process. Make the list as extensive as possible, covering your entire adult life. Do not limit the list to items you would list, or have listed on your curriculum vita. Rather, it should include everything that can help shed some light on you as an individual. This should, of course, include your educational and occupational accomplishments to date, but also team projects, extracurricular activities, volunteer work, and athletics, down to your handling of specific complex and difficult situations. Many find it helpful to ask friends, family, and peers at work or school for their insights. This will add a different perspective and help shed light on aspects of yourself that do not readily come to mind, perhaps because you have forgotten them, suppressed them, or see them as insignificant.

Following the listing of accomplishments, try to get at the primary personal causes or facilitators of the accomplishments. Which personal qualities and characteristics, knowledge, skill, and experience were most important for your success? These causes or facilitating aspects are your strengths. The list of accomplishments may have made some of your weaknesses (near causes or facilitators of failure) evident as well. Go beyond that, however, and develop a specific list of attempts and accomplishments that you failed in completing successfully. Again, the insights and input of family, friends and peers might prove most useful.

Upon completing these two lists and identifying the underlying causes, facilitators, and inhibitors of attaining the desired accomplishments, develop a self-rating tool such as that suggested by Sciarini (1996). Self-assessment tools will allow you to develop a comparative analysis of your strengths and weaknesses, and can help direct your efforts to the areas that can benefit the most as well as to areas that you can exploit the most, i.e., identify the weaknesses you can improve the most, as well as the strengths that you can apply most readily in your academic career pursuits. Following the documenting of strengths and weaknesses and the comparative analysis, you should match your strengths and weaknesses with the relevant accomplishments, and develop an anecdotal description of how the strength or weakness came into play. These descriptions will be useful later when you are applying for a position or graduate school and you are asked to list your strengths (and perhaps weaknesses) and elaborate on why or how you consider yourself to have said strength. More immediately the listing of strengths and accomplishments can be used to bolster self-esteem and self-efficacy, which in turn affects performance (for a discussion of performance see Locke and Latham, 1990; for a discussion of self-efficacy see Bandura, 1986). The list of weaknesses can be used to identify skills, knowledge, and abilities that can be improved through course work, self-study, or other training approaches.

Improving weak personal qualities is more difficult, although courses, such as interpersonal skills courses, that incorporate role play and other interactions and enactments can be helpful in improving interpersonal skills and related self-efficacy and self-esteem. If you identify a personal quality as particularly lacking and you wish to improve it, you may wish to seek the help of a professional career counselor or psychologist. In general, however, when you have identified your weaknesses, establish a plan of action for improvement with specific timelines for completion of the necessary work. Setting specific hard goals with deadlines will help ensure that you make progress and do not simply put your goals aside for later attention (Locke and Latham, 1990).

Interests and Values

The next step in the self-assessment process is to make salient to yourself your interests and values. Knowing your strengths and weaknesses is an important tool for proactive career development,

although your strengths and weaknesses do not necessarily reflect
what you like and prefer to do. Rather, they may be a reflection of
past interests and values that provided the impetus for your skill
development. In assessing interests and values it is helpful to maintain a hospitality focus. Try to establish your likes and dislikes, your
preferred pursuits and your aversions. In doing so, consider them in
light of the opportunities within hospitality and hospitality education. You may, for example, find that you enjoy planning events,
traveling by car, and preparing foods, but dislike air travel, and
working weekends and holidays. This may help direct your attention toward preferred career segments. Consider your values and
beliefs in the same way. If you are a teetotaler and believe in
abstinence, you should probably not pursue beverage management
as part of your teaching portfolio, as this would conflict with your
belief system and may lead to discomfort and behavioral or attitudi-
nal changes (Festinger, 1957; Heider, 1946, 1958).

The self-assessment should help provide a clearer image of who
you are and where you can take your career. The intent is to learn
about yourself by developing answers to question such as: "What
are your skills, talents, strengths, and weaknesses? What are your
beliefs and values? What lifestyle do you wish to achieve? What
environments appeal to you? What work experiences, clubs, student
organizations, research projects, internships, or volunteer experiences appeal to you? What is it about them that you like? Where
might your skills and interests fit in a career as hospitality academic?" (Vance, Potter, and Scheetz, 1993).

It is unlikely that you will know exactly how you want your
career to unfold, but the self-assessment can be used in guiding you
toward the best possible fit in choice of employer. To make the best
career choice it is essential that you research the array of educational institutions and positions available to the hospitality academic,
and that is where we turn our attention now.

Researching Organizations and Positions

Although the following could be used in searching broadly for a
career, we are assuming you have already made the decision to
become a hospitality educator, and will focus the discussion on

organizations and positions with primary relevance for hospitality educators.

The question you should now attempt to answer is what you need to know about hospitality education and research in terms of careers and occupations. In essence you are now moving to a consideration of external environmental opportunities and threats from the SWOT perspective (Sciarini, 1996). Since the hospitality industry, as well as hospitality education, is ever changing, it is important that your knowledge of the hospitality academy is current. Your local library can help; schedule a meeting with the reference librarian assigned to hospitality or business and explain that you are looking for information about careers and institutions relative to hospitality education. The librarian is likely to direct you toward some of the hospitality journals, such as *The Journal of Hospitality & Tourism Education* and *The Cornell Hotel and Restaurant Administration Quarterly.* In particular, the stream of articles that describe compensation and other characteristics of the hospitality academy may be helpful (see for example Cook and Yale, 1994; Pizam and Milman, 1988; Schmidgall and Woods, 1992; and Woods, 1994). Such articles can help differentiate the segments within the hospitality academy so that you can make the best possible choices in pursuing your career.

One can also contact relevant associations, such as the Council on Hotel, Restaurant and Institutional Education, the Educational Institute of the American Hotel and Motel Association, and the Educational Foundation of the National Restaurant Association (see Table 5.1). These associations can provide you with a wide range of information and publications regarding universities and colleges with hospitality programs. You may also seek out the recommendations of your local or state lodging and restaurant association. In addition to a traditional library search, you should consider a search of the World Wide Web if you have Internet access. There are a number of Internet sites that may provide relevant information (see, for example, Kasavana and Borchgrevink, 1997). In addition, a growing number of educational institutions are establishing their own Web pages. For example, the URL for the School of Hospitality Business at Michigan State University is http://www.bus.msu.edu/broad/shb and the URL for the Tourism and Convention Department at the University of Nevada, Las Vegas is

TABLE 5.1. Industry Associations and Addresses

The Council on Hotel, Restaurant and Institutional Education (CHRIE)
1200 17th Street
Washington, DC 20036
Phone: 202-331-5990
Fax: 202-785-2511
E-mail: alliance@access.digex.net

The Educational Foundation of the National Restaurant Association (EF-NRA)
250 South Wacker Drive
Suite 1400
Chicago, IL 60606
Phone: 312-715-1010
Fax: 312-715-0807
(Individual e-mail addresses only)

Hotel & Catering International Management Association
191 Trinity Road
London SW17 7HN
United Kingdom
Phone: 44-181-672-4251
Fax: 44-181-682-1707
E-mail: Library@hcima.org.uk

The Educational Institute of the American Hotel and Motel Association (EI-AHMA)
1407 South Harrison Road
East Lansing, MI 49926
Phone: 517-353-5500
Fax: 517-353-5527
E-mail: generalinfo@ei-ahma.org

http://www.nscee.edu/unlv/tourism. These Web pages will typically contain a great deal of information about the university, the hospitality program and faculty, and their research and publications, as well as general information about the geographic area in which the program is located, all of which may be relevant considerations. The latter Web site, in particular, contains a great deal of information about hospitality education, in general, and many links.

A good place to start in investigating programs is with the *Guide to College Programs in Hospitality and Tourism,* published by CHRIE. In investigating hospitality programs, you will find that they generally fall into four categories based on the level of degrees that they offer, including associate's, bachelor's, master's, and doctoral. The above guide categorized them as such but groups the master's and doctorate-granting institutions into one section.

The degrees offered at an institution will often determine the minimum degree the faculty must possess. Typically, educators need at minimum to have one degree higher than the degree their students are pursuing. Thus, if you wish to teach students pursuing a bachelor's degree, you will need to have a master's degree or higher in a field of study relevant to the bachelor's degree offered at the institution in question. Until recently, it was still possible to get a position teaching at some four-year programs with a master's degree. This is changing, however, and most four-year programs now require that their faculty possess a doctoral degree. An example of a position announcement is presented in Exhibit 5.1.

The type of position available will also vary across institutions and educators. The institutions may or may not have a tenure system, which protects faculty from summary dismissal after a specified period of satisfactory performance. The intent of tenure is to allow and encourage academic freedom in research and teaching, so that a faculty member can profess an opinion or pursue an avenue of research that is at odds with administration's or external entities' interests, and not be pressured to conform or desist due to employment concerns. Satisfactory performance is institution-specific and should be inquired into prior to employment. The tenure stream typically takes five to seven years with a midstream review. An institution may have positions that are not within the tenure system, such as visiting lecturer, instructor, or adjunct faculty. These positions are typically based on annual contracts and may provide part-time employment only. At some institutions time spent as a lecturer or instructor counts toward tenure, while others do not count such activity, but require a position within the formal hierarchy for it to count toward tenure. The formal hierarchy ranges from assistant professor, through associate professor, to (full) professor. Some universities may also have higher-level, more prestigious designations such as research professor or chaired positions.

Tenure is typically not awarded to faculty below associate professor. The above is descriptive of the U.S. educational system. In other parts of the world, the position titles may be used somewhat differently. For example, in Europe you may find titles such as senior lecturer or first scientific officer, which could equate with associate and full professor, respectively, depending upon the institution.

EXHIBIT 5.1. Vacancy Announcement

UNLV
UNIVERSITY OF NEVADA LAS VEGAS

4505 Maryland Parkway • Box 451026 • Las Vegas, Nevada 89154-1026

VACANCY ANNOUNCEMENT

POSITION TITLE	Assistant (tenure-track), Department of Hotel Management, William F. Harrah College of Hotel Administration. #591
RESPONSIBILITIES	HOTEL OPERATIONS/MANAGEMENT: Instruct undergraduate and graduate courses in lodging operations, hotel management, labor management, and organizational theory. Chair and serve on graduate thesis and dissertation committees. Conduct research and meet all service obligations.
QUALIFICATIONS	Doctorate in hospitality or related field required. Evidence of teaching excellence, research, and industry experience is highly desirable. Expertise in security operations is a plus.
SALARY RANGE	Competitive salary consistent with academic, industry experience and teaching backgrounds.

THE SETTING: UNLV is a premier urban university located in the vibrant city of Las Vegas and is surrounded by the Mojave Desert. UNLV is the state's largest comprehensive, doctoral degree granting institution with 20,000 students and more than 600 full-time faculty. UNLV provides traditional and professional academic programs for a diverse student body and encourages innovative and interdisciplinary approaches to teaching, learning, and scholarship. For more information, see the UNLV World Wide Web site at: http://www.unlv.edu.

APPLICATION DEADLINE & DETAILS	Submit letters of application, vita, and three (3) letters of recommendation, indicating position for which applying, to:
	    Dr. Tom Jones
	    Chair, Department of Hotel Management
	    William F. Harrah College of Hotel Administration
	    University of Nevada Las Vegas
	    Box 456021
	    Las Vegas, Nevada 89154-6021
	Application deadline is January 15, 1999, or until filled. Appointment is for Fall 1999. **POSITION CONTINGENT UPON FUNDING**

Affirmative Action/Equal Opportunity Employer. Minorities, Women, Veterans, and the Disabled are encouraged to apply.

Educational institutions vary also in terms of their research and teaching focus. Some are pure teaching institutions, and expect their faculty to perform little if any research, while institutions at the other end of the teaching-research continuum consider research to be the primary component of a faculty member's activity. Thus, teaching loads can vary dramatically from five courses to two courses per semester. Generally, as teaching decreases, research expectations increase. The expectations for community service will also vary across institutions. It is important to understand the targeted institution's focus, as it will affect the requisite skill and knowledge set, and your choices in educational preparation (see Chapter 6 for a more in-depth discussion of the roles of teaching and research).

In addition to the focus on teaching, research, and service, it is relevant to consider the college in which the hospitality program is housed, which may be a college of agriculture, business, human ecology, natural resources, or some other college, depending on the history of the institution. This will also influence the focus and direction of the program. For example, a program housed in a college of business is likely to have a different understanding of and approach to hospitality education and research than a program that has its origins in dietetics and nutrition. You need to establish what the relevant criteria are.

EDUCATIONAL PREPARATION

Which Degree to Pursue

If you decide that you wish to work at a research institution, developing good research skills will be essential and a PhD (doctor of philosophy) or a research-oriented EdD (doctor of education) are appropriate terminal degrees. Alternatives, if you hope to work at a teaching institution, might include tagged degrees (having a special designation versus a generic degree such as PhD) such as a DBA (doctor of business administration) or certain types of doctorates in education. This is not to suggest that there is rigidity in degrees, but that you should consider the wide range of degrees available, and pursue the degree best suited for you and your targeted programs. Sheldon and Collison (1990) asked deans and directors of hospitality and tourism programs in the United States to rank order their preferred degrees for faculty position applicants. The PhD or DBA was the first choice for all, while the EdD was second, followed by the JD (doctor of law), and finally a master's degree. In his study of hospitality faculty members, Woods (1994) reports substantial change in degree backgrounds from 1982 to 1992. Please see Table 5.2 for a complete description of hospitality faculty degree backgrounds.

It is particularly interesting to note the growth in PhD degrees in education and in the "other" category. The wide variety of degrees is a reflection of the multidisciplinary nature of hospitality management. The growth in education degrees, Woods (1994) suggests, may be due to hospitality programs seeking out candidates with doctors of education, while supplementing with specialists in the many relevant fields. Other potential reasons for the proliferation of degrees in education is their broad relevance and application. Furthermore, in some instances, they may be less quantitatively focused than PhD degrees in other disciplines, and may thus be better suited for those who are more inclined toward a qualitative focus in their research.

Lefever and Witham (1995) looked at actual hiring practices at CHRIE member institutions between 1992 and 1994. They found that among the ninety-seven reported hires, 53.6 percent held a doctoral degree, of which 36.1 percent had a PhD, 9.3 percent had a EdD, and 5.2 percent had an unspecified "ABD" (all but dissertation), and 3.1 percent had a JD. Of the remaining hires, 40.2 percent had master's degrees (unspecified) and 6.2 percent had bachelor's degrees. This shows that the bulk of recent hires have doctoral degrees. It is important to point out that this is not inconsistent with Woods (1994) finding a majority with degrees in education, as education doctorates can be either EdD or PhD.

In choosing a degree program, it is essential that you research your preferred organization and position, and uncover both latent and manifest expectations and desires within the program. Look at the research and publications of the faculty. Talk to the faculty at your targeted institutions, and ask them for advice and insights. Ask them to share their own experience and educational preparation.

TABLE 5.2. Hospitality Faculty Degrees

Hospitality	1992 Study			1982 Study		
	Bachelor s	Master's	Doctorate	Bachelor's	Master's	Doctorate
Hospitality Management	35	35	16	38	29	14
Arts and Sciences	16	5	4	21	8	11
Business	17	24	12	11	35	23
Education	7	11	40	3	8	24
Engineering	2	2	3	7	2	3
Food Science or Agriculture	1	1	1	6	2	6
Home Economics	6	3	3	9	12	6
Law	0	0	0	0	1	4
Other	17	20	22	5	5	6

Source: Woods, R.W. 1994. Ten years later: Who teaches hospitality in the 90s? *The Cornell Hotel and Restaurant Administration Quarterly, 35*(4), 68. Copyright Cornell University. Used with permission from Cornell University.

This may prove particularly helpful if you contact faculty members whose teaching and research background fit with your own interests and aspirations. According to Sheldon and Collison (1990), when hiring a new faculty member, more than 50 percent of queried deans and directors of hospitality and tourism programs expect that the candidate's degree must somehow be related to hospitality and tourism. Only 5 to 7 percent suggested that the candidates *must* have hospitality- or tourism-related majors, while the remainder had no particular subject requirement for the applicant's degree.

Overall this suggests that those who intend to pursue a degree for a hospitality career have a rather large latitude in choosing their degree, discipline, and subject of inquiry. The primary consideration is to establish the relevance of degree and subject of inquiry to hospitality and tourism through course work and dissertation; the actual degree and discipline is an important, but secondary, consideration.

Before you begin a degree program it would be beneficial to try to find work as an adjunct professor or visiting lecturer. This can often be done while you are still employed full-time elsewhere. It is an excellent way to test the waters and see if teaching is really something you wish to pursue. Many graduate degree programs will require that you teach while pursuing your degree and as such prior experience may be a consideration when your application to graduate school is considered.

Pursuing the Degree

Think carefully before you decide to pursue a new degree. Do you really need it? Do you really want it? Can you afford to make the commitments? A doctorate will typically take three to five years of graduate work to complete, while a master's degree may be completed in one to two years. Some doctoral programs will require you to have a master's degree prior to admission; others may provide a master's degree en route to the doctorate. Some graduate programs are very structured and have a predetermined set of courses that must be satisfactorily completed, while others are less rigid and negotiate an individual track of study based on the students' needs.

In most doctoral programs you will experience a great many academic hurdles the first year or so. You will be pushed and stretched a great deal. The intent is twofold. Primarily, and ostensibly, there is a need to establish that you have, or to provide you with, broad competency within the discipline. The second intent, often not voiced directly, is the need to establish that you really want the degree, and are willing to put in the effort needed. The graduate faculty and the department direct a great deal of resources in terms of time, people, and money toward doctoral students, and they wish to secure their investment, so to speak. The draw on resources per student is much higher at the doctoral level than it is for master's or undergraduate students. In contrast to master's programs and undergraduate programs, doctoral programs are not directly revenue-building programs for universities, although they may indirectly generate funds through recognition and research funding. As such, a great deal will be expected and demanded of you in the first years in the program. Consequently, a great many students drop out of doctoral programs in the first year. On a personal note, one of the authors started his doctoral program as part of a cohort of eight. Within a year the cohort was reduced to four, all of whom continued to complete all required courses and comprehensive exams. Eight years after starting in the program, only two have obtained their PhDs.

In a doctoral program, just about every class will require a research paper of some sort. It can be enormously helpful if early in your doctoral program you identify your potential dissertation topic, or at least the general area upon which you wish to focus your research. This will allow you to use every class and research paper to build your knowledge and understanding of said topic or area. In effect, you can build the literature review for your dissertation over time, while generating valuable feedback and insights from your professors.

Early in your program of study you will be expected to ask a professor to act as your primary advisor and to chair your dissertation committee. The professor may decline, due to competing commitments or perhaps a sense that other professors may better meet your needs. Have an alternate choice in mind, should your preferred professor not accept. Later you will be asked to choose additional committee members. The choices you make can dramatically influence your progress toward your PhD as well as sense of well-being. Choose carefully. Make sure that the professor has the expertise and interests needed for your intended inquiry. In addition it is wise to ascertain that your committee members get along, personally and academically. Otherwise you may experience obstructions that will delay your progress, and perhaps hamper your learning.

Typically doctoral students are expected to teach classes as part of their academic preparation. This is good and valuable experience. Unfortunately, most programs will not provide you with any instructions on how to teach. Apparently, the candidates are assumed to naturally know how to teach, or to acquire this knowledge as they acquire their needed academic content! Mill (1991) put it well: "If we as educators, can argue for the need for classes to prepare students to enter the hospitality management profession, how can we possibly deny the need for instructional technique classes for those about to enter the teaching profession?" (p. 183). If your doctoral program does not provide such classes, seek them out. Teaching does not necessarily come naturally for those who seek a doctoral degree. See Griffin (1994) for anecdotal evidence, and Reich and DeFranco (1994a, b) for some advice on how to improve your teaching.

The Dissertation

After completing the required course work and passing preliminary examinations or comprehensives, your attention will focus on producing your most substantial piece of work, that is, your dissertation. It is helpful for timely success if you do not think of the dissertation as an infinitely long and fully comprehensive document that is perfect and worthy of endless preparation. Think of it rather in terms of its distinct components and work closely with your committee chair and members, keeping them appraised of your progress as you go along. Before you invest considerable time in producing the components of your dissertation, make certain that the critical core of inquiry is sound and well-received by those truly qualified to guide, direct, and approve your dissertation—your committee members and chair. It can also be beneficial to inquire of experts at other universities if a great deal of research and writing within your area of inquiry has been produced by professors at other universities. Perhaps they can act as outside committee members. Considering logistics and expediency, you may opt to limit your committee to faculty at your institution. This does not preclude you, however, from soliciting input elsewhere.

The eighty-twenty rule applies to your dissertation—you are likely to find that twenty percent of your efforts will generate eighty percent of what actually ends up in your dissertation. It is, therefore, essential that you try to identify the most valuable twenty percent and direct your efforts accordingly. The good way to accomplish this is to schedule yourself rigorously, particularly in terms of when you will stop working on the dissertation on any given day. It is always hard to get started, but if you have established an ending time, starting is easier. Furthermore, scheduling your time will help you avoid wasting time, or taking time away from other important aspects of your life, such as your family. Miller (1996) suggests that those who have substantial, structured demands on time through job, spouse, children, etc., are usually more productive than those without limits on time.

Writing a dissertation is a slow, solitary activity, and you will find yourself with much reduced social interaction for the duration. It is impossible to do it all, and you will need to put on hold much you would normally wish to accomplish. Accompanying guilt and frustration is likely. You may find it necessary to take a "satisfizing" rather than maximizing approach to several aspects of your day. On the other hand, make sure to find time for some activities that are not related to your field of study, so that you can refresh and reinvigorate. Some recommend taking one day a week completely off from dissertation work (Miller, 1996). If you get stressed out and burdened with guilt, it will negatively affect your judgment and speed, resulting in poorer quality work. Focus on the successes and accomplishments of each day; try not to dwell on that which you are not pleased with. Above all, listen to and follow the instructions and recommendations of your dissertation committee. If well chosen, they will help bring you to your PhD; that is what they are there for!

A final note about educational preparation relates to increased diversity and globalization. Both within the hospitality industry and among the hospitality student body we are experiencing an increase in diversity, and drive toward globalization. Increasingly, hospitality companies are growing abroad as new markets open up or improve their business climate. An example would be the growth in the Pacific Rim and the opportunities for growth in Eastern Europe. Furthermore, hospitality programs in the United States are experiencing growth in students from abroad and a change in diversity among the student body at large. Although not likely to become a doctoral program requirement soon, doctoral candidates should consider learning a second and third language, and increase their understanding of the global hospitality and tourism marketplace. This would help minimize any tendency toward ethnocentrism among faculty and improve their ability to function as educators, researchers, and consultants within a wide variety of cultures, or with students, colleagues, and clients from said cultures. Casado's (1997) suggestion that undergraduate hospitality students be taught conversational Spanish is a first step in this direction.

Professional Experience

Hospitality programs are industry-driven in that they seek to provide a specific industry with management and leadership talent to meet their current and future needs. Some programs have started to focus more broadly on the service industries, while others have always had a broad business-based program. Considering that hospitality programs serve a definable segment of the business world, is it reasonable to expect, or even require, that hospitality faculty have practical (nonacademic) work experience from within this segment? This would provide faculty with a realistic point of reference, and would add credibility vis-à-vis students and other potential clients. Hospitality industry experience is a reasonable expectation, although it may not necessarily take the form of paid practical work experience. Much can be garnered by field research, reading of trade academic journals, and externships.

Regardless of the hospitality experience that new hospitality educators bring with them as they enter the profession, it is important to remember that this practical knowledge and experience will age. Some aspects will age rather fast. Consider the rapid pace of change in computer applications and hospitality Internet use. Faculty may need to return to industry for short spells, or attend short courses to upgrade their knowledge, in addition to staying in touch through academic and trade press and conferences.

Woods (1994) reports that hospitality faculty have increasing amounts of industry experience. In 1982, they had on average seven years of experience, while the 1992 average is ten years. Two-thirds of his sample report that they have experience above the department management level. In Lefever and Withiam's (1995) study of new faculty hires between 1992 and 1994, the mean, median, and mode for hospitality experience are reported as 3.8 years, two years, and one year, respectively. These findings are not contradictory in that the latter study looked at new hires, while the other study sampled the hospitality academy as a whole. Hospitality faculty members typically have some hospitality industry experience.

THE JOB SEARCH

Networking

During your academic preparation, as well as later as a faculty member, you will be expected to attend and participate at academic and professional conferences, trade shows, and association meetings. This is important for your professional academic development, as you will be able to listen to and take part in conference presentations, which are a component of the academic life. However, this activity may be even more important from the perspective of networking. Networking has been described as the intentional formation of relationships for the purpose of mutual empowerment (Lerner, 1992). Attendance at conferences, conventions, and association meetings provides significant opportunity for meeting people who are either in the hospitality academy, or connected to it somehow. Research has shown that networking is an important component of finding employment (Beatty, 1994). The old adage "it isn't what you know, but who you know, that's important" is true to some extent.

Throughout graduate school you should attend as many conferences and association meetings as possible. Networking should not start when a job is needed, but should be a continuous activity. Seek out and build new relationships constantly, while maintaining existing ones. Reciprocity and sincerity are key to sound relationship building. Show as much interest in your contacts as you wish for them to be interested in you. As the relationship develops, you may gain access to your contacts' broader networks.

Talk with the people you meet, let them know what you are up to, and how far you are into graduate school, or other activity. In other words, let them know what your primary interests are and when you will be in a job-searching mode. Trade business cards, and follow up with everyone.

It is wise to be focused and prepared to discuss your interests and career aspirations at all times, as it is impossible to know who will have a potential lead for you (Wessel, 1994). On the other hand, every contact is not a job lead. Most provide information, ideas, and referrals, some of which may at some point lead to a job offer.

Networking should not be limited to "in-person" contacts. The Internet provides a wide range of opportunity for establishing contacts and building a network. There are a wide range of e-mail lists, Usenet groups, and World Wide Web pages that may be useful (see, for example, Borchgrevink and Kasavana, 1995; Cho, Connolly, and Tse, 1995; Kasavana and Borchgrevink, 1997). Furthermore, it is possible to perform actual job searches on-line. Searches can be done using many search engines, or, if preferred, go directly to pages on the World Wide Web that support job search activity, such as http://www.job-hunt.org, or http://www.careersite.com.

Securing a Job

As academic preparation comes to an end and the actual job search is about to start, it is important that you revisit your analyses of self and organizations. A renewed analysis may be called for as you and your targeted employer may have changed. Knowledge about potential employers is associated with success in obtaining employment (Keenan and Scott, 1985). Therefore, make certain you have obtained and read all you can about your preferred educational institutions and their faculty. Reconsider the fit between your attributes and goals and those of the institutions in which you are interested in working.

It is beneficial to get organized and start the job search early. Research by Freeman and Schopen (1992) has shown at the undergraduate level that early organization and job search were more highly related to obtaining a job than academic success. It is likely that this "early bird gets the worm" effect takes place at the graduate level as well. This provides further argument for the consistent networking and discussion readiness suggested above. Moreover, it can be seen as supporting the notion of using cold calls in the job search. That is, do not wait until jobs are posted, but call on administrators and faculty at your preferred institutions when you are ready to begin the search. Finally, Freeman and Schopen (1992) suggest that targeting specific institutions with tailored messages is more effective than applying randomly using a standard cover letter.

Although one is advised not to wait for posting of positions before the job search starts, this is not to suggest that the print media should not be used in the job search. Two particularly useful sources are *The CHRIE Communiqué* and *The Chronicle of Higher Education.* They provide listings of open positions, as well as general information about institutions and positions that can be used for comparative analysis.

The Curriculum Vita

In academic settings the curriculum vita (CV) typically replaces the résumé. The CV is a detailed summary of qualifications, employment history, academic history, and professional accomplishments. It is very broad, and often attempts to be comprehensive. In contrast, the résumé is a personalized direct-marketing piece, which is specifically targeted to an individual organization and position. In either case, the intent is to describe you in the best possible way to improve your chances of a job interview and possible job offer.

Although a CV is not as narrow and targeted as a résumé, it should still be developed and composed with your intended audience or employer in mind. That is, make sure to include and emphasize what you know from your research the organization values and that you can provide. The following categories are typically included (Graduate School, 1997):

- *Personal data* such as name, address, and citizenship. Additional personal data can be included if you deem it relevant.
- *Educational history.* List all degrees, diplomas, and certifications you have received. Mention also the schools attended, particularly if *pedigree* is important for your targeted institutions. If you have attended schools outside of the United States, it may be helpful if you list the U.S. equivalency of the school and *document of completion.* Unfortunately, many educators and educational administrators in the United States are unfamiliar with foreign educational systems. Your description may be helpful. This is typically done in chronological order, but could be done in functional order if you wish to highlight specific skills and abilities. The latter may prove helpful if you are making a career change or are reentering the workforce.
- *Recognitions.* List all forms of fellowships, scholarships, and awards. Include all that you have received, not only those recently obtained. Describe them to the extent necessary to ensure that the reader of your CV knows what you are being recognized for.
- *Employment history.* List all jobs, assistantships, internships, and externships you have held. Here the order is also typically chronological, but should follow the format established for educational history. Make certain to describe your responsibilities, as well as the skills that were developed or refined.
- *Teaching experience.* This may be included as part of your employment history. However, as you are considering an academic career, it may be helpful to use a separate heading for teaching experiences to add emphasis. Describe all teaching experience, including teaching assistantships. If you have developed a teaching portfolio, cite it and attach it to the CV. If you have not developed a teaching portfolio, this is where you should discuss your teaching philosophy, and summarize your classroom accomplishments. That is, discuss briefly the courses taught, the innovations brought to the classroom, special workshops attended, etc.
- *Research experience.* Discuss all research, independent and collaborative, as well as research skills. Mention dissertation, theses, research projects, and other research activities such as grant applications. Include also your proficiency with relevant

software and hardware. If you developed a research portfolio, cite it and attach it to the CV. If you did not, discuss your research philosophy and (intended) research streams, and consider including brief descriptions of your primary research to date.

- *Publications.* List all publications you have produced. This can either be done wholly chronologically or chronologically within categories in descending order of importance such as peer-reviewed journals (refereed journals), nonrefereed journals, trade press, magazines, newspapers, etc. Books and book chapters could be mentioned here, or if extensive, given a separate category.

- *Conferences and professional meetings.* Mention all presentations you made at conferences or professional meetings. Discuss also all presentations of papers you co-authored. If you were an invited presenter, highlight this fact.

- *Service activities.* List all professional services and outreach activities, including committees, organizational activities, seminars organized, etc. Include a separate list of service activities not related to your discipline. If you developed a service portfolio, cite it and attach it.

- *Other.* Any and all other activities that you believe may interest others or that you believe may benefit you that they know. Do not forget language competencies, international experience, and computer skills.

In developing the CV, make certain that you do not leave any gaps in your academic and employment history. Explain what you have done. If a particular time period has not been listed, you are in effect highlighting it, and should expect questions about what you were up to. Multiple gaps are suspect. Highlight the depth and breadth of your experience in the CV as well as to a lesser extent in the accompanying cover letter. Establish that you are able to complete work in reasonable amounts of time. Have you published your dissertation? Did you complete your degrees within acceptable disciplinary timelines? If a degree was not completed within normal timelines, you need to acknowledge this and address it, as the readers of your CV are likely to notice, and will be left to wonder about your ability to perform.

Cover Letter

The cover letter should highlight what you want the search committee to focus on. As such, although the CV is broad, encompassing, and suited for multiple recipients, the cover letters should be specifically targeted to the institutions in question. That is, consider the research you performed regarding your targeted institutions and emphasize how you fit their mold and needs, so to speak. Furthermore, it should be addressed to one person in particular.

Mention your general and specific interests in the career, position, department, college, and university. Telling them why you want the job, emphasize your strengths relative to their needs. Cite specific accomplishments, capabilities, skills, and qualities that you can bring to the college. Try to establish your relevance and uniqueness relative to the other candidates.

If you have a preferred set of courses that you have experience teaching, mention them. Mention your teaching philosophy and your understanding of students, learning styles, and assessment techniques. If you do not have the precise experiences they are looking for, discuss what you would be willing to do to qualify yourself further. Mention your short- and long-term goals as to teaching, research, and service. Discuss the contribution you hope to make to the college. Above all, make sure you are realistic when you describe your potential. Finally, the cover letter should state how you plan to follow up on your job-search correspondence. Indicate how soon, and by which method you will follow up—by phone, letter, e-mail, or in person. It is then important that you do follow up as indicated. Keep a copy of all cover letters, and log when/how you said you would follow up.

Most institutions will require several letters of recommendation. As an applicant, it is your responsibility to ensure that reference letters arrive in a timely fashion. Follow up with those who promise to provide references.

Seeking Work

Seeking and securing work as an academic can be a frustrating and demoralizing affair (Iacono, 1981). This is further aggravated when there is a shortage of positions. What does the near future hold? It is hard to tell. Pavesic (1993) and Lefever and Withiam (1995) seem to suggest that the current state of affairs and the near future reflect no shortage of academic positions. Woods (1994) demurs, however, and argues that we will shortly experience a surplus of hospitality faculty, and suggest that a demand will exist only for highly qualified faculty. In fact, he reports a decline in the posting of hospitality faculty positions.

Another concern is the tendency to write job descriptions that are very narrow and specific, so that only a very few candidates meet the requirements. Iacono (1981) reported this as occurring for psychology faculty job descriptions. A look at recent hospitality job descriptions would suggest much the same. It appears that hospitality administrators and hospitality search committees have idealized images of the prospective candidate! Our advice is not to read the job description narrowly, but to apply if you feel that you provide a reasonable fit and are interested in the institution. If the recipients feel you clearly do not fit their criteria, you are likely to get a rejection letter quickly. As mentioned above, if you are interested in an institution, contact them even if there is no current posting.

The Interview

The first step toward success is to obtain an initial interview. Although many facets of an applicant are considered when determining who to interview, there is reason to believe that the number and perhaps quality of publications and conference presentations is a primary consideration and may be a determining factor in the interview decision process (Iacono, 1981; Sheldon and Collison, 1990). The adage "publish or perish" may be relevant even prior to employment. This is particularly the case at research universities. Institutions that emphasize teaching, however, are less likely to put primary emphasis on your publication record (Sheldon and Collison, 1990).

The initial interview to develop a short list of candidates may take place during a conference, or often by phone. The following advice draws primarily from Klomparens (1997):

- *Time and place.* You are likely to be contacted about the best time and place for the interview. Do not settle on a time and place that are not good for you simply because they are being offered. If you are not solicited for time and place, do not hesitate to be proactive and suggest what will work for you, or that the proposed time is not appropriate. It is essential that you be able to focus on the interview and think clearly without interruptions. Phone interviews may best be done from the privacy of your home. At a conference, be ready to offer a quiet place in the event your interviewer does not provide one.

- *Paperwork.* Have a copy of your application, including cover letter, CV, and portfolios on hand. It is helpful for you to refer to them during the interview. It will assist you in remembering the content of your targeted cover letter. If the interview takes place in person, bring several copies in the event the interviewer forgets to bring a copy, or brings an additional faculty member who would benefit from a copy. Besides, in the conference setting you may meet representatives of additional institutions looking for hires, and a copy may come in handy.
- *Refresh your memory.* As mentioned above, knowledge about the employer is related to success in obtaining a job offer. Refamiliarize yourself with the institution and the faculty prior to the interview. If you know who will be conducting the interview, knowledge about the interviewer's research may prove helpful. Develop a list of questions and information items to have on hand during the interview.
- *Conference calls.* If the interview takes place as a conference call, try to keep track of names and titles. Write them down as they introduce themselves. This will make it easier for you to remember who you are responding to, and may be helpful in developing questions. Your initial research should help you as you should be familiar with the interviewers and their work.
- *Be active.* Try to sound interested and alert. This is particularly important during phone interviews, as the assessment of the interview will be based on your verbal responses. Do not hesitate to take notes so that you can fill in the gaps, return to important issues, and ask your own questions. Typically the interviewer will lead the discussion, and leave time at the end for questions and issues. Jablin and Miller (1990) suggest that interviewees should not hesitate to take a more active role, and

ask questions throughout the interview, as this demonstrates assertiveness and communicative competence relative to information seeking. In addition, active participation in the interview allows the interviewee to exert some control over the interview, refocus and direct it onto tracks that are relevant and positive for the interviewee.

- *Follow-up.* Send a follow-up letter as soon as possible expressing your gratitude for the opportunity to be considered and restating your interest. It is also useful to volunteer to supply additional information that may be helpful in making their decision. An additional follow-up by phone a few days later suggests initiative, interest, and enthusiasm, and may be a factor in furthering the process (Sciarini, 1996).

The On-Campus Interview

Although you may take some first interviews in order to practice interviewing, the primary objective is to secure a second interview. The second interview is most often a series of interviews that take place in conjunction with a site visit and job talk. The purpose of the visit from the perspective of the institutional members is to further assess your competency and academic potential. Moreover, they serve as a vehicle to determine whether your personality and worldview fits within the department. The visit will cover one or two days, and is typically rather hectic. You may be scheduled to meet most every faculty member, and perhaps some staff members. At a large program you may only visit with select representatives from the various departments or disciplinary areas. A meeting with the dean may also take place. Save your questions regarding the department at large, salary, merit raises, travel and research funds, terms of appointment, and so on, for your meeting with the department chairperson or director. According to Iacono (1981) you will get the most candid and unbiased assessment of the department from other recent hires, that is, the assistant professors. They can help you develop realistic expectations. According to Wanous (1992), most newcomers have inflated expectations regarding the organization. The most serious expectation inflation takes place for the job factors that are most important to the potential new hire, excepting pay, which is concrete and easily verifiable. Thus, it is advisable that you seek as much relevant information as possible from a variety of sources. Do not hesitate to ask several of those interviewing you the same set of questions. This will help add validity to your expectations.

Consecutive interviews that last thirty to forty-five minutes with minimal time in between throughout the day is quite normal, as job candidates are expected to meet with quite a large number of people. To complement the interviews, you are likely to be invited to lunch and dinner with some of the faculty. It is important to keep in mind that although some of the encounters may appear relaxed, there is no "time-out," as you are constantly scrutinized and under examination. Something said casually during lunch or dinner may become an evaluation point.

Your job talk, sometimes referred to as your colloquium, is the most important part of your visit. During the job talk you will be scrutinized very closely. Particular attention will be given to how you conceptualize and define problems, analyze data, and present and tackle questions. Some questions may be considered "friendly fire" while other questions may come from faculty members who wish to see if you can handle "critical fire" and see if you really know your data intimately. A good presentation does not a guarantee a job offer, but it is likely that a poor presentation will be a detriment. This may be the only time the faculty get to see you present to and interact with an audience, much like what you hope to do in the classroom at their institution. As such, it is critical that you have a clear, concise, well-delivered job talk. Practice your presentation on a critical audience. If you have a choice about when you will present, try to schedule it as early as possible. Iacono (1981) makes the point that this will eliminate the need to divulge your presentation contents during preceding interviews, and if done well, will set a positive tone for the remainder of your visit. It will also allow you to expand on issues during the individual interviews that follow.

As to the topic of the job-talk, if you have a variety of subjects to draw from, consider your audience and choose a topic that is broadly relevant to their interests. If you are just at the stage of completing your doctorate, you may wish to present your dissertation research. If you plan to present the dissertation, but have not completed it yet, try to develop some summary data and analysis, so that you can demonstrate your competence as a researcher, and have some results and potential implications to discuss. It is advisable to avoid a topic on which one of your audience is an expert, particularly if your findings and interpretations differ from those of the expert.

Some programs will ask you to teach a class to their students as part of the evaluation and interview process. In such instances it is common for several of the faculty to be in the classroom as well. It would be wise to select a topic you are most familiar with and can show enthusiasm for. The students may be also be part of the evaluation process by providing feedback on your classroom performance.

Follow-Up

Immediately upon return from your visit you should send a follow-up letter, thanking them for the invitation and opportunity to visit with them. Reconfirm your interest in the position, and suggest you are looking forward to learning their decision. If possible try to reemphasize how your background profile fits well. Do this while drawing upon new information you garnered during the visit.

Offers and Rejections

If you are fortunate you should receive an offer of employment a few weeks following your visit. There will invariably be several qualified candidates, and you may receive a letter of rejection. Unfortunately most rejection letters are uninformative. If you are interested in learning from the rejection, you can call on the department head or the chairperson of the selection committee. Politely inquire into what they saw as the key issues, strengths, and weaknesses of your candidacy. Do not be defensive or hostile; your purpose is to gather information, not to argue about their decision. You may not be provided much information, but what you do learn may prove helpful for future job seeking.

On the other hand, if you receive a letter offering you a position, you will find that they expect you to make your decision within a few days. At best you will be given two weeks to respond. It is to the institution's advantage to have you respond quickly, as this decreases the odds of you receiving other more attractive offers. It is to your advantage to be able to consider two or more offers simultaneously. Occasionally this happens. In any event, when you receive an offer, call all other programs you have visited. Tell them you have an offer in hand, and would appreciate being able to decide with the knowledge of their decision to guide you. You may be able to solicit an earlier decision, or assess their relative interest in you as a candidate. If a program is seriously interested in you, they will wish to know that you have received offers from others. The more offers you get, the better bargaining position you have. This is the time that you should use to negotiate any outstanding issues or terms of employment. As Iacono (1981) points out, if they have a strong second choice that is eager for the job, they may not be willing to negotiate much.

Responding to the Offer

You should respond to the offer in writing. If you decide to accept, you should indicate your pleasure and excitement at joining their program. It is also essential to outline and confirm all terms and conditions of hire, including salary, benefits, research support, and so on. This is particularly important, considering that expectations are typically inflated, and that recruiters and interviewers are sometimes inaccurate in their description of the job and organization (Wanous, 1992).

Should you decide to reject the offer, thank them for the opportunity and interest, while telling them that after careful consideration you have decided to accept another offer. Since it is possible that you would ask to be considered for employment at this institution in the future, you want to leave as favorable an impression as possible, despite your rejection of their offer.

THE FIRST FIVE YEARS

Organizational Entry

Whenever starting employment in a new organization, you go through a process known as organizational socialization (Louis,

1980). This is the process by which new employees come to learn of and appreciate the values, abilities, expected behaviors, and social knowledge needed to assume a position and function adequately as an organizational member. Organizational socialization is typically seen as having three stages: anticipatory socialization, the encounter stage, and the adaptation stage. If Graen and Scandura's role theory (1987) is applied to the socialization process, we can identify a potential fourth stage, the routinization stage. The process of organizational socialization is most pervasive during and after organizational entry, but can be seen as relevant throughout an employee's tenure with an organization.

Anticipatory socialization is the first stage. It starts prior to accepting a position, during the period in which information about the organization in question is gathered, from initial search, through application process, potential offer, and acceptance of position. The inflated expectations discussed by Wanous (1992) develop during this stage. Following anticipatory socialization is the encounter stage. This is when the new hire passes from outsider to organizational member. Many describe the initial encounter as a reality shock, fraught with surprise and violated expectations (Louis, 1980) as their anticipations are tested against the reality of the workplace. Newly hired hospitality faculty are also likely to experience some surprise and have expectations violated. Most doctoral programs require research and presentation of research and teaching as components of the program. Thus, doctoral candidates should experience less encounter stress than in other occupations as they in effect have had an experience akin to a realistic job preview (for a discussion of realistic job previews see Wanous, 1992 and Meglino, 1988). The third stage is adaptation, in which the new employee adapts to the organization and becomes an insider rather than a newcomer. This stage will be discussed further from the perspective of role theory later.

Louis (1980) further points out that newcomers should expect to experience five forms of surprise when entering an organization. The surprises may be encountered relative to unmet conscious expectation about the organization, unmet expectations about oneself, unmet unconscious expectations or unanticipated job features, difficulties in assessing potential internal reactions to events, and cultural assumptions. Her findings suggest that newcomers should attempt to find insiders as mentors or buddies that can help ease the transition. They can assist in socialization and assimilation by sharing their insights. A mentor or buddy would have insights to use in sense making due to their greater knowledge of the organization's history and processes. In addition, they can act as a reference person for the purpose of comparing and testing perceptions and attributions. As a new academic hire, you should attempt to find referent others within the department to use for sense making. The work of Ashford and Tsui (1991), although it focuses on managers, has relevance for the new academic hire. Their research suggests that new hires should seek formal critical feedback, not positive feedback, about their performance and attempt to monitor the social cues they observe directed toward them. This would allow the new hire to self-regulate performance and behavior as needed. Furthermore, individuals who engage in such action are perceived as more effective and convey a more positive image than those who do not take such action. Miller and Jablin (1991) give some excellent suggestions regarding how new hires should go about seeking relevant information during the organizational entry process.

Graen and Scandura (1987) advanced a role theory consisting of three stages: role taking, role making, and role routinization, which is relevant for the new hire as well. From their perspective, when a new hire starts, or when an individual is given a new position within a company, they enter the role-taking stage. In this stage initial role expectations are communicated to the organizational member by the member's role-set (Katz and Kahn, 1978). The immediate superior is often a message transmitter in the role-set, because the leader tends to produce numerous role-specific messages. Other organizational members, such as peers, also convey much role information. The member receives the information and acts accordingly, providing feedback regarding role acceptance, role understanding, or both. During this stage the member is primarily a passive recipient and internalizer of role information. It is in the next stage, role making, that the negotiation process between the immediate superior and the member takes place.

Following role taking, which may take hours, weeks, or perhaps the entire relationship, the role-making stage starts. During this stage the organizational member is no longer a passive recipient of role information. Contrary to the previous stage, both the leader and the member as well as other referent persons are seen as communicating their understandings, preferences, and expectations regarding their respective roles, their relationship, and the organization at large. As such, they develop jointly how they will interact with each other, and they establish or discover the degree to which they are interdependent. This negotiation often takes the form of sequences of offers and counteroffers regarding work-related behaviors, tasks, or communication. The areas about which they talk and negotiate typically include: (1) access to inside information, (2) provision or use of influence within the organizational system, (3) task choices and behaviors, (4) latitude (power) to make decisions, (5) support of each other's activities and choices (i.e., intradyadic loyalty), and (6) individual attention. Upon implicit or explicit acceptance and settlement of this negotiation process the immediate superior and organizational member move into a role routinization process in which the role behaviors and dyadic interdependencies become increasingly routinized and ossified. This regimen allows for clear expectations to form so that the dyadic partners know what to expect from each other. There are likely aspects of either's role that are not salient and therefore not discussed or negotiated. From this perspective the relationship between superior and subordinate is typically described in terms of leader-member exchange (LMX). Borchgrevink and Boster (1997) have researched hospitality organizations within this framework, attempting to establish how positive LMX quality develops. Most of their findings focus on the immediate supervisor actions, but of value to new hires, they found that communication between the immediate supervisor and the subordinate about work and nonwork issues is critical for positive LMX quality to develop. Major, Kozlowski, Chao, and Gardner (1995) have considered LMX and TMX (team-member exchange) relative to organizational socialization, and report that LMX and TMX help ameliorate the negative effects of unmet expectations upon organizational entry. Combined, this suggests that new hires would be well advised to engage their supervisor and peers in conversation and exchange of information, and adds to the arguments above for seeking feedback and developing mentors.

The Faculty Caveat

In recent years hospitality faculty at large have experienced increased emphasis on research and expectations to perform research. This is so prevalent that even typical teaching institutions have started to include research as an assessment criterion for their faculty. Research shows that although institutions may suggest that they value teaching very highly, when asked to consider teaching relative to research, research is by far the most important (DeFranco, Ferreira, and Rappole, 1994). This research does not suggest that teaching and service are not considered, but that as research expectations have increased, expectations relative to teaching and service have not. These issues are explored further in upcoming chapters. New faculty should take care to establish what the institution truly rewards and direct their efforts accordingly. Focusing solely on teaching-related activities can be the impetus for a new job search. At times, junior faculty may feel overwhelmed by all of the activities in which they are engaged, but eventually most faculty members are able to strike a meaningful balance. The next chapter further defines the responsibilities of professors and specifically discusses the combined roles of teaching, research, service, and professional development.

REFERENCES

Ashford, S.J. and Tsui, A.S. (1991). Self-regulation for managerial effectiveness: The role of active feedback seeking. *Academy of Management Journal, 34,* 251-280.
Bandura, A. (1986). *Social foundations of thought and action: A social cognitive theory.* Englewood Cliffs, NJ: Prentice-Hall, Inc.
Beatty, R. (1994). *Job search network.* Holbrook, MA: Bob Adams, Inc.
Borchgrevink, C.P. and Boster, F.J. (1997). Leader-member exchange development: A hospitality antecedent investigation. *The International Journal of Hospitality Management, 16*(3), 241-259.
Borchgrevink, C.P. and Kasavana, M.L. (1995). Internet browsing. *The Hospitality and Tourism Educator, 7,* 31-35.
Casado, M.A. (1997). Conversational Spanish in the hospitality curriculum. *Journal of Hospitality and Tourism Education, 9,* 63-65.
Cho, W., Connolly, D.J., and Tse, E.C. (1995). Cyberspace hospitality: Is the industry ready? *The Hospitality and Tourism Educator, 7,* 40.
Cook, R.A. and Yale, L.Y. (1994). In search of a common body of knowledge for introductory tourism courses. *The Hospitality and Tourism Educator, 6,* 39-42.

DeFranco, A.L., Ferreira, R.R., and Rappole, C.C. (1994). Research, teaching, service—Where is the balance? *The Hospitality and Tourism Educator, 6*(4), 56-58.

Festinger, L. (1957). *A theory of cognitive dissonance.* Stanford, CA: Stanford University Press.

Freeman, B. and Schopen, A. (1992). Does the early bird get the worm? An analysis of academic success, early placement preparation and hiring. *Journal of Employment Counseling, 9,* 183-190.

Graduate School (1997). *1997-98 career guide.* East Lansing, MI: The Graduate School, Michigan State University.

Graen, G.B. and Scandura, T.A. (1987). Toward a psychology of dyadic organizing. In L.L. Cummings and B.M. Staw (Eds.), *Research in Organizational Behavior, 5,* pp. 175-708. Greenwich, CT: JAT Press, Inc.

Griffin, R.K. (1994). Teacher of teachers. *Hospitality and Tourism Educator, 6,* 71-72.

Heider, F. (1946). Attitudes and cognitive organization. *Journal of Psychology, 21,* 107-112.

Heider, F. (1958). *The psychology of interpersonal relations.* New York: John Wiley and Sons.

Iacono, W.G. (1981). The academic job search: The experiences of the new Ph.D. in the job market. *Canadian Psychology, 22,* 217-227.

Jablin, F.M. and Miller, V.D. (1990). Interviewer and applicant questioning behavior in employment interviews. *Management Communication Quarterly, 4,* 51-86.

Kasavana, M.L. and Borchgrevink, C.P. (1997). Taking a byte out of the internet: The best of cyberfoodservice. *Journal of Hospitality and Tourism Education, 9,* 56-61.

Katz, D. and Kahn, R.L. (1978). *The social psychology of organizations,* Second edition, pp. 183-221. New York: John Wiley and Sons.

Keenan, A. and Scott, R.S. (1985). Employment success of graduates: Relationships to biographical factors and job-seeking behaviors. *Journal of Occupational Behavior, 6,* 305-311.

Klomparens, K. (1997). The job interview. In *1997-98 career guide.* East Lansing, MI: The Graduate School, Michigan State University.

Lefever, M.M. and Withiam, G. (1995). Hiring hospitality faculty: Evaluation and experience. *The Cornell Hotel and Restaurant Administration Quarterly, 36,* 93-96.

Lerner, E. (1992). Word of mouth. *Meetings and Conventions, 27,* 186.

Locke, E.A. and Latham, G.P. (1990). *A theory of goal setting and task performance.* Englewood Cliffs, NJ: Prentice Hall, Inc.

Louis, M.R. (1980). Surprise and sense making: What newcomers experience in entering unfamiliar organizational settings. *Administrative Science Quarterly, 25,* 255-261.

Major, D.A., Kozlowski, S.W.J., Chao, G.T., and Gardner, P.D. (1995). A longitudinal investigation of newcomer expectations, early socialization outcomes, and the moderating effects of role development factors. *Journal of Applied Psychology, 80*, 418-431.

Meglino, B.M. (1988). Effects of realistic job previews: A comparison using an enhancement and a reduction preview. *Journal of Applied Psychology, 73*, 259-266.

Mill, R.C. (1991). Responsibilities of the hospitality educators. *The International Journal of Hospitality Management, 10*, 179-186.

Miller, J. (1996). How to survive the dissertation. Parts 1-3. *The Graduate Post, 3*(1), 17; *3*(2), 8, 22; *4*(1), 10-11.

Miller, D.T. and Olsen, M.D. (1990). Setting standards for faculty evaluation. *The Cornell Hotel and Restaurant Administration Quarterly, 29*, 46-47.

Miller, V.D. and Jablin, F.M. (1991). Information seeking during organizational entry: Influences, tactics, and a model of the process. *Academy of Management Review, 16*, 92-120.

Pavesic, D.V. (1993). Hospitality educator 2005: Curricular and programmatic trends. *The Hospitality Research Journal, 17*, 255-294.

Pizam, A. and Milman, A. (1988). Academic characteristics and faculty compensation in U.S. hospitality management programs. *Hospitality Research Journal, 12*, 93-105.

Reich, A.Z. and DeFranco, A. (1994a). How to teach so students will learn: Part one. *The Hospitality and Tourism Educator, 6*(1), 47-51.

Reich, A.Z. and DeFranco, A. (1994b). How to teach so students will learn: Part two. *The Hospitality and Tourism Educator, 6*(2), 43-47.

Schmidgall, R.S. and Woods, R.H. (1992). Does education pay? A comparison of total earnings of hospitality educators and industry practitioners. *The Cornell Hotel and Restaurant Administration Quarterly, 33*, 64-68.

Sciarini, M.P. (1996). Strategic career planning. In R.H. Woods and Y.Z. King (Eds.), *Managing for quality in the hospitality industry*, pp. 363-410. East Lansing, MI: Educational Institute of the American Hotel and Motel Association.

Sheldon, P.J. and Collison, F.M. (1990). Faculty review criteria in tourism and hospitality. *Annals of Tourism Research, 17*, 556-567.

Vance, M.L., Potter, K., and Scheetz, L.P. (1993). *Graduate and professional school preparation.* East Lansing, MI: The Graduate School, Michigan State University.

Wanous, J.P. (1992). *Organizational entry: Recruitment, selection, orientation and socialization of newcomers.* Reading, MA: Addison-Wesley Publishing Company.

Wessel, J. (1994). 'Tis the season to network, *Training and Development, 48*, 7.

Woods, R.W. (1994). Ten years later: Who teaches hospitality in the 90s? *The Cornell Hotel and Restaurant Administration Quarterly, 35*, 64-71.

Chapter 6

The Academic Life
of Hospitality Educators

Robert H. Bosselman

INTRODUCTION

This chapter will attempt to discuss the everyday life of an academic, specifically those in hospitality education. There is great confusion over what constitutes work life for a faculty member. There has been growing concern over faculty work life since the latter part of the 1980s, specifically focused on faculty productivity and the amount of money being spent on higher education. There are three major emphases of a faculty member's life; teaching or instruction, research or scholarly activities, and service. Depending on the faculty member, specific institution, specific academic program, and immediate supervisors, the three unique functions of faculty can change in relative importance even in a given year.

As one who has worked exclusively for public universities, I have seen firsthand the disdain for public higher education on the part of legislators. Certainly public officials have a duty and obligation to be sure taxes paid by the public are being spent wisely, and that state employees are not abusing the system. From the outside, it can be difficult to understand what faculty do. We do not punch a time clock, nor are we generally supervised directly. We can be observed leaving our workplace in the middle of the day. We sometimes dress casually for the office. Work in this country still measures pay on a basis of time, not for a job done. Since we are not paid for time, legislators and other education watchdogs are confused about how to assess what we do. With no other model, faculty are frequently required to fill out a form stating how much time is spent in class, preparing for class, grading class work, holding office hours, attending meetings, and so on. These quantitative methods fail to capture what we do, since what we do can not be quantified.

When people are asked to name the major influences in their lives, the answer most common after "parents" usually has been "teacher." This then, is what we do. At its simplest, the nature and substance of education is to impart knowledge and intellectual and professional skills, as well as enable students to develop their vision of who they are and how they fit in our society. This act is often not seen nor measured. Yet, just think of a time when you sat with a teacher discussing something. Did you gain something, a new skill, new confidence, new insight that could be used? Who will know of that besides the teacher and you? How can that be measured? There are no quantitative measures that can be applied uniformly in the classroom, as motivating students entails different styles, depending on the individual students. In fact, there rarely exists a moment in our lives as teachers when we are not working. We are never sure where an idea will come from that can be introduced in a classroom, and will influence students.

Scholarly work begs for a standard of measurement as well. Those outside academia seem bent on counting numbers of publications, presentations, and such; anything that has practical value. What good is an article if only a few hundred readers of a journal ever see the article? Like teaching, scholarly work has much to do with providing students (and others) some tools by which they can enhance their quality of life. Intellectual work is no less work just because it cannot be seen.

The previous chapter ended with a discussion of the first five years of employment in an academic institution. Here I discuss the tenure decision process (which typically occurs in the sixth or seventh year). The rest of this chapter is devoted to discussions of teaching, research, and service in the academic's life (this will serve as an introduction to these activities—an entire chapter is devoted to each one later in the book). The path from entry-level assistant professor to tenured associate professor, and finally promotion to full professor and how these levels relate to the various activities will be explored in detail.

THE TENURE SYSTEM

Most faculty will serve a long period of probation, usually five or six years, and receive a decision on tenure in their six or seventh year. Tenure in its essence is the protection of academic freedom. This should not be confused with a public employee's right to free speech, but rather focuses on the individual faculty member's unique competence. The faculty member's right to freedom to expose, test, and extend knowledge hinges upon lengthy professional training, the development of specialized skills, and the mastery of a particular discipline. As long as faculty members adhere to a professional standard, they will not be placed at risk because of something they have said. The conferral of tenure by an institution means that after a probationary period during which it has had opportunity to determine professional competence, it has offered a favorable judgment on the individual's professional excellence. Tenure is not a guarantee of lifetime employment. It does not and should not assure rewards or rank or salary, nor should it protect a faculty member from future evaluations.

So, what does it take to earn tenure? Over the course of your first six years as a faculty member, you will wonder if you have made the right career choice; at the same time, colleagues in your specific institution will be considering if they made the right choice by selecting you for the job. Different groups on campus actually take part in the tenure decision. First and foremost is your own department; second is the specific college or school in which your department is located; third is the institutional level, usually represented by a committee on tenure and promotion; and finally, college or university administration (this would include your department chair or head, dean of your college, provost, and president of the college or university).

Your immediate colleagues will have several criteria to judge your performance. While the university may dictate the standards of tenure, it is at the department level that the relevant materials are gathered for evaluation. A review committee of fellow faculty (usu-

ally the tenured faculty of the department) will examine your curriculum vitae, copies of publications, student evaluations, course syllabi, and other related items. The faculty committee will discuss
your case, and recommend you, hopefully, to the department head.
Recall that you were hired on the basis of potential; clearly the
evaluation will assess that potential. The review committee will
likely rank you with your peers in the field. They are also likely to
address your effectiveness as a teacher, and your qualities as a
colleague. If the review at this level is negative, usually upper
administration concurs, and you are given one year to seek opportunity elsewhere.

Essentially, the main question being addressed is whether you
will, over a lifetime, add to the reputation of the department and
university through your performance in the classroom and via publications. During the six years of probation, the individual faculty
member needs to prepare this demonstration of worth to the department. Research must be conducted that yields tangible results, such
as publications or funding; teaching must be rated as effective; and
you must perform as an able and responsible member of the academic community. In other words, demonstrate an upward path for
your career that tells colleagues you know what it takes to get
somewhere worth going. However, there is a fine line between
doing what is needed and what is required. If you volunteer too
readily for committees or large teaching sections, you may find
yourself without time to focus on what is important.

Once your department has passed judgment, the department head
signs off. Rarely will there be disagreement here, unless there are
intradepartmental politics at play. The department head will pass the
portfolio and recommendations on to a collegewide committee for
evaluation. Usually the only difference between a department and a
college review is the standards applied. If a college is broad-based,
there may be significant disagreement as to what standards apply. In
most cases, hospitality education is a department contained in a
college of business or home economics. There may be substantial
differences in what is considered acceptable performance between
the hospitality program and the parent college. A new faculty member would be wise to spend considerable time learning the culture of
his or her particular college and university. Be especially wary if the

hospitality program is perceived as weak by other college departments, or by the university administration.

Usually at the college or university level of review, research activities take center stage. While committees do not actually count pages, they do examine articles for quality. Letters from external reviewers carry substantial importance at this level. Thus, it is critical for the new faculty to establish a name quickly. New faculty should attend CHRIE functions, get involved with CHRIE, and seek to publish in the *Journal of Hospitality and Tourism Research* and the *Journal of Hospitality & Tourism Education*. The key question here may be, does the candidate's work really matter?

Once you pass this level, the remaining steps are cursory reviews by administration. Rarely will a college dean or provost disagree with a tenure and promotion committee; but recall, that is likely a political issue, not a performance issue. If your file contains mixed votes, then upper administration will want explanations of both sides of an argument. There could also be a period of financial exigency, in which tenure can be denied. The whole process takes six months to a full year, and is likely the most stressful time of your life. If the decision is no, there are always grounds for review and possibly arbitration. Hopefully the response is yes, and the work will have been worth all the effort. In all likelihood, you will go through the tenure process only once. However, should you leave your current position, your new position may not grant tenure automatically. This is surely something to consider when examining opportunities in the field.

THE ROLE OF TEACHING

Instruction, or teaching, is clearly the guiding principle of higher education. On some campuses that emphasis may be primarily show, rather than reality. However, a number of institutions are devoting more resources to teaching; in particular, rewarding excellence in teaching. The beginning assistant professor in hospitality education should be clear about the instructional goals of the particular institution he or she has joined. Most likely the institutional statement on teaching will read something similar to, "all faculty members are expected to excel in classroom instruction."

One way to quickly ascertain the role of teaching is to examine the means by which teaching is evaluated. Let's examine both from the perspective of excellence. Faculty are expected to exhibit command of their subject matter in the classroom, and present material to students in an objective, organized manner that promotes learning. Faculty display concern and respect for their students. Faculty strive always to broaden their own knowledge and understanding of their specific discipline, and to stay abreast of the latest developments in their field. Faculty constantly seek to improve their teaching methods, use technology in the classroom, and develop materials that are well-designed and current. Faculty can further enhance their excellence in teaching by engaging in scholarly activities such as publication of textbooks or articles on their specific discipline. Such scholarly work could also include laboratory manuals or software. Excellence in advising also serves to augment excellence in teaching, as faculty interact with students.

So how will teaching be evaluated? Usually by a combination of factors, which might include student ratings, department chair ratings, an evaluation by the dean of the college, a self-evaluation or report, a committee evaluation, opinions from colleagues, visitations to the classroom by an appointed committee, and review of course syllabi and exams. More than likely, the hospitality instructor will be teaching three full classes each term. A higher class load can be expected at a two-year program, while a lower course load might be characteristic of a research-focused institution. Hospitality faculty who teach laboratory or graduate-level classes may also receive reduced teaching loads.

Teaching is inevitable for a hospitality faculty member. More than likely, faculty members receive their teaching assignments in the previous semester; in other words, fall classes are assigned in spring, with spring classes assigned in fall. If summer school is part of the hospitality program, the faculty member will usually have a choice whether to teach then or not. Although teaching assignments are usually dictated by administration, one of the growing problems in academia is the scheduling of classes. Most faculty seek to minimize their time with students, to spend more time on research activities. Classes are often scheduled at the convenience of the faculty member, not the students. More than likely, untenured faculty will have little or no choice about what they teach or when. On the other hand, full professors likely dictate what they teach and when.

Our examination of teaching seeks to explain that teaching is not simply a three classes/nine semester hours schedule for a faculty member. Are there faculty who abuse their position of privilege, working only the scheduled number of class hours and recycling old material? Unfortunately yes, although that is certainly the exception and not the rule. In hospitality education, faculty generally carry some of the highest teaching loads in an institution. They also tend to spend more time with the students. My explanation for this is that we treat students as our guests/customers. Faculty who have worked in the hospitality field know what it takes to be successful. In fact, a growing concern among hospitality academics has been the insistence of upper administration to hire more doctoral-degreed faculty at the expense of those with more hospitality field experience.

What does it take to produce a three-credit class? Such a class likely meets for a total of 150 minutes each week, for approximately fifteen to sixteen weeks in a semester. That does not leave much time to accomplish the goals of the course. For a faculty member to do a good job in the classroom, preparation time is critical. To prepare a simple fifty-minute class requires of the faculty member a good 150 to 200 minutes of preparation. And that is if it is done effectively. A good teacher has actually scripted out the class, and is prepared for just about anything to occur.

In an effort to supplement the material presented in the following chapter, the remainder of the discussion on teaching will center on the competencies necessary for teaching effectiveness. Numerous studies have been conducted, and knowledge and understanding of their findings can greatly assist aspiring faculty members and graduate students. Essentially, I am suggesting that prospective faculty note the findings of previous work in the area of competencies. Several studies have been conducted on the topic, some oriented toward college teaching in general, and three specifically on hospitality education.

Seldin (1988) identified five key ingredients of effective teaching: deep knowledge of subject, ability to communicate with and motivate students, enthusiasm for the subject and for teaching, clarity of presentation, and fairness. Kellough (1990, pp. 73-87) described twenty-two characteristics for a competent college instructor:

1. Knowledgeable about the subject matter
2. Active member of professional organization (attend meetings, read journals)
3. Understand the process of learning
4. Be an "educational broker"
5. Use effective modeling behaviors
6. Be open to change, be willing to take risks and be held accountable
7. Be accepting of each student's background
8. Organize the course and plan lessons carefully
9. Be an effective communicator
10. Constantly strive to further develop your repertoire of teaching strategies
11. Demonstrate concern for the safety and health of students
12. Demonstrate optimism, while providing a constructive and positive environment for student learning
13. Demonstrate confidence in students' abilities
14. Be skillful and fair in assessment of student learning
15. Be skillful in working with colleagues, administrators, and classified staff, maintaining and nurturing friendly and ethical professional relationships
16. Demonstrate continuing interest in professional responsibilities
17. Demonstrate a wide range of interests
18. Share a healthy and enjoyable sense of humor
19. Be quick to recognize a student in need of special student services
20. Make an effort to demonstrate how the subject matter may be related to the lives of students
21. Be knowledgeable about career opportunities and share this with students
22. Be reliable

Smith and Simpson (1993, 1995) organized teaching competencies into six major skill areas: scholastic, planning, management, presentation and communication, evaluation and feedback, and interpersonal. Their list of thirty-four competencies associated with student learning can assist faculty in their individual approach to teaching (Exhibit 6.1).

Hu and Bosselman (1997) used Smith and Simpson's work as a foundation for their study of hospitality education. They studied a large sample of both two- and four-year educators to ascertain if differences existed with respect to importance placed on teaching competencies. Findings in this study were different from Smith and Simpson's in terms of the ranking of competencies. Hospitality educators ranked interpersonal, or communication-oriented competencies higher than educators in Smith and Simpson's study. In the former study, planning and management skills were ranked higher than in Hu and Bosselman's study. The hospitality study found two-year educators ranking the teaching competencies higher than four-year educators. A number of significant differences were found between the two groups of faculty. Planning skills were found to be ranked lowest, suggesting that faculty are not trained to be teachers. According to research on new and junior faculty (Fink, 1984; Boice, 1991), novices in the professoriate experience great stress from their teaching responsibilities, feel uncertain about how to improve their teaching, and typically have received little guidance in graduate school or from colleagues about creative and effective approaches to teaching. Two additional studies of interest to hospitality educators are Canterino (1990) and Avgoustis (1996). Both used a Delphi approach with hospitality educators to identify specific competencies for educators in this field. Canterino identified fourteen knowledge competencies, six skill competencies, and six learning experiences for hospitality educators. Avgoustis identified five knowledge competencies, ten abilities competencies, and ten skills competencies. These studies obtained results similar to those described in this chapter. Interested readers should seek out the references.

THE RESEARCH PARADIGM

Unless you are employed in a hospitality program exclusively oriented toward teaching, you will be expected to engage in research activities. For those choosing a career at a traditional four-

EXHIBIT 6.1. Teaching Competencies by Skill Category

Scholastic Skills

a. Demonstrate mastery of subject matter
b. Recognize and accept teaching as a fundamental and challenging dimension of scholarship
c. Enhance motivation of students by demonstrating relevance to future needs and goals of students*
d. Communicate important values inherent to the specific discipline
e. Demonstrate relationships between the course and the broader liberal education curriculum
f. Advise students of career opportunities in the specific discipline

Planning Skills

a. Promote individual involvement of students through learner-centered teaching methods*
b. Encourage cooperation and collaboration among students*
c. Select course material suited to the background, ability level, and interests of students
d. Match varying teaching methods with specific instructional objectives
e. Accommodate different learning styles of students by using a variety of teaching methods
f. Present material that is sequenced and paced appropriately for learners
g. Enhance motivation of students by demonstrating relevance to future needs and goals of students*
h. Use research in teaching as it applies to instruction in one's field
i. Design courses that challenge students to pursue higher levels of learning

Management Skills

a. Communicate and manage appropriate expectations for achievement in the course
b. Manage the learning environment so that optimum learning will result
c. Manage the process of planning, teaching, and evaluation in a timely manner
d. Deal appropriately with matters of discipline, academic honesty, and legal information
e. Communicate important departmental policies that relate to the goals of the course
f. Communicate and implement important safety measures in the classroom
g. Manage administrative responsibilities such as ordering books, and complying with other departmental requirements

*Skill found in more than one area.

EXHIBIT 6.1 (*continued*)

Presentation and Communication Skills

a. Communicate effectively in both written and oral formats in English
b. Promote individual involvement of students through learner-centered teaching methods*
c. Encourage cooperation and collaboration among students*
d. Enhance motivation of students by demonstrating relevance to future needs and goals of students*
e. Lead class discussions that stimulate learning and enhance the goals of the course
f. Build confidence in students by helping them to successfully meet learning objectives
g. Use technology to enhance learning

Evaluation and Feedback Skills

a. Provide helpful feedback to students in a variety of ways
b. Develop a reflective approach to teaching through collecting feedback and continually modifying instructional approaches
c. Construct valid and reliable tests and fairly administer other evaluative measures

Interpersonal Skills

a. Exhibit respect and understanding for all students
b. Enhance motivation of students through personal enthusiasm for the subject
c. Demonstrate a general belief that all students are capable of learning
d. Be accessible to students
e. Enhance motivation of students by demonstrating relevance to future needs and goals of students*
f. Deal appropriately with issues that relate to diversity
g. Project a sense of warmth and humor to the students

---

*Skill found in more than one area.

year hospitality program, your research efforts are likely the key to your long-term success. Indeed, it would be unlikely to earn tenure without a modest effort at scholarly pursuits. Why has research assumed such a powerful position in academia? At its roots, the university (and academia) is a place of learning. Therefore, for a university or college to function effectively, it must be staffed by those who are excellent learners. This group of learners (faculty) are constantly pushing the boundaries of knowledge in all fields, hospitality education included. If we were to teach only what we knew from history, students graduating from our programs would not be prepared for the challenges awaiting them in tomorrow's world. A faculty member's ability to pursue these boundaries of knowledge will therefore be a measure of personal worth, and also a measure of the worth of the respective academic program. Your research is what my colleague John Bowen (Director of Graduate Studies and Research in the William F. Harrah College of Hotel Administration) calls your passport in higher education. Research establishes your reputation as a scholar, both in the United States and internationally. You carry that reputation everywhere you go. Thus, it can open doors for you, and for your institution. Another factor, which has been previously noted, refers to the measurability of research as compared to teaching by administrators.

While the words research and scholarship have been used in the discussion, there has been debate over what term to utilize when discussing "research." Many land-grant schools use the term "research and discovery," which suggests creation and preservation of knowledge that benefits the many constituencies of the university. Most of the public thinks of scientists in laboratories when they consider research. Yet a great deal of scholarly work takes the form of books, many written in humanities and the liberal arts. Artistic creativity can also be classified as research, since the artist conceives and performs work, often for the public. It is quite possible that hospitality education contains examples of all of these types of research. Boyer (1991) suggested that scholarship encompasses integration, application, and dissemination of knowledge as well as its discovery. Getman (1992) provides us with definitions of major terms in the discussion:

- Publication: academic writing, essentially a restatement of others' thinking
- Scholarship: writing that introduces or challenges concepts
- Research: the effort to discover something significant about the way the world works

Perhaps rather than getting hung up on definitions, it is far better to focus on what is important. A faculty member who keeps current by reading literature, but does not actively engage in generating new knowledge, is not conducting research. Research is not simply a process, but a completed product. Publication is essential. The products of research—journal articles, books, exhibitions—become tools of teaching. These tools can then be used outside the faculty member's institution. This leads to greater credibility of the institution, and the hospitality program, among peer programs and institutions.

Many hospitality programs, and institutions in general, are wrestling with standards regarding research. The best suggestion is to set your standards high. Tenure requirements appear to be stiffening. As an example, one program in our field in 1997 noted it took six refereed articles to be considered positively for tenure (it was expected the faculty member would average one refereed publication a year for each of the six years of probation). This year the number has been removed, and the word now circulating is quality of work (note the more subjective approach allows universities to control faculty more). So what should you do to prepare for this academic exercise? You should demonstrate the ability to conduct research that reflects original scholarship and makes a contribution to knowledge. This can be accomplished by conducting research with proper methodological techniques; conceptualizing and theorizing in original ways; demonstrating ability to synthesize, criticize, and clarify existing work; provide innovation in data analysis; and relate research to solutions of practical problems. Such work can be demonstrated through journal articles (ideally refereed), books, book chapters, citations of your work, research grants and proposals, papers presented at professional conclaves, editorial positions, consulting, invitations to speak at professional meetings and other institutions, and reviews of your work by other academics.

The emphasis thus far has been on the individual, but the hospitality program itself has a key role to play also. As a faculty member you have a right to expect time to conduct research. This freedom to engage in scholarly pursuits comes via reduced teaching loads, sabbaticals, summer breaks, and any other ways to maximize your time management. There are also the tools of research. A good library is essential, although the development of technology may alter this in the future. A computer would appear to be a minimum, although there are academic programs that cannot provide one to the faculty member. Research costs money, and your program will not have much to offer, considering all the other expenses inherent to an organization. However, some form of monetary support may be available, such as graduate assistants, computer accounts, in-house grants, or consulting opportunities. One opportunity for newer faculty would be to pair up with an established senior faculty member in collaborative research efforts. Younger faculty might also consider seeking a senior faculty member as a mentor for their research; someone who can act as a reviewer and guide to their work.

There are other secrets to success here. For example, becoming known in hospitality education circles will lead to more opportunities for you as a faculty member. Hospitality education is still a newer academic field, and has a limited number of programs. Everyone knows the better programs, and students from those programs seem to enjoy an edge in getting published, or having papers presented at hospitality conferences. Faculty should get to know editors of major hospitality journals. If you can't walk up and introduce yourself, have a colleague introduce you. Be sure to read the hospitality publications and be cognizant of what type of writing each journal seeks. It is probably best not to pursue writing a textbook until after receiving tenure, unless your program encourages it. Many institutions strongly encourage grants and refereed articles to earn tenure.

One point to remember is that research is not just a means to earn tenure. Let me again cite my colleague John Bowen. John directs students to keep their research pipeline full. In other words, while you should always be writing up a result, another study may be in literature review, and still another project is at the proposal stage. Faculty members are expected to show growth beyond graduate school. Work begun in graduate school should propel an assistant professor forward, further developing ideas on topics from a dissertation. It is hard work, and requires dedication. This commitment may mean you pass up some opportunities. New faculty should keep their priorities straight, and remember that once you earn tenure, more opportunities will present themselves.

SERVICE: THE THIRD WHEEL OF ACADEMIA

Service (see Chapter 9) is always included in the triad of academic responsibilities, but its importance varies by institution. If you join a research-oriented program, service responsibilities will be quite limited. Conversely, a program with little or no research mandate may place a strong emphasis on service. Service in hospitality education has always been a strong component of programs. One of the reasons for the development of hospitality education has been the strong relationship between industry and academia. A significant danger to the long-term success of hospitality education would be a focus exclusively on research, and minimal emphasis on industry.

What exactly is service? One branch might be referred to as institutional service, or what I refer to as academic citizenship. These activities help maintain the hospitality program itself, as well as the parent college and the university. The university by nature requires faculty participation, usually expressed via committees. It would be expected that senior-level faculty would carry more of a service role than newer faculty. However, all faculty are expected to contribute in some way. A new faculty member needs to recognize the difference between making an expected contribution and being too involved. It would be wise to seek counsel from your department head with respect to service assignments.

A second form of service is professional. This type of service could take place locally, nationally, or even internationally. Recall from earlier work that peer recognition will distinguish you from others in the field. In hospitality education, professional service can be best experienced through CHRIE. There are numerous opportunities to participate in CHRIE activities or committees. One advantage of this participation is the networking among colleagues and industry professionals. A third type of service is public service, sometimes referred to as community service. The purpose of community service is to communicate what happens in academia to the lay world outside the academic walls. There are numerous ways to be involved here: membership on local/regional boards; production of written materials; consulting with state/regional officials; organizing workshops for the public; or testifying to a state legislature. Public universities in particular have a role in this type of service. Their outreach activities can assist states with economic or social issues. Such activity helps in a positive impression of the institution by the public at large. A fourth type of service is private or individual service. It is unlikely this type would be considered as part of a faculty member's portfolio for tenure and promotion. Most often, one thinks of consulting here. In the hospitality field, there are numerous opportunities for such work.

For newer faculty in particular, balancing service responsibilities with teaching and research requirements can be tricky. It is recommended that new faculty take the service role easy in the first two to three years. It might be wise to let your department head nominate you for specific assignments. This way, they are taking responsibility for you, and mentoring you in the way they desire. On the other hand, be careful that such an administrator knows the institutional culture. You want to do your part, but you also want to do what is right, and best for you. Certain committees are considered more prestigious than others, such as curriculum committees, or promotion and tenure committees. Other committees are considered low prestige and heavy workload, such as an admissions committee. Working with student groups as an advisor may also be a double-edged sword. How student groups are perceived may differ depending on the college or university. Students may praise your efforts, but remember that students do not decide your tenure and promotion.

A Faculty Activity Report

Before you accept that first position, get hold of the annual faculty review form used for evaluating faculty. By examining this form, you can quickly tell what activities are of importance to the institution. A sample form follows in Exhibit 6.2.

CONCLUSION

In this chapter, I have attempted to paint a picture of life as an academic. It is not as easy as imagined by those outside the academic world. Yet, with proper planning, life as an academic can be constantly invigorating. Students are always changing, and their youth and vitality stimulates you to be a better teacher. Your curious nature leads you to constantly seek more knowledge, so you stay on the cutting edge of the hospitality field. And, finally, we are in the hospitality field. This means dealing with people. Through service we maintain our touch with industry and practical solutions to real issues. Each of these activities requires time—you may find there are not enough hours in the day to accomplish all you had hoped for.

EXHIBIT 6.2. Annual Report Form

Personal Data

Name, university address, phone, highest degree earned, date of initial hire, date of tenure award, current position, length of time in current position.

Instructional Activities

Courses taught, credit hours, numbers of students in courses, any special courses such as independent study or thesis/dissertation, student evaluation scores, advising responsibilities, graduate students you serve as major advisor, graduate committees you serve on.

Research Activities

Publications—journals, books, monographs, book chapters; papers presented; grant proposals and funded research; research in progress.

Service Activities

Institutional service—department, college, university.
Professional service—activities in professional organizations; professional memberships; editorial or reviewer activities; participation in workshops; professional travel.
Public service—local, regional, state, national.

Other

Anything that does not fit under existing categories; possibly future plans.

REFERENCES

Avgoustis, S.A. (1996). *The design of a job specification model for hospitality management educators: Using the Delphi method to analyze competency requirements.* Unpublished PhD dissertation. Terre Haute, IN: Indiana State University.

Boice, R. (1991). New faculty as teachers. *Journal of Higher Education, 62,* 150-173.

Boyer, E.K. (1991). *Scholarship reconsidered: Priorities of the professoriate.* Princeton, NJ: Carnegie Foundation for the Advancement of Teaching.

Canterino, J.T. (1990). *Necessary competencies and learning experiences for hospitality educators: A Delphi study.* Unpublished PhD dissertation. Ames, IA: Iowa State University.

Fink, L.D. (1984). The first year of college teaching. *New directions for teaching and learning.* San Francisco: Jossey-Bass Publishers, No. 17.

Getman, J. (1992). *In the company of scholars: The struggle for the soul of higher education.* Austin, TX: University of Texas Press.

Hu, C. and Bosselman, R.H. (1997). Validating teaching competencies in hospitality education: Faculty members' perspective. *Journal of Hospitality and Tourism Education, 9,* 39-46.

Kellough, R.D. (1990). *What are my current competency levels? A resource guide for effective teaching in postsecondary education: Planning for competence.* Lanham, MD: University Press of America, Inc.

Seldin, P. (1988). Evaluating college teaching. College teaching and learning: Preparing for new commitments. In *New directions for teaching and learning.* Young, R.E. and Eble, K.E. (Eds.), pp. 47-56. San Francisco: Jossey-Bass Publishers, No. 33.

Simpson, R.D. and Smith, K.S. (1993). Validating teaching competencies for graduate teaching assistants: A national study using the Delphi method. *Innovative Higher Education, 18,* 133-146.

Smith K.S. and Simpson, R.D. (1995). Validating teaching competencies for faculty members in higher education: A national study using the Delphi method. *Innovative Higher Education, 19,* 223-234.

Chapter 7

Curriculum and Instruction

Robert H. Bosselman

INTRODUCTION—WHAT MAKES A GOOD TEACHER

An inevitable component of a faculty member's professional life is teaching students. With research and service choices can be made; whether to do it, how much, when, and what type. A teaching assignment, however, is usually handed down via administrative fiat. Although teaching has long been ignored or downplayed in importance relative to research, the basic role of academia lies with instruction of students. This is particularly true in hospitality education.

How are we able to identify an effective teacher? Centra (1990) reported that over 90 percent of faculty judged their colleagues' teaching as "excellent" or "very good." Yet repeatedly we hear reports of dissatisfaction with instruction. When one considers the broad range of classroom environments (lectures, discussion sections, seminars, institutes, workshops, media presentations, laboratory instruction, in-service training, media courses, correspondence courses, individual tutorials, advising and counseling, and consulting), it becomes clear that no one teacher can be expected to be equally proficient in all situations. However, one should clearly demonstrate proficiency in those situations germane to one's individual teaching responsibilities.

What then makes a good college/university-level teacher in hospitality education? For a topic so controversial, there is little hard data that relates teacher quality to objective measures, such as test scores. A number of researchers focus on personality traits, such as enthusiasm, a love of teaching students, an inquiring manner, a democratic perspective; while others concentrate on knowledge of subject matter (intellectual excellence) as the critical factor. There is a growing sentiment that a good teacher, and thus good teaching, results from a combination of traits and behaviors. These would include those characteristics indicated above, as well as creating a comfortable learning environment, having an ability to relate to students, and showing a caring attitude. If we examine the knowledge of subject as a base, that leads us to our training in graduate school—developing a sense of inquiry. The good teacher is curious; the good teacher challenges himself or herself; the good teacher is open to change. From this approach, one can grasp how a hospitality management instructor can develop a specific class, or series of classes, which link objectives/outcomes to the curriculum as a whole. The other approach apparent from the characteristics given is that the good teacher has a positive perspective, an anything-is-possible, can-do approach. From this perspective, the teacher is a leader. This should not surprise those of us involved with hospitality management education. Some educational theorists suggest that the role of the teacher is responsible for approximately 20 percent of the student's actual achievement. In fact, a teacher often does not know when or where his or her influence starts, or stops.

Another approach to good teaching is recognition of the needs of the core constituency. Does this sound familiar to hospitality professionals? Of critical importance here is the attribute of interpersonal rapport (Lowman, 1995), which includes speaking ability and interpersonal skills. This attribute encourages contact between faculty and students, both in and out of the classroom. When faculty show interest in the students, students are more likely to remain motivated and involved in the class. Good teachers are cheerfully available to students outside the classroom. A second aspect of the attribute is developing a cooperative environment among students. Students learn more in a collaborative and social setting, and this also prepares them for work situations outside academia. A third parameter of the interpersonal style is an active learning classroom. Learning is not a one-way process, and is less effective when only the teacher is active. Students want to talk about what they are learning, and in particular, apply it to their individual lives.

We have a real advantage in hospitality education; our students usually are working in their chosen field. This should lead to very active class discussions. The good teacher also gives students feedback promptly. With feedback, students sharpen their learning and benefit from a class. This not only applies to exams and papers, but to frequent opportunities that may arise in a classroom setting. In conjunction with this pattern of assessment, students expect good teachers to communicate their expectations. Students want high expectations. The more faculty members expect and demand from their classes, the more they will get and the more students will benefit. Teachers who push students to produce better work, while also coaching them on how to produce, will consistently receive high praise from students. This reference to coaching includes emphasizing the importance of time on assignments. Deadlines should be established for all course work, and adhered to, with exceptions for certain extenuating circumstances. This challenge to students also respects the many different talents present in the students. Chances are that the hospitality management classroom of tomorrow will be more diverse than today's. People bring different talents and styles of learning to higher education. When we as teachers can provide our students with the opportunities to demonstrate their talents and learn in an appropriate manner for them, then we will have succeeded at teaching.

To become a good teacher is an ongoing challenge. Although it is expected that all teachers are good, reality tells us this is a false assumption. What we know is that a good teacher is many things. Not every one of us can always be that good teacher. However, if one plans on spending time in a college/university classroom, one needs to consider the factors discussed. For most of us, the intellectual component, or subject knowledge, is the easy part. We received training in hospitality management or a particular discipline, and probably conduct research in that area. Students look to us as the experts in the field. Most likely it is the interpersonal component that challenges most faculty. One cannot be forced to exhibit enthusiasm, or a caring attitude. Good teachers take pride in their work, and in their positions at their respective institutions. For those not sure of their interpersonal style, one alternative way of figuring out who you are in the classroom would be to look inward at your own values, and in particular, your philosophy of teaching.

DEVELOPING A PHILOSOPHY OF TEACHING

No single theory of teaching/learning can account for the complexity of the classroom learning environment. Indeed, any particular learning theory does not, and cannot specify all aspects of the practice of teaching. Therefore, whether or not a specific educational exercise is valid does not depend on its having a theoretical basis.

Traditionally, there have been three particular theoretical approaches to education; cognitive, behaviorist, and humanistic. A cognitive approach views students as active seekers of new information and skills. The best teachers are those who motivate students to tap their own natural ability to attempt solving problems and making decisions. Hospitality management teachers who follow this perspective favor the work of Piaget, whose work on constructivism implies that each individual creates his or her own knowledge. Behaviorists tend to structure students' environment to aid in the learning process. Like B.F. Skinner, they believe in the use of reinforcers. Behavioral objectives guide students in their acquisition of content. Humanistic teachers focus on helping students learn how to learn. This student-centered approach follows Carl Rogers's perspective of self-actualization, that teachers are merely facilitators in the learning process.

In examining approaches to teaching, one must be aware of the environment influencing both students and faculty. In the 1960s, for example, the unprecedented number of young people seeking education transformed institutions of higher education. Accompanying this growth was a wave of social activity centered on race, gender issues, and an unpopular war. This created a concern for community, and a more significant role for sensitivity. In the 1990s, corporate downsizing and reengineering, coupled with an obsessive focus on the stock market, has created a cohort of students (particularly in hospitality management and business administration) focused on achieving "the best jobs, making lots of money." This has led to an increase in students seeking more vocational skills. Witness the growth in enrollment in two-year and culinary arts programs, including high schools. Perhaps the best educational theory is the one that encourages students to acquire a competence based on an understanding of ecological, social, and cultural problems. Students will need an education that allows them to solve the social, ecological, cultural, and political problems that they inherit.

For hospitality faculty, certain considerations should be included in developing any principle of teaching. First, always put the student's need first, and the institutional need second. Encourage diversity of opportunity rather than uniformity. De-emphasize time and course requirements in favor of competence and performance. Ask yourself, are you satisfied with your beliefs about education? Are you tradition-bound, or do your beliefs help you to meet the needs of today's students? By identifying and clarifying the role values play in your life, you can recognize how your own values affect the choice of instructional methods, your relationship with students, and the degree to which you are willing to experiment with innovative approaches in the classroom. Values represent the important and stable ideas, beliefs, and assumptions that affect our behavior. These have been freely chosen from among alternatives and after much contemplation. As such, these values are cherished, affirmed to others, and incorporated into our everyday behavior. Thus, our values are repeated on a regular basis. A good teacher will help students do the same. Personal values are not forced upon students. The teacher creates conditions that help students find values if that is their choice. This process can be discomforting. Who are you as a teacher? How can you discover, and develop the part of you that is a teacher? You need to envision the ideal you as a teacher. Based on this vision, what do you need to do to move yourself from today's reality to your perception of ideal?

Planning a Course

Begin by asking yourself, "Why am I teaching hospitality management?" and "How do I want my students to change?" Be specific. In other words, defend your course. The primary goals, essential to your class, are probably easy to develop. There may also be secondary goals important in the overall curriculum. These goals are likely cognitive or affective, and may involve oral or written skills.

The starting point is the students (Brinko, 1991). Who are they? Is this an introductory class, or a capstone class? Are students traditional college-age students, or nontraditional/older adult students? Why are they taking this class? What level of skill or knowledge will students bring to your class? Other questions to ask yourself before composing your syllabus and class lessons include specifics such as length of the class (number of weeks, i.e., quarter or semester; minutes for each class meeting, i.e., fifty minutes three times weekly, seventy-five minutes twice weekly, or 150 minutes once a week), location of the class (on campus, off campus, which building and room, condition of the room—desks, chairs, audiovisual equipment, etc.), and what your expectations for students will be. The last point refers to the level of responsibility you will share with the students. For example, will you require a textbook, or will there be a reading list available from the library? Will the class be straight lecture, or will you require discussion of readings and/or current events? What type of assignments, quizzes, papers, and/or exams will be included in the class? Will you emphasize oral or written work? Keep in mind that all material should enable students to reach the objectives clearly delineated for the class (Cross and Angelo, 1993).

One of the more critical points to consider today is choice of a textbook (Johnson, 1990). Critics argue that textbooks quickly become outdated and do not provide the most current innovations in a field. In addition, an instructor may rely solely on a textbook for course content and objectives. On the other hand, many hospitality management texts are written by the foremost experts in the field, and students benefit from exposure to these primary sources. A number of textbooks in hospitality management are complemented by well-designed student workbooks or study guides. These can help students apply the theories presented to real problems. Should a course not utilize a textbook, there are alternatives such as a library reserve list, or a course packet designed by the instructor. With the growth of electronic communication, students can access numerous sources of material via the Internet. Again, the teacher must decide if a text adds value to the class, and meets the objectives set for the class. If the answer is no, then an alternative to a textbook should be considered.

Preparation of the syllabus is an exercise many faculty handle poorly (Lowther, Stark, and Martens, 1989). Many campuses now dictate certain components of a syllabus, in order to limit misunderstandings that often lead to grievances. Since the syllabus may be the first impression of you, and your course, it would be foolish to ignore the opportunity of making a favorable impression. The word syllabus is defined most commonly as an outline of study. However, the primary purpose of a syllabus is to let students and faculty know their destination in the course.

A syllabus should contain an outline, and a schedule of topics. But, an effective syllabus communicates to students what the course is about, why the course is taught, and what are the student's responsibilities in order to successfully complete the course. A syllabus, then, can be regarded as a written agreement between the faculty member and students. You could make the agreement binding by adding a brief final page, "I have read the syllabus, understand its implications, and will abide by it," and have students sign. This would formalize the contract between parties (Matejka and Kurke, 1993). If it is necessary to change the direction of the class, or alter the material examined in some way, the instructor should do so in writing to the class.

The Syllabus

Let us examine a model syllabus. It is quite possible that some material may not be applicable to certain classes or hospitality management programs. However, one should include all the information students need to have at the start of the class, and all this information should be in writing (Altman and Cashin, 1992). Course information can serve as an introduction: course title, course number, and number of credits. It might also be appropriate to include the location of the classroom and the meeting times for the class. Personal information about the instructor should include instructor name, title, office location, office phone, fax, and e-mail address, and office hours. You may also want to include other contact numbers, such as a department office/phone/fax, graduate assistant information, and a home telephone number (be careful with the latter; use a restriction such as no calls after 9:00 p.m. and before 8:00 a.m.). When you discuss the syllabus with the class, these items can be clarified. For example, how do you wish to be addressed? Is your office easily accessible, or do you need to describe how to get there? Will you meet with students outside of scheduled office hours?

A clearly worded course description can be included, and may be similar to that provided in the university catalog. This also presents an opportunity for the instructor to describe his or her feelings about the course. Instructor enthusiasm draws students into the course and starts motivation immediately. Course objectives should be clear and convey to the students what will be accomplished in the class. This part of the syllabus should present students with an intellectual challenge that will relate the purpose to real-world application. Students should be clear about what they will know, and be able to do at the end of the class.

The course calendar provides approximate dates for class topics, exams, and projects, and may be presented in a daily or weekly format. Stating that the schedule is tentative and subject to change based on the class frees the instructor from liability concerns. Remember that it is important to communicate any changes in writing. If you expect students to meet deadlines, then you must give them necessary information for planning. Be sure to emphasize critical due dates and assignments. Course requirements make it clear what students are required to do to successfully complete the class. All issues related to the evaluation process should be spelled out. Poor student performance often results from confusion over expectations. Do you have a policy on attendance? Is class participation included in grading? How many quizzes or exams will take place? A well-designed course will offer multiple opportunities for students to demonstrate performance. A class with but one type of evaluation limits success to those students most adept at that style of learning. The textbook and other materials has been noted earlier in this section. Information on the text should include title, author, edition, publisher, and where available. The instructor may also want to inform students why the particular text was selected. The syllabus should also indicate which readings from the text are required. If other materials are used in the course, the teacher should make it clear how to find the readings, and again explain why they are relevant to the course.

Course grading should be handled as a separate topic, and considerable effort must be given here by faculty. Since grading policies often tend to be a focus of confusion or misunderstandings, take special care to articulate grading criteria. Avoid misunderstandings by reminding students of their responsibilities in the course. The instructor should indicate what percentage of the course grade will be assigned to each evaluation activity (homework, papers, quizzes, exams, lab reports, etc.). Recall that a good teacher places emphasis on specific course requirements; if students know the relative importance of these at the start of the class, it will likely help them budget time and effort. On the first day of class, spend time on the grading section. Be sure students recognize what level of work corresponds to respective grades (A, B, etc.). Students will want to know if you curve grades, or if you make adjustments as the semester moves along. Another consideration is how quickly you grade class material. Again, a good teacher makes every effort to evaluate student work as quickly as possible. Students will be amazed, and you will show you care, if you can return material by the following class period.

Course policies are a final area to consider for a syllabus. These policies may be dictated by your institution. Of consideration here are policies related to attendance/lateness, missed exams/assignments, academic dishonesty, and the availability of student support services. The instructor needs to be quite clear with respect to such policies, and not make exceptions. Once students know you make exceptions to rules/policies, it will be quite difficult to enforce such rules/policies consistently. One example is plagiarism. In fact, some students may not know what plagiarism actually is. It is the instructor's responsibility to explain policies on the first day of class.

Now the instructor is ready for class. Keep in mind that you are now beginning an educational journey with a new group of students. The syllabus, and your first day of class, are critical to the overall success of your course. Recall that the first impression of your class conveys a powerful message to students (Hockensmith, 1988). Ask yourself if your syllabus conveys your appreciation of the course content. Would you be excited and motivated to take the class?

Developing Goals and Objectives

As we have indicated, the good hospitality management teacher designs a syllabus that is clear in its mission. Students and faculty both have an understanding of what will be expected from them. One of the challenges in preparing the syllabus (and in planning the course itself) is the development of goals and objectives. Initially, the goal of education was to teach each new cohort all the knowledge accumulated from history. Today, the overriding purpose of education would more likely be described as developing students in such a way that they are better able to meet their needs in our ever-changing society.

The development of students usually involves new knowledge, intellectual skills, affective patterns, and also psychomotor skills. These are commonly delineated into three domains: cognitive, affective, and psychomotor objectives. Since the goals of education (particularly hospitality management education) are student-oriented, educational objectives should be stated in terms of desired student behavior. The cognitive domain includes objectives related to the recall of knowledge, and the development of intellectual abilities and skills. The affective domain refers to those objectives dealing with changes in a student's emotional state, or a degree of acceptance/rejection of some value/attitude. The psychomotor domain includes objectives that primarily involve motor skills.

Bloom's (1956) taxonomy is well known as the organizing philosophy of the cognitive domain. The taxonomy consists of six subdivisions, categorized by degree of increasing complexity: knowledge, comprehension, application, analysis, synthesis, and evaluation. The affective domain is characterized by the process of internalization. Five categories have been identified by researchers (Krathwohl, Bloom, and Masia, 1964); receiving, responding, valuing, organization, and integration. Classifying objectives is more difficult in the psychomotor domain, although Harrow (1972) designed a six-level continuum based on observable movement. The stages include reflex movements, basic fundamental movements, perceptual abilities, physical abilities, skilled movements, and nondiscursive communication. Psychomotor activity involves both cognitive and affective influences.

Objectives may vary in terms of specificity. Some are quite general; that is, the aim or goals of the process of education. Three levels of objectives have been identified. The first deals with long-term goals, such as self-realization. The second level represents objectives attained when students complete a course of study. The third level is composed of very specific objectives, derived from those of the second level. An example of the first level would be the goals stated by a college/university in its catalog. The second level would be characterized by a curriculum from a hospitality management program in higher education. The third level might be commonly referred to as instructional objectives, and are course specific. Since our focus is on the course level, we need to address how to develop these specific objectives.

Mager (1962) defined objective as a description of a performance you want students to be able to exhibit before you consider them competent. In other words, he suggests it describes the intended result. Without the objective, how do we know what was accomplished in our course? In addition, without the objective, there can be no basis for instructional materials, course content, or teaching strategies. The basic components of an instructional objective are performance, conditions, and a criterion measure. Performance describes what the students will be able to do. Conditions refer to circumstances under which students will complete the performance. The criterion identifies the level of performance considered acceptable in the course. Performance is best described using action words. Can you observe and/or measure the required action? How do we prepare the objectives? Start by identifying the knowledge, behavior, or skill you want demonstrated after your instruction is completed. Then identify the situation in which students will demonstrate the knowledge, behavior, or skill when the instruction is completed. Finally, identify a real-world test environment that will demonstrate if the student has achieved the necessary competence.

The course goal is broad-based; course objectives are specific. The number of course objectives are unlimited, but should cover each major component of the course. The objectives should be written in the order in which they will be learned. An acceptable alternative is to present them in the order of importance to the course. A student should be able to see that successful completion of course objectives will lead them to achievement of the course goal.

Examples of words to use in preparing objectives include to write, to identify, to solve, to compare, to contrast. Words that should not be used for preparing objectives include to know, to understand, to appreciate, to believe. When writing objectives, avoid certain common mistakes. One is preparing what appears to be an objective, but is not; i.e., "be able to think critically" or "be able to understand." A second problem results from use of the word "given," which may not describe conditions of learning; i.e., "given one week of instruction on," or "given sufficient training." A third common error is to describe teacher performance instead of student performance, i.e., "the teacher will demonstrate." One final example is the use of false criteria, i.e., "to the satisfaction of the instructor."

The best teachers design their classes to offer a wide range of challenges for students. You must consider what you want your students to learn about each topic relevant to your course. Time will be your greatest challenge, for the average college course has but forty hours in a term. When you subtract for administrative duties on the first day and closing day of classes, and factor in exams, suddenly the time is even shorter. There are other specific challenges to the instructor, such as the size of the class and the type of material in the course. An instructor can keep students focused and motivated by reminding them when an objective has been achieved. Once you know your objectives, you can begin to develop the methods portion of your class; that is, how you will deliver the material.

STUDENT LEARNING STYLES

Learning style consists of distinctive and observable behaviors that provide clues about the mediation abilities of individuals. People, through their behavior, tell us how their minds relate to the world. These mind qualities emerge as dualities—abstract and concrete perception, sequential and random ordering, deductive and inductive processing, and separative and associative relationships. While everyone has all the qualities, most people have innate tendencies that show toward one aspect of the duality. These qualities are manifested as behavior and register as preferred means of learning. These behaviors allow instructors to identify styles through observation, interviews, and paper-and-pencil testing.

Kolb, Rubin, and McIntyre (1971) suggest two elements of learning; the manner by which one perceives information, and how that information is processed. Information can be perceived as a concrete experience, or as an abstraction. For example, hands-on approaches are concrete, while theories are abstract. Most people fall somewhere in between the two extremes. Kolb, Rubin, and McIntyre (1971) created a scale for describing learning styles, similar to the Myers-Briggs scale for personality. The first quadrant describes divergers, those who perceive best through concrete experience and then reflect on their activities. Individuals in this category tend to be social, interested in people, and need to be involved in learning. They need a reason to learn, and usually ask "why?" Assimilators make up the second quadrant; these are people perceiving through abstract concepts and processing the information through internal reflection. The classic lecture format of most traditional higher education programs fits this quadrant. People are given the facts ("what") and incorporate the information privately. The third quadrant, convergers, perceive information through abstract concepts but process through active experimentation. These are people who need to know how things work, and they are best taught by letting them try it themselves. Laboratory classes are appropriate for these individuals. Accommodators represent the fourth quadrant, where people perceive information in concrete form and process with an active, hands-on approach. These individuals learn best by teaching to others. While individuals utilize the skills of all four quadrants, most feel comfortable operating in one or two specific areas.

Further complicating understanding of learning styles are principles based on age, gender, and culture of the learner. For example, there are group patterns in learning style preference. Females and individuals of color tend to prefer connected learning styles, which utilize collaborative approaches. Anglo-European, and some Asian cultures, prefer a separate style of learning, which is individually (competitively) based. Adult learners are typically self-directed, and desire to control the learning experience. This concept of andragogy is based on the premise that the learner is the center of the learning process. Adult learners view an instructor as a resource, not as an authority figure.

Mann et al. (1970) has provided much of the information on college classroom learning styles. Eight styles of learning were identified:

1. Compliant students: task-oriented, concerned with understanding the material
2. Anxious dependent students: very grade conscious due to feelings of incompetence
3. Discouraged students: personally dissatisfied, blame themselves
4. Independent students: older, self-confident
5. Heroes: feel superior to others, often male, usually productive and/or creative
6. Snipers: hostile, rebellious, usually little involvement with the class
7. Attention seeking: want to please, concerned about their relationship with teacher and others in the class
8. Silent students: do not verbally participate, exhibit helplessness

Traditional college classrooms usually force students to adapt their learning styles to the teacher's style. Often the highly structured classroom inhibits students' growth as individuals, as they strive only to please the instructor. While faculty may prefer a particular learning style (quite often this is abstract reflective), most of the general population are concrete active learners. The danger here is obvious: if the faculty member teaches the way he or she learns best, only part of the class will learn properly. Berger (1983) studied hospitality students, faculty, and alumni working in management to ascertain learning style via Kolb's Learning Style Inventory. She found no significant differences between faculty and managers, although she noted students changed from entry to graduation. She suggested that educators convert students who were more like managers on entry into graduates who are more like faculty than managers.

Students learn best when various approaches are utilized in the classroom. This allows students to make the most out of any situation. This approach matches with the hierarchical pattern for learning (Bloom, 1956). Bloom's systematic progression from simple to complex learning activities can guide teaching strategies and develop specific classroom activities.

TEACHING STRATEGIES

We have noted that an understanding of learning styles can assist a teacher in reaching different students, whatever the instructor's own preferences for learning might be. Characteristics of good teachers have also been identified, and how these teachers reach a wide cross-section of students. The question facing hospitality management instructors is when to utilize particular teaching strategies. For the instructor, deciding which teaching technique to utilize in a specific class can be based on the stated objectives of the course. All too often, due to inadequate training in graduate school, faculty simply emulate their own teachers, believing this to be the appropriate method. Typical in college/university environments is the lecture, which presents a topic, concept, or theory, with the student left to reflect on the presentation. Since most faculty (including hospitality) are products of such a system, they are adept at this process. There is little incentive for faculty to experiment with other methods, yet a more integrated approach to teaching would encourage students to utilize a variety of learning styles.

There is no single best teaching format. A good teacher can make a class interesting by utilizing any one of a number of methods. On the other hand, a poor instructor can limit the potential of any class through improper methods. Prior to 1900, teaching consisted primarily of recitation. By the early part of the twentieth century, this learning "by heart" method was gradually replaced by active methods and those centered on problem-solving. Around 1930, individualized teaching methods were introduced. The 1960s witnessed developments in cognitive psychology, leading to teaching formulas that were centered on the student and his or her in-depth treatment of the information. In this discussion of teaching strategies, it is important to distinguish between teaching method and teaching material. A teaching method is a particular way to organize pedagogical activities that are consciously implemented according to certain rules. The goal is to help students attain the given objectives as effectively as possible. Teaching materials are technical objects used by the instructor or students within the framework of a teaching method, such as computers, written documents, or audiovisual aids.

Teaching methods can be divided into three major classifications: those based on different forms of presentation; those based on group-oriented activity; and those based on individual learning. In the first category are formal and informal presentations. The lecture is the prime example of a formal presentation. Informal presentations may consist of a demonstration, a case presentation, or a presentation by students. The primary difference between the two processes is that involvement with/by students is usually associated with informal presentations. However, a lecture can involve student participation; it just takes adjustment by the instructor. The second category, group work, includes seminars, debates, and case studies. The process allows for collective exploration and thorough study of a specialized subject. The third category is individual learning. Examples include distance learning, learning contract, and programmed teaching. The role of faculty member is critical as you are supervising the student's development.

There are five criteria that are likely to influence the selection of teaching method: the levels of cognitive objectives targeted; the degree to which a method promotes independent and continuous learning; the degree of control exercised by the student; the number of students a method can accommodate; and the number of hours of preparation, student contact, and correction that a method requires. Levels of objectives refer to Bloom's (1956) taxonomy, and are characterized as low (knowledge, comprehension, application) or high (analysis, synthesis, and evaluation). The degree to which learning is promoted depends on whether students are encouraged to acquire and develop work skills; the level of degree is characterized as low, medium, or high. How much a student controls his or her learning influences quality of learning, and is classified as low, medium, or high. The number of students that can be accommodated varies, but the more students, the fewer possibilities for interactions (low = 1-15 students; medium = 16-30 students; high = 31-60 students; very high = more than 60 students). Different methods will require variable hours of preparation, contact, and correction, and can be labeled as low, medium, and high. Lectures target only lower-level objectives. All other methods permit students to attain upper-level objectives. However, such methods work best with modest-size groups. One exception is individualized learning. Once it is set up, it can accommodate a large number of students.

Research on teaching methods has not demonstrated that any one method is superior to the others. It appears that effectiveness of method depends on a combination of factors: the nature of students in the class, subject matter, professor's personality, physical and material conditions, and targeted objectives. Not all students benefit from a method in the same manner. It is important to choose methods that correspond to the characteristics of students. While Haywood (1989) proposed more active learning approaches for hospitality and tourism education, Trowbridge (1997) recently reported that a study of seven different hospitality programs revealed that instructor teaching style was not what students preferred. Instructors seemed to agree with Haywood, but students preferred to be entertained, and not engage in writing or in-depth work. While the sample was small in the study, the results indicate the difficulty hospitality management instructors have in selecting the right approach for a class. Grasha (1996) has developed a cluster system which links teaching styles and learning styles that faculty may find useful.

THE ROLE OF EVALUATION AND ASSESSMENT

There has been a growing interest on the part of parents, students, employers, and the general public in higher education programs during the last decade. In general, the public has demanded accountability from educational institutions and faculty receiving public support. In addition, all major regional accreditation associations require an assessment program to be a regular part of academic operations.

In education, assessment is used interchangeably with testing, evaluation, and measurement. Assessment itself refers to the gathering and assembling of data into interpretive form. Traditional assessment data might include number of doctoral degree faculty, volume of books in the library, research dollars received from federal agencies, amount of endowment dollars received, and so on. Astin (1990) postulated a model that incorporates inputs, the environment, and outcomes. Inputs are the personal qualities the student brings to the specific academic program. Included in these qualities are demographic characteristics, test scores, life goals, and personal values. The environment deals with the student's experiences while on campus. This includes courses, faculty, student clubs, other extracurricular activities, and even living arrangements. This component is often the most difficult to measure, since the student often creates much of his or her own environment. Outcomes, the critical part of the assessment process, are often viewed as dependent variables, while inputs and environment are viewed as independent variables. Examples of outcomes include academic achievement, awards, and professional accomplishments. For a hospitality management program, the most important outcome question might be, "Would you enroll in this program if you had to do it all again?"

Ideally, an assessment program involves a database that is a longitudinal study of a cohort of students. Both short-term and long-term measures will be utilized (Elfrink, Agbeh, and Krause, 1995). An example of data used might include input information of admission test scores, environmental data of which courses were taken, and an outcomes measure of degree completion and when. This file could be expanded by adding other outcome data over time, such as career progression. Faculty play the key role in this assessment process. While the information is primarily focused on student outcomes, it is clear that faculty accountability is also being measured. Instructional objectives for each class have to be designed that are the competencies necessary for entry-level success as a manager in the hospitality industry. Pre- and posttests can be applied to any course in the curriculum. While most faculty think of multiple choice tests as the only format for such an exercise, interviews, essays, and portfolios have all been successfully used.

Although the discussion thus far has focused on assessment, the role of faculty evaluation remains a critical component of the process. The same pressures driving higher education's movement toward assessment are prompting examination of evaluation criteria. Traditionally, evaluation of faculty performance has guided administrative decisions on retention, promotion, tenure, and merit. Classroom teaching has long been a major factor in evaluating overall faculty performance. In some institutions, research and publication activity may also rank as high. It has often been said of higher education that faculty are paid to teach, but rewarded for research and publication. Although research and publication activity can be assessed through a variety of quantitative measures, such as number of grants funded or research dollars awarded, assessing teaching often proves elusive.

What is clear is that the assessment of teaching is becoming more structured. The main sources of information continue to be ratings by students, departmental administrators, and college-level administrators. Student evaluations of faculty performance appear to carry the most weight, although some believe such a dependence has led to grade inflation. Examples of other data that could be employed in evaluating teaching performance include classroom visits, course syllabi, exams, colleagues' opinions, alumni opinions, and a self-evaluation. When one considers the focus on student learning experiences, examination of instructional materials and the performance of students on exams becomes increasingly relevant. A recent study (Hu and Bosselman, 1997) should give cause for some alarm in the field of hospitality education. While hospitality educators ranked teaching competencies as important, they rated planning skills involved with teaching lowest. Research on newer faculty (Boice, 1991) revealed that novices in the professoriate experience significant stress from teaching, feel uncertain about how to improve their teaching, and have received little guidance from their graduate program or current colleagues about effective approaches to teaching.

With the trend toward more structural information gathering in the evaluation of faculty, and the concerns of faculty about teaching, the self-assessment tool presents an option for hospitality management faculty to consider. The self-evaluation process allows a faculty member to examine instructional objectives and classroom performance. An example of this process is the teaching portfolio, which can provide evidence (i.e., accountability) of teaching effectiveness.

THE TEACHING PORTFOLIO
AND CAREER PROGRESSION

This chapter has focused on components of curriculum and instruction, with specific attention on what makes a good hospitality management teacher. Like Boyer (1991), I am concerned about how teaching is treated in the hospitality curriculum. Too many faculty and institutions undervalue teaching in today's institutions of higher education. Several studies have suggested that the public, specifically legislative entities, will demand accountability concerning teaching (Daly, 1994; Edgerton, 1993; Gilbert, Keck, and Simpson, 1993). Higher education has long utilized student evaluations as a means of quantifying teaching, yet such a singular focus provides insufficient evidence of teaching quality. Teaching portfolios have been identified as a means to assess and improve teaching by providing more reliable evidence of teaching, including student evaluation data (Braskamp and Ory, 1994).

A teaching portfolio is highly personal, and provides flexibility to the teacher. Seldin and Annis (1990) refer to it as a collection of instructional materials that document the faculty member's performance over time. This presentation allows faculty to illustrate their instructional skills and accomplishments to others. It is, in reality, a unique measure of self-reflection for teachers. The main purpose of such an exercise is to improve performance. As faculty members construct their portfolios they are forced to consider how their teaching has actually fared to date. It may help hospitality management teachers rethink their role as instructors, and plan for the future.

The preparation of a teaching portfolio should not be solely the work of the individual faculty member. The institution must first define effective teaching in order to establish criteria and standards for evaluating portfolios. Centra (1992) reported on teaching portfolio evaluation by peers and deans, noting varied results. Centra concluded that each evaluator approached the portfolio with individual criteria and standards for evaluation. A good starting point for characteristics of effective teaching can be found in Eble (1976). In addition, development of portfolios can occur only in arenas of collegiality. If reflecting on a weakness creates an opportunity for abuse in the evaluation process, then it would be advised to delay the use of an innovative evaluative tool such as the teaching portfolio.

There is no one best way to prepare a teaching portfolio. However, if the hospitality instructor includes all of his or her work, it is quite possible that the result will be a fragmented, unorganized effort that prevents identification of the best work. It is therefore selective, and should focus on the teacher's best work. If the purpose of the portfolio is truly to improve performance, and the operating environment is collegial, then reflections on problems uncovered in teaching would be appropriate. The fears of those concerned about the amount of work needed to actually construct a teaching portfolio appear unfounded. Most faculty have the contents of a portfolio available, just not organized all together. Several researchers have identified components of a teaching portfolio (Seldin and Annis, 1990; Centra, 1993; Edgerton, Hutchings, and Quinlan, 1991; Wolf, 1991), which are compiled in Exhibit 7.1.

While the physical material itself is necessary for the portfolio, those evaluating need additional commentary from the individual teacher to guide the evaluation. As indicated, improvement in performance should be the end result of the teaching portfolio. The portfolio should conclude with a plan for improvement. What areas has the faculty member identified as needing improvement? How can this improvement be successfully completed? Perhaps most critical is support from institutional sources. If there is no administrative/institutional support, then improvement of teaching will not occur.

EXHIBIT 7.1. Teaching Portfolio Design

1. Institutional Data

   - A listing of all courses taught, including level of course, when taught, number of students, elective or required course, description of grading
   - A summary of goals for each course
   - A description of how each class fits into the overall curriculum
   - Institutional student survey results for each class taught

2. Teaching Philosophy

   - A statement on teaching beliefs
   - What you expect students to achieve in your classes and why it is important
   - A list of teaching strategies utilized and why they were chosen
   - Examples of assignments and exams
   - Course materials prepared for students

3. Assessment of Effectiveness

   - Pre- and posttest scores
   - Testimonials from students, current and former
   - Peer review of teaching
   - Peer review of teaching materials
   - Sample student work
   - Audio- or videotape of an actual class, if available
   - Test scores on standardized exams
   - Student comments from course evaluation forms
   - Testimonials from employers of students/alumni
   - Teaching awards won
   - Samples of unique or innovative teaching material such as texts, lab manuals, computer programs, etc.
   - Any research conducted that focuses on learning

4. Teacher Development

   - Comparison of same class syllabi to illustrate changes
   - Comparison of same class evaluations over time
   - Scholarly work on teaching
   - Attending and/or participating in professional workshops/conferences that focus on teaching
   - Examples of new teaching strategies employed and why
   - Samples of teaching materials and student work that demonstrates impact of change
   - Discussion of changes resulting from self-reflection

REFERENCES

Altman, H.B. and Cashin, W.E. (1992). *Writing a syllabus.* Idea Paper No. 27. Kansas State University: Center for Faculty Evaluation and Development.

Astin, A. (1990). *Assessment for excellence.* New York: Maxwell McMillan, Inc.

Berger, F. (1983). Disparate learning styles of hospitality students, professors and managers. *International Journal of Hospitality Management, 2,* 15-23.

Bloom, B.S. (Ed.). (1956). *Taxonomy of educational objectives: Handbook 1: Cognitive domain.* New York: David McKay.

Boice, R. (1991). New faculty as teachers. *Journal of Higher Education, 62,* 150-173.

Boyer, E. (1991). The scholarship of teaching. *College Teaching, 39,* 11-13.

Braskamp, L.A. and Ory, J.C. (1994). *Assessing faculty work.* San Francisco: Jossey-Bass.

Brinko, K.T. (1991). Visioning your course: Questions to ask yourself as you design your course. *The Teaching Professor,* February, 3-4.

Centra, J.A. (1990). Evaluating college teaching: Some reflections. *Department Advisor, 5* (Winter), 1-5.

Centra, J.A. (1992). *The use of the teaching portfolio and the Student Instructional Report [SIR] for summative evaluation.* SIR Report No. 6. Princeton, NJ: Educational Testing Service.

Centra, J.A. (1993). *Reflective faculty evaluation.* San Francisco: Jossey-Bass.

Cross, K.P. and Angelo, T.A. (1993). *Classroom assessment techniques: A handbook for college teachers.* Second edition. San Francisco: Jossey-Bass.

Daly, W.-T. (1994). Teaching and scholarship: Adapting American higher education to hard times. *Journal of Higher Education, 65,* 45-57.

Eble, K.E. (1976). *The craft of teaching.* San Francisco: Jossey-Bass.

Edgerton, R. (1993). The re-examination of faculty priorities. *Change, 25,* 10-25.

Edgerton, R., Hutchings, P. and Quinlan, K. (1991). *The teaching portfolio: Capturing the scholarship of teaching.* Washington, DC: American Association for Higher Education.

Elfrink, J.A., Agbeh, A., and Krause, F. (1995). A survey of student assessment in hospitality education: Implications for the future. *Hospitality Research Journal, 18,* 143-153.

Gilbert, J.P., Keck, K.L., and Simpson, R.D. (1993). Improving the process of education: Total quality management for the college classroom. *Innovative Higher Education, 18,* 65-85.

Grasha, A.F. (1996). *Teaching with style: A practical guide to enhancing learning by understanding teaching and learning styles.* Pittsburgh, PA: Alliance Publishers.

Harrow, A.J. (1972). *A taxonomy of the psychomotor domain.* New York: David McKay.

Haywood, K.M. (1989). A radical proposal for hospitality and tourism education. *International Journal of International Management, 8,* 259-264.

Hockensmith, S.F. (1988). The syllabus as a teaching tool. *The Educational Forum, 52,* 339-351.

Hu, C. and Bosselman, R.H. (1997). Validating teaching competencies in hospitality education: Faculty members' perspective. *Journal of Hospitality and Tourism Education, 9,* 39-46.

Johnson, G.R. (1990). *First steps to excellence in college teaching.* Madison, WI: Magna Publications.

Kolb, D.A., Rubin, I.M., and McIntyre, J.M. (1971). *Organizational psychology: An experiential approach,* Third edition. Englewood Cliffs, NJ: Prentice Hall.

Krathwohl, D.R., Bloom, B.S., and Masia, B.B. (1964). *Taxonomy of educational objectives: Affective domain.* New York: David McKay.

Lowman, J. (1995). *Mastering the techniques of teaching,* Second edition. San Francisco: Jossey-Bass.

Lowther, M.A., Stark, J.S., and Martens, G.G. (1989). *Preparing course syllabi for improved communication.* Ann Arbor, MI: University of Michigan National Center for Research to Improve Postsecondary Teaching and Learning.

Mager, R.F. (1962). *Preparing instructional objectives.* Palo Alto, CA: Fearon Publishers.

Mann, R.D., Arnold, S.M., Binder, J., Cytrynbaum, S., Newman, B.M., Ringwald, B., Ringwald, J., and Rosenwein, R. (1970). *The college classroom: Conflict, change, and learning.* New York: John Wiley and Sons.

Matejka, K. and Kurke, L.B. (1993). Designing a great syllabus. *College Teaching, 42,* 115-117.

Seldin, P. and Annis, L. (1990). The teaching portfolio. *The Journal of Staff, Program, and Organizational Development, 8*: 197-201.

Trowbridge, E.H. (1997). Preferences of instructional styles used by faculty and their acceptance by students at collegiate schools of hospitality management. *Journal of Hospitality and Tourism Education, 9,* 41-46.

Wolf, K. (1991). The schoolteacher's portfolio: Issues in design, implementation, and evaluation. *Phi Delta Kappan,* (October), 129-136.

Chapter 8

Hospitality Research and Scholarship

Harsha Chacko

INTRODUCTION

As was discussed earlier, the three major roles for hospitality educators are often defined as teaching, research, and service. All of these demand continuous personal development and lifelong learning experiences, but while the role of teaching is to communicate knowledge to students and requires a breadth of knowledge of the subject matter, research requires a depth of knowledge of a topic so that an educator becomes an expert in that topic. Publication of research articles is also an essential part of the faculty evaluation process, especially when the time arrives for promotion and tenure. In many universities, a copy of a hospitality faculty member's curriculum vita, listing all the refereed research publications, is sent to other hospitality educators for external evaluation. Thus, the research efforts of educators must also stand up to the scrutiny of their peers in other institutions.

Although creating experts enhances the reputation of a university, faculty research also plays an often overlooked role in the functioning of an institution. In times when public funding for higher education is tight, the overhead expense rate (ranging from 25 to 80 percent of the total value of a grant) charged to research grants can be used to augment the budget of the university. In addition, public universities that conduct more research and produce more doctoral students receive more state and public funding than those that have only limited or no doctoral programs. Thus research is important not only from the viewpoint of an individual faculty member but also from that of the university as a whole.

Research requires hospitality educators to select a particular topic and to study and examine it intensively. Although research is often the basis of developing and testing new theories it can also be used to provide valuable information to hospitality organizations. This is even more important as the hospitality industry becomes more competitive and as customers become more experienced, sophisticated, and demanding. No more can hospitality organizations conduct their operations based on hunches and intuition. Rather, they must seek answers to many questions that can only be obtained by well-conducted research.

APPLIED VERSUS PURE RESEARCH

Research can be classified as applied or pure. Applied research has findings that can be applied to solve problems and answer questions of immediate concern. Much of the research conducted by private hospitality and tourism organizations and by many academics is applied. This type of research produces results that are needed to make relatively short-term business decisions such as the Host example that follows (Marriott Corporation, 1993). Marriott Host/Travel Plazas, which provide food service at many airports in the United States, found that many people walk by their airport facilities but only a very small proportion of them actually stopped to buy something. The question they asked was, "What can we do to attract those people?" So they started looking at research with a focus on customer needs. Host conducted over 2,000 customer interviews and discovered that there was a relatively small number of things customers wanted from airport facilities. These were convenience of location, speed of delivery, and friendliness of service. Host decided to examine the convenience issue first. They found that at an airport, customers preferred the food and beverage facility to be within sight of the gate-hold area. If they could not have that, they preferred it to be along their path from the entrance to the counter. Unfortunately, this preference was not always factored into existing airport facility design. To counteract this limitation, Host decided to test a concept in which snack bar attendants would walk the gate-hold area selling a variety of beverages and snacks, an upscale version of the traditional "hawking" found at stadiums and arenas. The goal was the same: Take the product to the customer. Without research Host would never have uncovered the fact that convenience of location meant that customers wanted be in sight of their gate-hold areas. Thus research was used to properly understand customer wants and needs before matching products and services were created.

Hospitality educators can conduct similar applied research projects as consultants or obtain funding and grants. Recent research proposals have been requested by the American Hotel Foundation for research on employee turnover and on managing cultural diversity. Other examples include tourism advertising conversion studies, hotel performance surveys, market segmentation analysis, and so on.

Pure research, on the other hand, involves developing and testing theories and hypotheses that are intellectually interesting to the researcher and might have some application in the future, but do not answer questions of immediate concern. In this case, research often involves the testing of hypotheses developed from abstract and specialized concepts. Hospitality researchers who wish to do pure research generally must have studied the concepts intensively so that they are aware of the research that has been previously conducted. Pure research will then expand or add to the body of existing knowledge.

Hospitality and tourism research, whether applied or pure, still must withstand the scrutiny of the industry and fellow researchers. Dann, Nash, and Pearce (1988) discussed several weaknesses of tourism research that are not strongly built on a foundation of theory combined with suitable methodology. These weaknesses include research that describe theories but have no empirical foundation, research based on anecdotal evidence, and research using complex data analyses without theoretical foundations. They proposed a four-quadrant rendering of the various possibilities of combining theory and method (Figure 8.1) and contend that Quadrant 4 should be the goal of academic researchers.

QUALITATIVE VERSUS QUANTITATIVE RESEARCH

Qualitative Research

Qualitative research often has the natural setting as the direct source of data and the researcher is the key instrument. It is largely

FIGURE 8.1. Theory and Method in Tourism Research

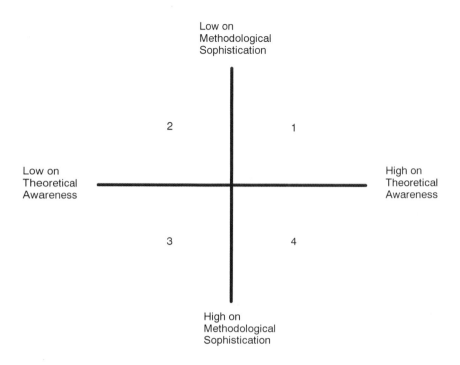

Source: Dann, Nash, and Pearce, 1988, p. 5.

exploratory in nature and the findings cannot be generalized to a larger population. Its purpose is usually to learn more about a subject, to understand how consumers use a product, to test a new product concept, or to provide information for developing further quantitative research.

A common form of qualitative research used in the hospitality industry is the focus group. A focus group consists of six to ten people who are screened to match the population under study. These people are brought together in a room where a skilled moderator leads them in discussion. As illustration, suppose a restaurateur was considering a radically new menu. He has a mock-up of the menu made but before he goes ahead with the change he wants to see how his customers might react. He invites eight of his customers on each of four different days of the week to have a free dinner if they will agree to participate in a two-hour focus group. He hires a skilled moderator (he would not do this himself because of his lack of skill and potential bias) who leads the group in discussion. The moderator not only asks questions but also attempts to build a rapport with the group and spends a lot of time "probing." The relationship between the moderator and the group is important because a reluctant group will not provide thorough information.

It is not uncommon to audio- and/or videotape focus groups. Thus, more complete analysis is possible after the session is over. Also, while the session is being conducted, the restaurateur and some of his staff may sit behind a one-way mirror and observe the proceedings, watching for special nuances and signs that the moderator might miss.

Another form of qualitative research in the hospitality industry is the personal interview. An example of such a project is one that I am currently conducting on how the acceptance of service quality as a competitive force is affecting the organizational structure of hotels. This research consists of a combination of structured and unstructured exchanges in which the interviewer probes for specific comments and reactions from hotel front office managers. There are a number of pragmatic reasons for using qualitative research such as:

- It is relatively economical
- The environment can be tightly controlled
- It permits direct contact with subjects
- It permits greater depth by probing for responses
- It permits subjects to "open up"
- It develops new creative ideas
- It establishes subjects' vocabulary
- It uncovers basic consumer needs and attitudes
- It establishes new product concepts
- It interprets previously obtained quantitative data

The major problem with qualitative research is that the data analysis and interpretation are difficult and the results cannot be generalized. It does, however, help in "getting inside the subject's mind." It helps to better define concepts and often forms the basis for quantitative research to follow. Although qualitative research has been conducted for many years in business management, it became more widely accepted as a result of Peters and Waterman's (1982) best-selling book *In Search of Excellence*, in which they describe organizational factors that led to excellence in certain U.S. corporations. Chacko and Nebel (1990) have also discussed the efficacy of qualitative research in the hospitality industry.

Quantitative Research

Quantitative research deals with numbers. It measures, quantitatively, what people say, think, perceive, feel, and do. Descriptive quantitative research is the most common type. It describes how many, how often, and what percentage, such as how old people are, their sex, their income, their education, or whether they like or dislike something. Frequencies and percentages can be calculated to show, for example, that there are 362 females in the sample (48 percent), they ate in a restaurant 2.3 times last week, and 36 percent of them have at least a college education.

Results may also show how many persons in each age bracket ate out how many times and the relative percentages. From this information it can be determined, statistically, if any differences in eating-out patterns by age category were likely to have occurred by chance. However, it would not show how these factors interact, for example, does the age of an individual predict how many times that person will eat in a restaurant in a given week? As an example, a guest comment card might show that customers thought the food and service were fine but it would not predict whether they would return.

Inferential quantitative research can be used to infer to a larger population based on the findings from a probability sample, a sample in which each person in the population being studied (e.g., business travelers) has an equal chance of being selected. With inferential statistics, it is possible to draw conclusions about the population on the basis of the sample data. At the same time, inferential methods permit the analysis of interaction effects. An example is the measurement of various reasons why members of a particular market segment might choose a particular restaurant. A sample of the members of the segment could be surveyed and asked to rate the importance of food quality, service, ambience, location, and price in their decisions. In inferential analysis, each of these attributes would interact with the others. The analysis would then reveal "weights," that is, the respective importance of each attribute in choosing the restaurant. This could show the relationships of the various attributes as well as the predictive capability of each in choosing the restaurant. Thus inferential data is far more powerful and useful than descriptive data. It is also more complex, takes more skill to obtain, requires the use of a computer, and is more expensive both in collection and analysis. Further, while more powerful, inferential data are also more susceptible to misinterpretation. One of the best ways to avoid faulty conclusions is to ensure that the researcher follows the guidelines of the research process discussed earlier.

THE HOSPITALITY RESEARCH PROCESS

Much of the research conducted in organizational sciences, including the areas of management, marketing, accounting, and finance, traces its roots to the "mother" sciences of sociology, psychology, economics, mathematics, and others. Hospitality and tourism research is no exception and is often seen as an extension or derivation of both the social and organizational sciences. According to Lundberg (1997), the hospitality reality is complex and he advocates a variety of research designs, methods, and participants to provide a "multistream" inquiry of hospitality phenomena. Examining research journals in tourism and hospitality reflects this variety, and although each research strategy is unique the steps in the research process are fundamentally the same. Although Figure 8.2 shows the entire research process, it must be remembered that these steps are not only interconnected but they also often overlap.

Research Purpose

The first step in the research process is the establishment of the purpose of the research, which is derived from the particular questions that need to be answered. For example, the purpose of a research study may be to find out if a tourism advertising program was

FIGURE 8.2. The Research Process

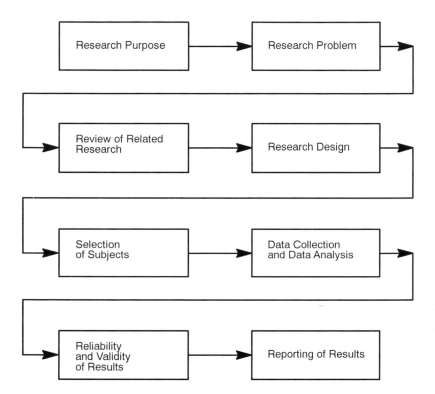

effective, or why hotel occupancy is declining, or what specific benefits are required by our customers, and so on. The research purpose is the end product that is expected to be attained on the completion of a project. Often the purpose of applied research indicates what actions are needed—that is, what kinds of business decisions are planned after the results are obtained. A new advertising campaign can be developed, the menu can be changed, or the decor could be refurbished. Thus the research purpose establishes the parameters of everything that follows in the research process. Exhibit 8.1 describes the parameters of a typical applied research problem, which was to evaluate the effectiveness of a tourism advertising campaign.

EXHIBIT 8.1. Applied Research Case Study

Louisiana Tourism Advertising Effectiveness

Each year the Louisiana Office of Tourism spends approximately $8 million to promote the state as a place to visit. The advertisements are placed in various media including radio, television, magazines, and even the Internet. Each of these advertisements provides potential visitors with a response mechanism, such as a toll-free telephone number, business reply mail card (BRC), or reader service card (RSC) with which Louisiana tourism information can be requested. The advertising campaign has resulted in over one million inquiries from potential visitors. At the end of each fiscal year, research has to be conducted to evaluate the effectiveness of the campaign. This evaluation includes an examination of the effectiveness of each medium and also that of specific media vehicles such as a particular magazine or television channel. This applied research case study will be used as an illustration of the various phases of the research process.

Research Problem

Formulation of the research problem is often a difficult task because of the complexities of conducting organizational, social, and behavioral research. The study subjects are often human and it is difficult to control for all exogenous factors. Take the example of gauging the effectiveness of tourism advertising. The objective of tourism advertising is to bring more visitors to a destination. In addition, these visitors should be spending enough money in the destination to more than offset the costs of the advertising. The research problem is now framed in the form of questions. "How many potential visitors who saw the advertising were influenced to visit the destination? How much money did they spend? Which magazines were more effective?" From a practical standpoint, there are enormous difficulties in establishing a clear and direct connection between tourism advertising, visitation, and tourist spending.

Review of Related Research

A review of the literature is essential in the effort to clarify concepts, identify variables, and if the research is theoretical, to formulate hypotheses. Hospitality researchers use many different sources to conduct this review, including books, periodicals, journals, reports, theses, paper presentations at professional meetings, and even the Internet. A partial list of hospitality and tourism journals is shown in Exhibit 8.2. Not only can the items on this list be used to review previous research, but they also serve as outlets for publishing new research papers. Although the list is by no means exhaustive it is being used by a major university as the recommended list to guide faculty members in their publication efforts. These and other journals are compiled in Purdue University's index of lodging, restaurant, and tourism, which is also useful in locating previously published research. In addition, Coopers & Lybrand, an international consulting firm, is trying to develop an Internet Web site (www.lodgingresearch.com) to provide lodging industry data.

Using the case study in Exhibit 8.1 as an example, a review of the marketing literature showed that it was very difficult to establish a direct and conclusive relationship between advertising and sales of a product/service. It also showed that it was very expensive and practically impossible to locate everyone who was exposed to advertising for each of the media vehicles used to ask them how much they were influenced by the advertising. However, a review of the tourism literature showed that different types of "conversion" studies were used to evaluate tourism advertising effectiveness. Since the Louisiana Office of Tourism had the names and addresses of all inquirers for each media vehicle it was possible to ask these inquirers if they visited the state after receiving the information (i.e., "converted"). Thus the variable under study was the conversion rate. In addition, there had to be a way to screen and remove inquirers who had already made up their minds to visit Louisiana even before they were exposed to advertising. This example shows the complexities of hospitality research because of the many intervening variables that may result in faulty conclusions. Once the variables were identified the next step was to select a research design for the advertising effectiveness case study.

Research Design

The different types of research design are exploratory, descriptive, explanatory, and causal. Exploratory designs are useful when studying phenomena that have not been extensively studied previously. A study may utilize qualitative research to try to uncover variables and to clarify the concepts. For example, Nebel (1991) studied ten general managers by observing them at their workplaces and through in-depth interviews. He was then able to identify the day-to-day activities of these managers and also their individual leadership styles. On the other hand, descriptive studies try to obtain results that are generalizable to larger populations. A logical continuation of Nebel's study would be to assess the leadership styles of all general managers in the United States. Descriptive research provides pictures of variables, but it cannot be used to infer that there is an implied causal relationship between them. For example, descriptive data does not identify the real reasons customers behave as they do and make the decisions they make. The frequency of hotel customers naming an attribute, for example location, does not necessarily indicate its relative determinance in the product choice process.

The purpose of explanatory studies is to attempt to explain a social phenomenon by specifying how and why it happened. Explaining why and how a hotel or other service was selected would require an explanatory research design. In addition, this type of design may also result in identifying variables that could be used to predict results with some degree of accuracy. The final type of design is the causal research design. Such research is conducted in controlled environments using laboratory or field experiments. Medical research to assess the effect of new drug interventions uses this type of design. Usually, subjects are studied before and after receiving treatment, with other variables remaining constant. However, this type of research is difficult in the hospitality field since the subjects and the environment are not easily controlled. Thus it becomes problematic when trying to assess the cause and effect of any intervention such as an advertising campaign. Nevertheless, once the researcher has selected the design of the study the next step is the selection of subjects.

Selection of Subjects

Selection of subjects requires the researcher to achieve balance among timeliness, cost, and accuracy of a study. When the total number of subjects is small it is possible to collect data from every individual, namely a census. However, in large populations, such as a nationwide study, it is expensive, difficult, and often unnecessary to include all the individuals in the population. A sample of subjects can be carefully selected and although there will be a margin of error the results will be reasonably accurate. Sampling is commonly used by researchers and most widely seen in political polling.

A probability sample is one in which every member of the population has an equal chance of being selected. This means that the sample is collected randomly without any bias as to who is selected. A simple method of randomly selecting a sample group of fifty might be to put all the names in the population in a bowl, reach in, and pick out fifty names one at a time. Statistically, it can be shown that a random sample will closely approximate the true characteristics of a population. This is why results can be inferred from a sample. It can also be shown, with a certain degree of confidence, that results could not have occurred by chance, given a certain error tolerance. It is only with probability samples that one can legitimately use inferential analysis. A probability sample can also be stratified by separating elements into nonoverlapping groups and then randomly selecting subjects from within each stratum. This was the procedure used in the tourism advertising case study where specific advertisements could be connected to names and addresses of people who requested information from the Louisiana Office of Tourism after being exposed to advertising. Subjects for the study were selected from this population.

A nonprobability sample obviously means just the opposite— that is, everyone in the population does not have an equal chance of being selected. This is called a convenience sample, in which subjects are selected simply because they are conveniently available. The researcher might choose to sample the first fifty people who check out of the hotel one morning. This does not allow researchers to generalize the findings to anyone else who stays at the hotel. People who check out later, or on another day, might have very different characteristics from these first fifty.

Another kind of nonprobability sample is called a judgmental sample. In this case, it might be decided that some specified variation is needed such as a mixture of sexes, age groups, travel purpose, and method of arrival at a hotel. The first ten of each category who check into the hotel every evening may be selected.

A common method of creating judgmental samples in tourism research is the visitor intercept survey. This means, essentially, that we go to a tourism attraction and intercept people. If they will respond (many will not), then they will be screened, by asking, for example, "Do you live more than 100 miles away?" If the answer is no, then the interviewer moves on; if it is yes, then further questions will be asked.

Another type of nonprobability sample is composed of the people who fill out guest comment cards in hotel rooms. This is a biased "default" sample. Although one could argue that everyone who stays in a hotel has the same opportunity to fill out the comment card, this does not constitute a probability sample because the researcher has no means of controlling the probability. This results in a default selection. The bias comes from the fact that the sample would represent only those people who are prone to fill out comment cards. These people may differ drastically from people who never fill out comment cards.

Data Collection and Analysis

The three common methods used to collect data are examination of secondary data, observation, and direct communication. Secondary data have been collected for some other purpose. For example, Smith Travel Research collects data on hotel occupancy, average room rates, and revenue per available room. In addition, many tourism destinations keep track of airport deplanements, convention bookings, visitors to tourist information centers, and so on. These data are very valuable but it is difficult, for example, to show a clear and definite relationship between an increase in these secondary data measures and tourism advertising. There may be intervening variables that confound the relationship. Direct communication with subjects provide primary data since it is obtained directly from the subjects of the study. This is by far the most commonly used method in hospitality research. Direct communication could be in the form of a telephone, in-person, or mail survey. In the Louisiana tourism advertising effectiveness study it was decided that a mail survey would be used especially since the names and addresses of the entire population of inquirers were available.

Researchers must be aware that sample selection and data collection methods are closely related. If subjects' names and addresses are available it may be more practical to collect data via a mail survey. If subjects' telephone numbers are available a telephone survey may be more appropriate. Usually written preparation is required before the data is actually collected. For example, a questionnaire has to be prepared if the data is collected by telephone, personal interview, or mail. A mailed questionnaire will require more care in preparation in terms of format, design, appearance, and other factors that will both induce respondents to complete it and make it easier for them to do so. It is also important that the data collected be easy to tabulate or enter into the computer for analysis.

Questionnaire design is not as simple a task as it may sometimes seem. Questions must be clear and unambiguous. Each question should have the same meaning for all respondents. This means that if an abstract term such as *quality* is used, the word *quality* should be defined so that everyone interprets it in the same way.

The subject of questionnaire design is covered in research textbooks and will therefore not be discussed here (for example, see Dillman, 1978). However, it must be remembered that many hazards are involved which, if not carefully avoided, result in invalid data and findings. For this reason, it is always necessary to pretest the questionnaire. This means trying it out on people to get feedback on wording, the time it takes, clarity, understanding of terms, possible omissions, and other factors that might confuse respondents or invalidate the findings.

The decision whether to use personal interviews, mail, telephone, or other data collection methods (such as comment cards or individual intercepts) is an important one in the research design. Each one has its trade-offs in terms of time and money. While the budget is always a limiting factor, the most important criterion is the method that will provide the most reliable data for the problem at hand. There is no one answer to this because each case is individual and must be weighed on its own merits. The data obtained must, of course, be analyzed very carefully. The methods of analysis and analytical techniques to be used should be predetermined, since these will affect the way questions are asked, the type of response solicited, and how they are measured.

Reliability and Validity

The research design, sampling, data collection, and data analysis must be all rigorously controlled when doing research. Each step is critically important, none more or less so than the others. Two supreme tests are applied to research findings: reliability and validity. Reliability in research means that the findings can be projected to a larger population if that is one of the intents of the research. It means that if a study is conducted using a similar sample from a similar population the results would be similar. It means that if the same questions were asked in a different way that similar results would be obtained. Even if reliable, the findings may or may not be valid.

Findings must be reliable if they are to be valid. Validity means that the data must support the conclusions. The conclusions must be valid in that they are based on whether the research actually measured what it is presumed to have measured. Anyone who wants to use research for decision-making purposes should always verify its validity first. Lack of validity is the most common cause of faulty research.

Research Dissemination

Although there are many ways to disseminate and share research findings with others, the three commonly used vehicles are journals, conferences, and technical reports. Of these, publication of research in peer-reviewed academic journals is of greatest value because it is often a major criterion in evaluating university faculty, especially those who are involved in graduate teaching and guidance of doctoral students. Although there has been a move away from the heavy priority placed on research over teaching, the "publish or perish" syndrome still exists in many universities. This means that educators are required to publish quality articles in journals that are relevant to the tourism and hospitality industry. In addition, pure research is valued over applied research when it comes to evaluating the performance of faculty for promotion and tenure. Exhibit

8.2 is an example of the journals and their quality ratings used by a major university to guide faculty in research and publication.

The process of book publishing is quite different from that of journal articles. Several major publishers have tourism and hospitality divisions with editors who review proposals for books that are likely to have some market demand. Generally, publishers favor books that have a potential to be used as a textbook for classroom use and thus do not lean toward publishing scholarly work that has a limited audience.

EXHIBIT 8.2. Examples of Hospitality and Tourism Research Journals

---

Group 1—Top-Ranked Refereed Research Journals

Annals of Tourism Research
International Journal of Hospitality Management
Journal of Applied Recreation Research
Journal of Hospitality and Leisure Marketing
Journal of Hospitality and Tourism Research
Journal of Leisure Research
Journal of Restaurant and Food Service Marketing
Journal of Travel and Tourism Marketing
Journal of Travel Research
Tourism Management

Group 2—Second-Tier Refereed Journals

Cornell Hotel and Restaurant Administration Quarterly
FIU Hospitality Review
Hospitality and Tourism Educator
International Journal of Contemporary Hospitality Management
Journal of College and University Food Service
Journal of Gambling Studies

FUNDED RESEARCH

There are several sources for funding of tourism and hospitality research. These include university, government, foundation, and corporate funding.

University Funding

Colleges and universities may provide funding for research projects that enhance the reputation of the school and of the researcher.

Government Funding

Federal, state, and local governments award grants and contracts for research in tourism and hospitality, but these are mainly applied research projects. Examples include: economic impact studies, tourism advertising conversion studies, and other industry-related research projects.

Foundation Funding

Both the Statler Foundation and American Hotel Foundation provide funding for applied research projects based on submitted proposals. These foundations have specific criteria to evaluate the proposals in order to decide whether to fund research projects. Proposals to the American Hotel Foundation need to include a narrative listing the objectives, significance, methods, time frames, and budgets.

Corporate Funding

Large corporations have programs for funding university research on topics that are of interest to the corporation. This is not very common in the tourism and hospitality industry, where much of the research is conducted by private research companies.

CONCLUSION

Hospitality and tourism research is necessary for many reasons. The principle of lifelong learning is based on the belief that there is much to be discovered and unearthed. Exhibit 8.3 shows a partial list of subject areas that are potential research topics for hospitality educators. The fact that university educators are often judged by

EXHIBIT 8.3. Potential Topics for Research in the Hospitality Industry

---

Management and conservation of natural resources

Public safety and security issues

Career awareness

Impact of developing industry trends

Study of problems currently being experienced by the industry

Methods for advancing technological innovation

Organizational development

Workforce diversity issues

---

pure research that extends the knowledge in a field creates a motive to conduct research. However, this motive has resulted in a plethora of research that will never be read by anyone other than the reviewers of journals and overanxious doctoral students. This "publishing game" is entrenched in the culture of the higher education environment and perpetuated by the evaluation requirements of the tenure and promotion process. Nevertheless, research helps to lessen uncertainty and replace intuition with facts. It allows researchers to stay current with the market, determine needs and wants, and locate segments and target markets. Hospitality managers can use research to plan strategies and tactics and make better business decisions while educators can keep in touch with the industry and also expand their depth and breadth of knowledge.

REFERENCES

Chacko, H. and E.C. Nebel III. (1990). Qualitative research: Its time has come, *Hospitality Research Journal, 14*, 383-391.

Dann, G., D. Nash, and P. Pearce. (1988). Methodology in tourism research, *Annals of Tourism Research, 15*, 1-28.

Dillman, D.A. (1978). *Mail and telephone surveys: The total design method,* New York: John Wiley and Sons.

Lundberg, C. (1997). Widening the process of hospitality inquiry: Toward appreciating research alternatives, *Journal of Hospitality and Tourism Research, 21*, 1-13.

Marriott Corporation. (1993). Empowerment provides a "host" of ways to capture customers on the go, *Marriott World,* Jan./Feb./Mar., p. 10.

Nebel III, E.C. (1991). *Managing hotels effectively: lessons from outstanding general managers.* New York: Van Nostrand Reinhold.

Peters, T. and R. Waterman. (1982). *In search of excellence: Lessons from America's best run companies.* New York: Harper & Row.

Chapter 9

The Service Responsibility
of Hospitality Educators

Clayton W. Barrows

INTRODUCTION

University professors are accountable for a multitude of responsibilities. Depending upon the college or university, the extent of these responsibilities may vary considerably. Generally, the student population believes that teaching is a professor's primary responsibility. And teaching is certainly an all-important activity that has profound consequences. In academe, however, universities often place more emphasis upon research. This is particularly true of "research institutions," where many hospitality programs are found. Together, teaching and research account for the bulk of most professors' job responsibilities. In addition to teaching and research, however, there is the often overlooked area of service, which is the focus of this chapter. Of these three areas, the latter seems to receive the least attention while also seeming to be the most ambiguous. In particular, service can demand a large amount of time and effort while it rarely results in the same level of recognition or reward for the individual as do teaching and research. These are among the many issues surrounding service.

At many universities, service seems to be a catchall category that includes whatever is not directly related to a professor's teaching or research responsibilities. This might include such varied activities as student advising, serving on university committees, or serving on the editorial review board of an academic journal. Precisely because the range of activities can be so wide, it would be impossible to list everything that might fall under the category of service. Perhaps more important, though, it can often be difficult to quantify service activities when an attempt is made to evaluate the overall performance of professors in this area of responsibility, especially in comparison to one another. Theoretically, decisions regarding tenure, merit, and promotion should be based upon an evaluation of overall performance in all three areas. However, this is not always the case. In fact, Cornett (1993) has suggested that most merit decisions are based upon performance in teaching and research, with service getting the least attention. While Cornett was generalizing across disciplines, there is no reason to believe that the evaluation process is any different in the field of hospitality education. It will be argued in this chapter, though, that service is often a very important component of hospitality educators' responsibilities, which not only can take up a significant amount of time but can result in significant benefits to hospitality programs. As a result, it will be contended that the service component must first be more clearly defined and, second, carefully considered during periods of performance evaluation.

Service, however, remains somewhat ambiguous from the perspective of both administrators and professors themselves. The purpose of this chapter is to better define what the service component of a professor's job entails, to discuss the various forms that service can take, and to describe how service responsibilities are accounted for and evaluated by program administrators. If nothing else, the reader will quickly discern the importance that this often overlooked activity has to the success of the program, the university, and to the individual's livelihood.

SERVICE DEFINED

University faculty handbooks clearly state that the duties of a faculty member will include teaching (or instruction), research and scholarship (resulting in grants or publications), and service. While teaching and research guidelines and expectations are generally spelled out quite clearly either at the university, college, or departmental levels, service is more open to interpretation and may be more flexible in scope. Broadly defined, service is any activity in which the faculty member offers his or her professional expertise or time to others, either within or outside of the academic community.

Certainly, when defined as such, service could be interpreted to include just about anything—even including research and teaching! In fact this has been one of the problems with the way that service has been defined in the past—it can and has included a great variety of activities, not always directly related to the academic mission of one's program or to one's own academic agenda. In this respect, it could be argued that the more clearly this activity is defined, the more carefully professors might choose their service obligations and the more productive they would be in them.

To more narrowly define service commitments, the broad category of service can be broken down to internal service and external service. Internal service includes activities directly related to the administration of one's academic unit as well as the greater college and/or university. The best example may be serving on committees. Keeping in mind that faculty are very much involved in the management and governance of universities, particularly in such matters as curriculum, faculty are expected to serve on a variety of committees that are assigned to manage such matters. Internal service goes beyond committee assignments, though, and can be further divided into service to (1) the department; (2) the college; and (3) the university. Each of these areas will be discussed later in the chapter. Meeting one's internal service obligations may be accomplished in a variety of ways including: advising hospitality majors or organizing a student scholarship program; serving as administrative liaison with support departments; or even planning and managing a departmental function, such as a fund-raiser. Such internal service assignments can obviously take a variety of forms, but these are a few of the more common examples. A more comprehensive list is provided later in the chapter. In sum, the primary goal of internal service is for faculty to take an active role in the proper functioning and management of the university and its various academic units.

External, or professional, service may be even more broadly defined. Crosson (1992) states that "Professional service activities are those which bring the professional knowledge and expertise of faculty members off the campus and into the larger arenas in which governments struggle for solutions to complex problems, businesses seek new products and technologies, and people seek healthier and more satisfying living and work environments" (p. 1596).

External service activities, then, include not only providing professional assistance to the community at large, but also participation in professional societies, service on academic and industry boards, and making presentations to groups and associations. Again, as with internal service, the list of related activities goes on. In contrast to internal service, though, external service can be even harder to delineate, and as a result, evaluate.

Together, these two forms of service represent a very important contribution that faculty members make to their institutions and the external environment. However, service is rarely considered when the issue of faculty performance is discussed. Oddly enough, at one time, service was the pillar upon which higher education in the United States stood. Crosson (1992) emphasizes that professional service, at one time, was judged to be an integral part of the university's mission, going back to the 1800s. In the United States, and particularly at public institutions, this was an outgrowth of university reliance upon the state and federal government's support, financial and otherwise. In fact, having faculty provide some sort of professional service off-campus may actually be part of a university's written mission statement to this day, such as with an agricultural extension service at land grant institutions (Crosson, 1992). Professional service became increasingly important in the early 1900s as populations and state universities increased in size and states looked to their respective universities for additional professional assistance. Crosson also suggests that after a period of increasing service activity in the 1900s, emphasis upon professional service decreased as a result of universities' renewed focus on research. This perhaps accounts for the current view of service in our institutions. To compound matters, Crosson also points out that there is no universally agreed-upon definition of professional service.

Together, these two types of service activities, which universities expect of faculty members, can result in faculty members committing a large portion of their workday and workweek. Given the fact that university professors' workload has been scrutinized of late, it is not surprising that several studies have been conducted in an effort to reveal exactly how much time they spend working each week and how that time is allocated. As is pointed out in other chapters, one common misconception is that the majority of professors' time is spent teaching. One recent study, which looked specifically at hospitality educators, is quite revealing, particularly with respect to service responsibilities. That study, by Schmidgall and Woods (1996), looked at how hospitality educators allocated their work time and found that, on average, respondents spent a total of just over forty-eight hours per week on work-related activities. This was broken down as follows: 26.8 hours on teaching, 8.9 hours on research, 11.6 hours on university service, 5.9 hours on industry service, and 12.4 hours in other areas (p. 10). Total service activity represented a significant portion of the average work week. Of the total, respondents who were engaged in ongoing service activities indicated that they spent an average of almost twelve hours per week on internal activities and almost six hours per week on external activities. It should be noted that a higher percentage of respondents reported having internal service responsibilities (88 percent) than external (62.4 percent). In addition, one-fourth of the respondents reported spending an average of over twelve hours on "other" activities. Presumably, accepting the rather broad working definition of service, many of these other activities could conceivably fall under the service category. If Schmidgall and Woods's study is reflective of how hospitality faculty actually spend their workweek, it is clear that service activities consume the equivalent of one workday, at the minimum, and as much as two days for some faculty members, during a typical five-day work week.

Thus, faculty members can and do spend a significant portion of their time on service activities and yet, across disciplines, do not appear to be rewarded equitably when compared to research and teaching. Although no discipline-specific statistics are available, to my knowledge, it is not uncommon for the service component to contribute 20 percent or less to performance evaluations, and usually closer to 10 percent. Accepting the fact that service is often under-rewarded, let's take a closer look at the actual types of service activities in which hospitality faculty members engage.

INTERNAL SERVICE

Internal service, or institutional service, is often discussed in terms of service to one's university, college, or department. Flood and Moll

(1990) state that much of the time spent on institutional service is devoted to maintaining the integrity of the academic community. The various levels of internal service are discussed in turn.

Service to the University

Public universities, where most hospitality programs in the United States are found, are essentially government entities. As a result, the institutions are managed by persons in positions of authority that have been granted by the government entity responsible for the institution (usually the state). These institutions fall under the jurisdiction of state boards that exercise control over certain administrative activities such as planning, degree programs, and budgets. The chief executive officer for the university (president or chancellor) acts under the authority granted by the state boards. He or she is responsible for the overall governance of the institution. However, the internal governance of the institution, primarily relating to academic matters, falls under the jurisdiction of the faculty. Decisions affecting the university as a whole are made within a faculty senate, or other university-level committees, while lower-level decisions are made at college or department levels. Sometimes decisions are made at the lower levels but require approval at the university level, as with curricular issues. As a result of this arrangement, individual faculty members have extensive responsibilities for university governance.

The chief governing body representing faculty is often known as the faculty senate. Its primary scope is in maintaining standards relating to academic matters including curriculum and policy. The faculty senate is composed of representatives from each college. It may also include administrators, staff members, and students, despite what its name would suggest. The number of representatives per college is usually based the total number of faculty members within each academic unit so that larger colleges invariably have more representatives. Faculty terms are staggered and vary in length, assuring change while maintaining a certain level of continuity. Individual representatives are elected and must participate in the regular senate meetings, which are generally held once each month. In addition, representatives have voting privileges. They also are responsible for attending their respective college meetings and informing their colleagues of any decisions that might affect their colleges. Further, issues arising during senate meetings will often be sent to committee for further discussion. These smaller committees are made up of the representatives and obviously require an additional time commitment until such issues are resolved. Such committees may be standing committees or may be formed on an ad hoc basis. Recommendations are generally made by committees and passed on to the university senate for approval or disapproval. Ad hoc committees are formed when decisions must be made regarding a topic that has unexpectedly surfaced. Faculty members are expected to participate on both standing and ad hoc committees, as the need arises.

In addition to the faculty senate and related subcommittees, several other faculty committees exist at the university level and operate in either a policy making or advisory capacity. These, too, may be either standing or ad hoc. Typical standing committees within the university structure might include policy, graduate and undergraduate curriculum, research, library resources, lecturers and speakers, and grievance, among others. A more comprehensive list is provided in Exhibit 9.1. Although it is beyond the scope of this chapter to describe the roles and functions of each of these committees, two will be used as examples.

One fairly common committee that exists across college campuses is the university committee for courses and curricula. Similar committees exist at both departmental and college levels, but the university-level committee is responsible for approving or denying requested course-related changes that have been forwarded from individual colleges. These changes may include something as simple as a course name change or as major as the addition of a new course. A similar committee would exist for graduate-level courses. The university committee for courses and curricula obviously plays an integral role in the internal governance of the university.

Another example of a fairly common university-level committee is the university grievance committee. This committee is charged with assuring that faculty are treated fairly and equitably in their employment. Grievances often relate to tenure, promotion, and merit pay decisions. Essentially, this committee listens to grievances that have been filed by the faculty member, which may lead to a full grievance procedure, which may ultimately result in a hearing. This

EXHIBIT 9.1. Typical-Level Standing Committees

Faculty Senate

Graduate Council

Policy Committee

Courses and Curricula Committee

Grievance Committee

Research Council

Committee for the Protection of Human Subjects

Student Judicial Committee

Library Resource Committee

Committee on Artists, Lecturers, and Speakers

Committee on Faculty Honors

Student Publications Board

Promotion and Tenure Committee

---

portion of the procedure will vary from university to university. In the end, the committee, usually acting in an advisory capacity, will make a recommendation to the president or chancellor, who usually makes the final ruling. Obviously, this committee too plays an important role, and is another good example of how faculty are involved in the overall governance and management of the university.

Service to the College

Faculty also have service responsibilities to their colleges. Hospitality programs may be housed in a number of different settings including colleges of business, human ecology, agriculture, professional sciences, and others. Also, some of the more prominent programs in the field are independent colleges, including the Hilton College at the University of Houston and the Harrah College at the University of Nevada at Las Vegas. No matter where programs are housed, decisions must be made regarding course requirements;

new courses must be approved; faculty development issues must be addressed; and college missions need to be periodically reviewed. As with university-level committees, college committees allow faculty input into college-level decision making. Such committees might focus on incorporating new technologies into the classroom, mission effectiveness, and special programs. A more comprehensive list of college-level committees from one state university appears in Exhibit 9.2.

Ad hoc committees may be convened as needed to discuss impending issues. Examples of ad hoc committees might include a search committee for a dean or to explore changing needs of undergraduate students in a particular topic area. Finally, college-wide faculty meetings are frequently held as a means of keeping faculty informed about college activities. These meetings occur as needed and may be held as often as monthly or as infrequently as once a semester. Again, faculty participation is expected. Generally, faculty involvement is greater at the college level than at the university

EXHIBIT 9.2. College-Level Committees

Undergraduate Program Committee

Graduate Program Committee

MBA Program Committee

Committee on Faculty Development

Committee on Mission Effectiveness

Academic Review Board

Scholarships and Awards Committee

College of Business Executive Council

Strategic Planning Committee

Computer Use Committee

Summer Research Grant Committee

Promotion and Tenure Committee

level. Faculty members, especially in the early stages of their careers, might be on several college committees and not be placed on
a single university committee. This makes sense in that it is usually
to the professor's advantage to learn his or her way around the
university for a few years before getting involved in the actual
decision-making process at the higher levels.

In the same way that college representation is desired on university committees, departmental representation is desired on college-
level committees. This would mean that in a typical college made
up of several departments, each department would be represented
on the committees identified above. It only makes sense that each
academic unit within the college should have input on the selection
of a dean, makeup of the core curricula, or major college capital
purchases such as computers.

Service to the Department

As one moves down the university hierarchy, the degree of faculty involvement generally increases. Individual departments, while
having appointed a chief administrator (e.g., director, chairperson,
or department head) also need additional faculty administrative
assistance and input. Individual departments must not only look
after their own internal affairs but must also be represented on
college committees, as colleges are represented on university committees. Internal departmental service responsibilities may include
advising students (which may be included under teaching responsibilities), serving as the faculty advisor to student organizations,
planning and participating in a variety of departmental events, and
handling routine administrative duties. Departmental service also
includes serving on departmental committees. Depending upon the
size of the department, the size and scope of the committees are
likely to vary significantly. In larger departments, these committees
may include courses and curricula, promotion and tenure, and research committees (the same as at the college and university levels).
In essence, many of these committees are identical to committees
with the same names at both the college and university levels—in
some cases they are entirely redundant and accomplish nothing
more than to add another layer to the decision making process. In
other cases, the decisions made at the departmental level need only

meet with college approval before they may be implemented. Other departmental service responsibilities may be very different in scope, including working with a department's alumni or contributing to the department's newsletter.

A final responsibility, albeit a very important one, applies to faculty teaching in graduate programs. These faculty are likely to have the additional responsibility of serving on their students' master's and doctoral degree committees, which borders on service and teaching. These responsibilities include directing students during their graduate studies, reviewing and evaluating qualifying exams, and directing theses and dissertations. While the programs that offer graduate degrees are still relatively few, the advising and directing of graduate students can be very labor intensive. Normally, faculty who advise and teach graduate students receive appropriate reductions in their undergraduate teaching responsibilities. Graduate education is discussed in more depth in Chapter 11.

In programs both large and small, departmental service activities contribute to day-to-day administration, serving the students enrolled in the program and helping to make key decisions that affect long-term viability. For these reasons, it could easily be argued that, as internal service activities go, departmental assignments are among the more important.

Summary of Internal Service

Internal service activities, which contribute to the internal functioning of the department, college, and university, are extremely important in assuring the achievement of the academic mission of each academic unit, as well as maintaining their integrity. Such activities demand a significant portion of a faculty member's workweek. In essence, the majority of faculty members in hospitality programs (at least those on tenure track), have this administrative component built into their jobs to a greater or lesser degree. According to Schmidgall and Woods' (1996) study, on average, respondents spend almost twice as much time on internal service activities as on service to the industry.

EXTERNAL SERVICE

In addition to the various internal service activities, there is the expectation that faculty will provide support and assistance outside of the immediate academic environment. Whereas internal service is focused more on administrative tasks, external service is more broad based and is more likely to vary in scope. In an effort to simplify the broad range of activities that might be included, external service activities will be classified as one of three types: (1) service to the academic community; (2) service to the industry; and (3) service to the lay community. These will be discussed in turn.

Service to the Academic Community

University faculty are members of an exclusive club, in a manner of speaking. Attaining one's terminal degree also means achieving a level of membership in the academic community. But each discipline represents a separate club of sorts, and another level of membership. Hospitality educators are members of their university community but they are also members of the hospitality education community, which is a relatively small field as academic disciplines go. This is what Flood and Moll (1990) have referred to as the "invisible college." When one compares the field of hospitality to any of the more established disciplines such as math, engineering, or even business, it appears small indeed.

There are many elements with which a community member may become involved. In hospitality education there are, as with other disciplines, associations, journals, the accreditation process (see Chapter 4), special interest groups, and a host of other ways to give something back to the community. In the course of an individual's career, his or her contribution to the field is expected to increase. One reason for this is that the beginning of one's career is mostly spent satisfying departmental requirements and expectations in an effort to gain tenure and promotion (see Chapters 5 and 6). At some point in one's career, however, faculty members are expected to make their contribution to the academic community. The various ways that professors can contribute are discussed in turn.

Association Work

Many associations are in one way or another involved with hospitality education. Some are trade associations while others are professional associations. Some are geared to the industry while others are more for academics. As we tell our students, an association is beneficial to its members for a variety of reasons. And for the same reasons that hospitality students should join associations, so should faculty members. But just maintaining membership in an association is usually not enough. It is expected that faculty members will actively participate, or even take leadership roles in these various associations. As an example, with such industry associations as the American Hotel & Motel Association, National Restaurant Association, and Club Managers Association of America (just to name a few), there are opportunities to make presentations at conferences, conduct training sessions for certification purposes, serve on local or national committees, or even hold an office. The opportunities are endless and the more educators become involved with industry associations, the more positive exposure the individual (and discipline) gets. The best way to start is to join the association, attend its meetings, and then ask how to get more involved! Industry associations will be discussed in greater detail in the section on service to the industry.

The other type of association in our field is primarily academic. These include the Council on Hotel, Restaurant and Institutional Education (CHRIE), the Association of Casino Educators (ACE), and the Society for Travel and Tourism Educators, among others. Like the industry associations mentioned earlier, most of these groups also have opportunities for involvement. Of all of these associations, CHRIE is probably the one that elicits the greatest level of involvement from hospitality faculty. Aside from the CHRIE staff, based in Washington, DC, the organization depends upon volunteers to sit on various committees, serve as officers, plan the annual conference, chair special interest groups, moderate sessions at the conference, and act as liaisons to their allied associations. There is no shortage of ways to become involved. In fact, a quick glance at the association's monthly publication, the *CHRIE Communique*, will generally reveal solicitations for assistance in each of these areas. In short, for individuals who want to offer their time, there are ample opportunities with the associations mentioned here as well as many others.

Hospitality Journals

Another way that hospitality faculty can involve themselves with the academic community is by serving as a reviewer, or even editor, of one of the many hospitality journals. Most of the journals in the field (at least those that are refereed) rely upon the assistance of the academic community to review manuscripts that are submitted for publication. The average journal may have as many as twenty reviewers on call, to whom the editors can send manuscripts for review. Serving as a reviewer offers many benefits including gaining access to cutting-edge research before it is even published, gaining valuable editorial skills, and becoming more visible in the academic community. It also gives the individual a firsthand glimpse at the editorial process, which can help one to better understand how to get manuscripts published. As such, journal involvement is clearly beneficial to all involved. Journals also represent another area that is entirely dependent upon volunteer efforts. Without editors and reviewers, the journals, as we know them, would surely not exist.

Accreditation

Academic institutions may be accredited at several levels, including the university, college, and departmental. As discussed in Chapter 4, accreditation serves as a form of quality assurance. Not much can be added here except to say that content experts must be available to serve on accreditation commissions and conduct site visits. Such activities are very time consuming and are a clear example of external service to the academic community. Because of the time commitment involved, however, individuals would be advised to determine whether such activities are, first, recognized as legitimate service activities and, second, whether such activities are rewarded by their departments.

Other Service Opportunities Within the Academic Community

Finally, there are some other functions that fall under the external academic umbrella but do not fit with any of the previously discussed activities. From time to time, colleagues will call on each other for assistance in certain matters, which can vary greatly in degree and take a variety of forms. These activities often do more to maintain collegiality than to fulfill a performance requirement. In other words, these encompass the various ways that we are able to "help each other out." Nonetheless, these activities can be important in and of themselves. Some of the more common instances might include:

• Serving as an external reviewer for a colleague's dossier for tenure and promotion consideration
• Writing recommendations for colleagues for special projects, grants, or job applications
• Serving as a moderator or panelist at an academic conference
• Reviewing manuscripts for colleagues before they are submitted to journals
• Conducting external curriculum reviews (not relating to accreditation visits)
• Disseminating information to colleagues on one's area of expertise (through guidebooks, manuals, or workshops at conferences)
• Coordinating and hosting an academic conference (an example would be the Conference on Graduate Education and Graduate Students Research sponsored by several hospitality programs)
• Publishing/contributing to in-house publications that are distributed to other academic programs (e.g., the University of Houston's *Innsider*)

There are probably many more areas in which hospitality educators contribute to the greater good. These are just a few of the more common activities.

Service to the Industry

The second broad area of external service concerns service to the hospitality industry. Crosson (1992) has suggested that what was once a primary mission of the university, public service, is moving toward more of a "professional" service orientation where faculty members are more likely to engage in activities that capitalize upon their professional abilities. This same change seems to be occurring in the hospitality discipline as well. One reason for this may be that one of the factors that sets our discipline apart from others is that there is an entire industry that exists and which helps give us our identity. The relationship between the hospitality industry and the academic community has always been characterized by give and take. The service we provide to the greater hospitality industry is one of the primary ways that we give back to it. Some of the ways that hospitality educators provide service to the industry are discussed below.

Industry Associations

Association work has already been mentioned. Professors can get involved in any of the aforementioned professional and trade associations at the national, regional, or local levels. For instance, CMAA has regional chapters around the country that have their own officers and boards of directors. Many faculty serve as faculty advisors to their students and work closely with the regional chapters as a result. The Hospitality Sales & Marketing Association International (HSMAI), the American Hotel & Motel Association (AH&MA), the American Society of Healthcare Food Service Administrators (ASHFSA) and the American Culinary Federation (ACF) are just a few of the national organizations that have either regional and/or local chapters with which faculty may want to get involved. Association involvement, among other things, allows individuals to gain a better understanding of a particular segment of the industry and the greater hospitality industry to gain a better understanding of hospitality education.

Trade Journals

Another means of providing service to the industry is to contribute articles to the various trade publications. Hospitality educators have long contributed to such publications as *Club Management Magazine, Nation's Restaurant News, Hospitality Marketing Review,* and *The Consultant,* among others. There are a whole host of journals in circulation that actively seek contributions from academic experts. Some authors even contribute regular columns to such journals. Educators habitually develop two different types of articles from a single research topic—one more academically rigorous piece for submission to a refereed journal and another version, written for a larger audience, for submission to a trade journal. Along with these journals, there are also various newsletters and periodicals that accept contributions. One caveat must be mentioned at this point. Some programs will accept trade journal publications as part of a professor's research efforts, depending upon the nature and scope of the article in question. Other programs view them as an extension of a faculty member's service activities, and for that reason, they have been included here.

Industry Seminars

In much the same way that faculty members must engage in some form of professional development, so must industry professionals. One of the ways that industry practitioners accomplish this is by attending workshops and seminars geared to their area of expertise. Faculty members are a logical choice to develop and deliver these types of sessions and many do. Most of the same associations identified earlier actively seek individuals to conduct workshops and seminars and many faculty members comply. Sometimes this is accomplished on an individualized, as-needed basis. Other times, hospitality programs will enter into formal agreements with industry groups to prepare and deliver a certain number of programs. Sometimes faculty members are paid for their services. When they are paid, the lines between providing true "service" and "consulting" become blurred. However, some would argue that even consulting is a form of service and should be treated as such.

Other Industry Service Opportunities

While association involvement, contributions to trade journals, and the delivery of seminars represent some of the more common services that professors provide to the hospitality industry, there are other means of performing service. Some of these activities might include:

- Engaging in applied research projects involving the industry
- Serving as an expert witness
- Serving on boards of directors
- Participating in hospitality-related industry events/benefits
- Providing answers to questions or providing reference materials to industry practitioners
- Collaborating on special projects

Other Community Service

Although the trend seems to be moving from broad-based community service to more professionally oriented service, as discussed earlier, some universities (and colleges and departments) still allow and/or expect that faculty members will provide such service to the community at large. Such activities may range from serving as a leader with the Boy Scouts to serving on a board of directors for a nonprofit association. Some other possible activities might include:

- Speaking to local business or civic associations
- Serving on the school board
- Coaching youth sports
- Getting involved with political associations
- Managing a government-sponsored function

Obviously, such activities can be even more far reaching than those categories previously discussed. Programs that encourage involvement with the community at large do so in the belief that faculty members should also be good citizens. The question here is whether or not they should also be rewarded for such activities.

CONCLUSION

The service component of a hospitality educator's job plays a critical role in professional development, in a faculty member's level of visibility in an institution and the greater hospitality industry, and contributes significantly to the effectiveness of the various academic units. In recent years, service has been a relatively underappreciated aspect of faculty responsibilities. However, the role of service may finally be getting some of the attention that it has deserved for so long. A recent report by the Carnegie Foundation for the Advancement of Teaching focused on the assessment of scholarship in the university (Glassick, Huber, and Maeroff, 1997). Among other things, the researchers looked at how professors were evaluated with respect to teaching, research, and service. Service was broken down into the areas of "applied scholarship," "service to the institution," and "professional activity." In general, it seems that more institutions are putting a greater emphasis on these areas. Specifically, one-third (or more) of responding institutions indicated that new methods of evaluation had been developed in the areas of applied scholarship, service to the college, and service to the industry (p. 18). In addition, across institutions, it was revealed that over 40 percent of respondents count applied scholarship more in faculty evaluations than they did five years ago. Also, about one-fourth of respondents indicated that institutional service and professional activity count more toward faculty evaluations than they did five years ago (pp. 100, 101).

That same study argues that the traditional definition of scholarship must be broadened and that institutions must begin to develop clearer performance standards. Hospitality education is a relatively young field of study and is struggling with these very issues at this time. But the time is now to establish specific standards in all areas, including service. The clearer the standards are, the easier it will be to evaluate the performance. It then follows that perhaps service will receive the consideration it deserves come evaluation time. Service is clearly as important, if not more so, in the hospitality discipline because of our direct ties to industry. It is also clear, judging from at least one study, that hospitality faculty spend a significant portion of their time on service-related activities.

A simple method of standardizing service activities is to begin with the model presented in this chapter. Categories can be developed, activities can be categorized, and weights can be assigned. Weighting will obviously depend upon the scope and the mission of the program (see the discussion of program missions in Chapter 1). It must be remembered, however, that no list will ever be exhaustive. Because of the very nature of service, there will always be at least one activity that has not been accounted for in the standards.

Faculty members should choose their service activities responsibly. They must identify service activities that allow them to apply their scholarly abilities, are consistent with the missions of their academic units, meet with their long-term professional development objectives, and are recognized and rewarded by their institutions. If all of these things can be accomplished, then all of their constituents should be satisfied—which should be one of the objectives of the service process.

REFERENCES

Cornett, J. (1993). Consideration of service in the merit process for university faculty. In James J. Van Patten (Ed.), *Understanding the many faces of the culture of higher education.* Lampeter, UK: Edwin Mellen Press.

Crosson, P.H. (1992). Faculty and professional service. *The encyclopedia of higher education*, In Burton Clark and Guy Neaves (Eds.), pp. 1596-1605. Oxford, UK: Pergamon.

Flood, B.J. and Moll, J.K. (1990). *The professor business: A teaching primer for faculty.* Medford, NJ: Learned Information, Inc.

Glassick, C.E., Huber, M.T., and Maeroff, G.I. (1997). *Scholarship assessed: Evaluation of the professoriate.* San Francisco: Jossey-Bass Publishers.

Schmidgall, R. and Woods, R. (1996). Work effort of hospitality educators. *Hospitality & Tourism Educator, 8,* 9-14.

Chapter 10

International Perspectives: A Comparison of U.S., U.K., and Australian Hospitality Education and Their University Systems

J. S. Perry Hobson

INTRODUCTION

Just as there has been an explosion of hospitality programs in the United States over the last twenty years, so too has there has been an international revolution in the provision of hospitality-level education over the same period. Although the hospitality program at Cornell University in the United States can trace its roots back to 1922, the reality is that most of the growth in the numbers of programs and students has occurred globally in the 1980s and 1990s. However, it is difficult, if not impossible, to get an accurate number of students or institutions worldwide offering hospitality and tourism education.

The primary focus of this chapter is on hospitality management education. But the developments in hospitality education have often overlapped with those in tourism education (Stear and Griffin, 1991). Consequently, overlapping developments will be presented here.

In terms of preparing people to work in the hospitality industries, it is often seen that each country has its own national focus. An old joke in the hotel industry runs something like this:

Heaven is where the French are the chefs, the Italians are the waiters, the Swiss are the managers and the British are the accountants. Hell is where the British are the chefs, the Swiss are the waiters, the French are the accountants and the Italians are the managers!

While stereotypical, it does point to the fact that many countries place different cultural emphases on their hospitality and hospitality training.

For a number of reasons, universities and colleges that provide hospitality and tourism education are having to become more aware of the international context in which they are operating (Samefink and Smetana-Novak, 1994; Hobson and Josiam, 1995). One major factor has been the movement of millions of tourists between countries and cultures, which requires an understanding of foreign cultures and customs. Furthermore, the globalization of major companies within the hospitality and tourism industries has necessitated a move away from a narrow domestic focus to a broader international focus in operations. In addition, universities are seeing an increasing number of foreign students in their enrollments (many of whom are applying for credit for prior study). Another factor has been the desire by many universities to offer their own students (and staff) an international exchange opportunity. Understanding the details of other systems and programs is crucial to the success of such exchanges. Finally, academic conferences are now an international marketplace in which ideas and views about education and "best practice" are being constantly exchanged. Consequently, there is increasingly a need to have a firmer understanding of program structures and developments in other countries.

Hospitality Management Programs

It is all but impossible in one short chapter to review the development of hospitality education from a national, let alone international perspective. Rather, the aim of this chapter is to put into perspective three different systems and types of hospitality, and associated tourism degree programs offered in the United States, United Kingdom, and Australia. These three countries have been specifically chosen for geographic as well as cultural reasons. They cover the continents of Europe, the Americas and Australia. They are all English-speaking countries, with numerous cultural and academic links. This means that some meaningful comparison can be achieved. However, despite a shared cultural heritage, their education systems have developed quite differently. Even the same academic terms may have quite different meanings. As Winston Churchill once pointed out, "Britain and America are two countries divided by a common language." So, not only has the decision whether to use British English, American English, Australian English been a challenge—but also the use of certain words has proved troubling. For example, an individual component of a degree program might be called a "course" in the United States, a "module" in the United Kingdom, or a "unit" in Australia. Consequently, I hope that the reader will bear with the attempts at establishing a form of "global English" in this chapter.

In order to understand overseas hospitality and tourism degree programs, it is important to know something of the education system within which each program operates. Universities and colleges operate within a national education environment and framework, subject to government funding and some form of controls. Even institutions that operate in the private sector have to follow some form of government guidelines, registration, or accreditation. As a result, a knowledge of the education system and how it has evolved is crucial to understanding some of the basics of why hospitality programs are structured differently, and why they occur in the institutions that they do.

Throughout this chapter, there is a need to generalize about education systems, universities, and the programs offered. As a result, many of the points made may not apply to each and every individual institution or program within a country. Rather, the objective here is to give an overall impression. Specific details on the development of hospitality education in various countries can be found in the literature, though it is very limited. However, in recent years, specific articles on the development of hospitality education have been written on the United Kingdom (Hughes, 1991), Australia (Hobson, 1995), and Italy (Formica, 1997).

UNDERSTANDING THE U.S. SYSTEM

As one of the world's largest countries, the United States offers a diverse range of programs within its higher education system. The tertiary system is divided into two types of colleges: (1) community colleges that offer up to two-year programs and can confer an associate degree, and (2) universities and colleges that offer a four-year under-graduate-level degree and above. Americans tend to talk about "going to college" as a collective term. Such colleges (and universities) can be grouped into three broad categories, and hospitality and tourism programs can be found in all three. The categories are (1) state universities, such as Michigan State University, (2) private universities, such as Boston University, or (3) a hybrid, such as Cornell University. Of the private universities, some are operated as educational foundations that may have a religious base, such as the Roman Catholic Mercyhurst College. Others may be operated on a more commercial (or proprietary) basis, such as Johnson & Wales University.

Depending on their financial circumstances, students may obtain low-interest loans, though there are many who still aim to work their way though college rather than accumulate extra debt. Many students now hold some form of part-time job during the semester and cut down on the number of credits they are taking. Perhaps not surprisingly, the average American is now taking much longer than the traditional four years to graduate from college. In fact, the average American student takes closer to five years to graduate.

American academics are often employed on a nine-month contract basis. Academic staff can often earn extra salary by teaching during the summer semester, or through consultancy work. The academic scale in the United States varies somewhat by institution, but is typically lecturer, instructor, assistant professor, associate professor, or professor. However, in the United Kingdom and Australia, the term lecturer is used for quite senior staff. In the United States, the term lecturer tends to be used for only the most junior academic positions.

Academics may be employed on a short-term contract basis, or tenure-track basis. In the case of tenure track, after approximately five to six years the department makes a recommendation through its college/faculty to the university as to whether the academic should receive tenure. Failure to achieve tenure means the staff member is given one year to pursue employment elsewhere. Such a system tends to put considerable pressure on junior academic staff to "publish or perish" during a time when they may typically have higher teaching loads. Once tenure is granted, it is very difficult to remove academics from their jobs. Consequently, stress levels of junior U.S.

academics may be very high, while older tenured academics may rarely be seen on campus. This system is now in sharp contrast to the situation in the United Kingdom, where tenure no longer exists.

Most American universities operate on a two-semester basis, of fifteen weeks each. A third summer school semester (with reduced subjects) is offered by a number of institutions. The academic year tends to run from early September to December and January to May. Students are expected to study for a minimum of four years full-time, though a degree can be completed in less time if the student takes on extra credits during a semester or studies in summer school. Universities operate on a credit-based system—each discrete individual unit or course of study is given a credit weighting that reflects the number of contact hours. Traditionally most courses are three credits, which would normally be made up of three one-hour lecture periods weekly. Students take an average of fifteen credits per semester to graduate with a 120-credit four-year degree. Not all units are worth three credits, though, as they often vary from one to six credits. For example, food and beverage units might carry a higher number of credit hours to reflect the extra hours of contact as a result of "laboratory" work, such as working in a training restaurant.

Students can often apply directly to the program of their choice (known as their "major") from high school. The majority of students at public universities study within their home states, as in-state fees are cheaper. At a number of universities, it is possible to apply as an "undecided major," and students can then shop around within the university for a program that suits them, while they take their general education courses. Unlike the United Kingdom and Australia, a large proportion of American students change their major several times while they are at university. All students are expected to take a range of general education courses (often referred to just as gen eds or GEs). Students are allowed some choice in the courses, they can take but must take units from the sciences and humanities as well as English and mathematics. The GE units often represent around a third of the degree, though this varies by university. Students then take a core of units for their majors, and then electives. Electives may be structured into a minor field of study though this may involve taking additional credits.

Students' grades are based on a grade point system (GPA) normally allocated as follows: A = 4, A − /B + = 3.5, B = 3, C = 2, D = 1. Students whose GPA drops below 2.0 are usually temporarily suspended. They may be readmitted but cannot graduate until the GPA gets above 2.0. The student's GPA determines his or her degree standing. Students who do well, for example have a semester or continuous GPA of 3.5 or above, might be entered onto the "Dean's List," or have their academic achievement acknowledged in some other way. Some universities operate an honors system of units that are only open to high-performing students.

There are currently over 130 institutional U.S. members of CHRIE (the main association for hospitality and tourism educators), offering a variety of hospitality and tourism degree programs. Within universities, the majority of hospitality and tourism programs are offered through a college of business (e.g., the University of New Orleans program), though others are offered though a college of human development (e.g., University of Wisconsin–Stout), or a college of agriculture (e.g., Southern Illinois University). The predominant focus in the United States is therefore on the business aspects, and more on hotel management or hospitality management than on tourism. In fact, there are relatively few undergraduate degrees offered purely in tourism in the United States. In a 1996 study of the names of seventy-seven U.S. programs in this area, only two exclusively used the name tourism management and only one exclusively used the term travel industry management. However, another nineteen used the words tourism or travel in combination with the terms hospitality or hotel (Bloomquist and Moreo, 1997).

To complete a degree, most students have to satisfy a minimum number of hours of internship (work experience), which are often completed during the university vacation periods. It is unusual for students to be visited by a university staff member during an internship, though students are usually expected to submit a report upon completion. Degrees awarded tend to be bachelor of arts (BA), or bachelor of science (BS).

In terms of graduate programming, U.S. institutions offer master's (MA, MS) and doctoral degrees. These may be doctorates in law (JD), education (EdD), business (DBA), or philosophy (PhD). Master's are usually some thirty-plus credit hours of further study beyond a bachelor's, and PhD some seventy-plus credit hours. The master's degree is predominantly coursework based, as is the PhD degree. A PhD dissertation may constitute about only 25 percent of the degree. Until the 1990s there were relatively few universities offering PhD-level programs in hospitality management. This has changed quite substantially and there are now a number of institutions offering PhD programs.

Sample U.S. Program: University of New Orleans

The School of Hotel, Restaurant and Tourism at the University of New Orleans* is part of the College of Business. The school offers a Bachelor of Science in Hotel, Restaurant and Tourism and at the graduate level, a concentration within the Master's of Business Administration.

Bachelor of Science in Hotel, Restaurant, and Tourism Administration

The School of HRT offers a four-year bachelor of science degree in hotel, restaurant, and tourism administration within the college of business administration. HRT students receive the same intensive background as other business students. This management-oriented program prepares HRT graduates for entry-level management positions within the industry. They are equipped with the critical thinking, problem-solving, and decision-making skills that lead to success.

The curriculum gives students broad exposure to general education courses, a foundation in the fundamentals of business, and an understanding of the hotel, restaurant, and tourism industries.

The curriculum includes the following:

General education courses	47 hours
Business requirements	42 hours
HRT requirements	25 hours
HRT electives	15 hours
Total hours required	129 hours

*Details provided by UNO.

Curriculum in the School of Hotel, Restaurant, and Tourism Administration

Non-College of Business Administration course requirements:

English 1158	3 hours
English Literature*	6 hours
Humanities*†	6 hours
Humanities or Social Sciences*†	3 hours
Mathematics* 1111, 1140	6 hours
Non-Business Electives*	6 hours
Sciences*	11 hours
Social Sciences*†	6 hours
Total	47 hours

College of Business Administration course requirements:

Accounting 2100, 2130	6 hours
Business Administration 2780	3 hours
Economics 2203, 2204	6 hours
Finance 3300	3 hours
HRT or Business electives	6 hours
Management 3401, 3467, 3471, 3478	12 hours
Marketing 3501	3 hours
Quant. Methods—B&E 2785	3 hours
Total	42 hours

HRT course requirements (see following list for course titles):

HRT 2000, 2020, 2030, 2050	13 hours
HRT 3002, 3003, 3015, 3016, 3017, 4000	12 hours
HRT electives at 3000 or 4000 level	15 hours
Total	40 hours

Total	129 hours

*See General Education Course Requirements on page 62 of the UNO General/Graduate Catalog.

†At least six hours must be at or above the 2000 level.

HRT course titles:

HRT 2000 Introduction to HRT Administration	3 hours
HRT 2020 Hotel Operations	3 hours
HRT 2030 Principles of Food Preparation I	4 hours
HRT 2031 Principles of Food Preparation II	3 hours
HRT 2050 Principles of Travel and Tourism	3 hours
HRT 3011 Tourism and Hospitality Marketing	3 hours
HRT 3015 Hospitality Industry Accounting	3 hours
HRT 3016 Legal Environment in the Hospitality Industry	3 hours
HRT 3017 Service Organization Management in Hospitality	3 hours
HRT 3135 Commercial Food Service Operations	3 hours
HRT 3140 Cost Control of Hospitality Operations	3 hours
HRT 3141 Management of Beverage Service	3 hours
HRT 3145 Layout, Design, and Maintenance of Hospitality Facilities	3 hours
HRT 3150 Tourism Planning and Operations	3 hours
HRT 3240 Club Management and Operations	3 hours
HRT 3295 Independent Study in Hotel, Restaurant, and Tourism Administration	1-3 hours
HRT 4000 Policy Issues in Tourism and Hospitality	3 hours
HRT 4110 Tourism and Hospitality Research	3 hours
HRT 4120 Advanced Lodging Operations Management	3 hours
HRT 4155 Management of Hospitality Destination Systems	3 hours
HRT 4160 Theories of Casino Gaming	3 hours
HRT 4165 Management of Gaming Enterprises	3 hours
HRT 4230 Advanced Food Service Management	4 hours
HRT 4250 International Tourism	3 hours
HRT 4290 Special Topics in HRT	3 hours
HRT 4299 Senior Honors Thesis	1-6 hours

HRT 3002-3003 Hotel, Restaurant, and Tourism
Experience   —0 Credits

This course is a required work experience that may be completed prior to, during, or after completion of course work. The
program consists of two different hospitality industry experiences of 400 hours each for a total of 800 hours of approved
work experience. The students in this course must submit a
report on each work experience and the employers will be
required to submit an evaluation of the student's performance.

HRT 3290 Hospitality Internship—3 hours

Under the supervision of an HRT faculty member, the student will complete an internship at the site of a participating
organization that directs the intern in a specific research project. Readings and other research activities may be assigned.
Students desiring to take this course should apply a semester
in advance for school approval. Open to Hotel, Restaurant, and
Tourism Administration majors with overall grade point average of 3.00 and above. A minimum of eight hours per week at
the site of a participating organization will be required.

UNDERSTANDING THE U.K. SYSTEM

Unlike the relatively slow evolution of the U.S. system, the U.K.
higher education system has undergone a rapid metamorphosis in the
last thirty years. Following the Robbins review in the 1960s, the
United Kingdom's higher education system was split into three levels: universities (that only offered degree and above level education
and focused on research), polytechnics (that offered degree and higher diplomas), and colleges of higher or further education (that offered
higher diploma and diplomas). University education was essentially
only offered to an elite few, and in the 1970s less than 10 percent of
the population went to the thirty or so universities. While universities
were granted the power to offer their own degrees, the polytechnics
were governed by the Council for National Academic Awards
(CNAA), which was a national government accreditation body that
oversaw all the polytechnics and colleges. Student fees were paid by
the government, and students could receive a maintenance grant

from the government that was means tested on parental income, and did not need to be repaid. To keep national standards uniformly high, the CNAA fostered a degree of cooperation between the various polytechnics and universities by insisting that courses had external advisers from another institution, who monitored students' work and exam results.

Over the years the polytechnics sought to shift from offering higher diplomas to offering more degree awards. In 1984 there were some twelve institutions in the United Kingdom offering hospitality degrees, though this had risen to twenty by 1990 (Hughes, 1991). During the 1980s, Thatcher's Conservative government encouraged this, as polytechnics were a much cheaper place to educate students than the more traditional and expensive research-focused universities. A blurring of the lines between universities and polytechnics continued, and finally it was decided to allow polytechnics to become universities. In the early 1990s the renaming of polytechnics and other colleges began. Today, there are some ninety-seven chartered universities in the United Kingdom, of which only one, the University of Buckingham, is private. However, a number of international colleges also offer programs in the U.K., such as Schiller International University, though their degrees would be accredited elsewhere.

Given the expansion of student places and the rise in numbers, the former Conservative government moved from a system of state subsidy of students to a "user pays" model. While university attendance was still free, instead of giving students a nonrepayable grant to cover basic living costs, low-interest loans were offered. In 1997 the New Labour government took this one step further, and announced that students would also now have to pay fees as well.

Prospective students have traditionally applied from school for a specific university and course through a single national clearance center. Nontraditional students can apply directly to the university and course of their choice. The traditional time to obtain a degree in the United Kingdom's higher education system has been three years, though there have always been notable exceptions such as for degrees in medicine and architecture. Most hospitality and tourism degrees are four years in length, with one year of the program being set aside for supervised work experience (known as an industrial placement or internship). These degrees are known as "sandwich" degrees. Unlike U.S. degree programs, there are no general education courses. Students are required to focus from the first day on subjects that are directly relevant to their degree program.

Traditionally, the individual courses within a degree program are a year in length, and students are faced with major exams at the end of each year. Departments have an exam board where each student's exam results across all the subjects taken are looked at. At the end of the first year, students might be told they can proceed to the next year, resit a subject, repeat the year, or be unable to progress. At the end of the third year, a student's overall degree classification is assessed by the board. There are four classes of degrees in the United Kingdom, with the second division being split into two categories: a first-class degree; a second-class degree, first division (commonly referred to as a two-one degree); a second-class degree, second division (commonly referred to as a two-two degree); or a third-class degree. Marking of the individual courses or models may be done on the A B C D system, or on a system mirroring the degree classification.

It is also common in the United Kingdom to see the term "Honours" listed in the name of the degree, and a graduate with such a degree would write BA or BSc (Hons) after their name. Some universities only offer an ordinary degree, while others offer an honors degree. While it is hard to generalize about honors, it often means that students would have undertaken some sort of individual research project as part of the course. In the late 1980s the system moved toward offering students discrete modules based on the U.S. system. Oxford Polytechnic (which is now Oxford Brookes University), was one of the pioneers in offering such a system in the 1970s. However, while a system of modules is now more commonly offered, most universities still have exam boards where a student's overall progression is still reviewed by academic staff. Degrees awarded to students in this field are either a bachelor of arts (BA) or bachelor of science (BSc).

In the 1980s, most of the United Kingdom's hospitality and tourism programs were located in the former polytechnics or colleges of higher education. The two notable exceptions were the University of Strathclyde in Scotland and the University of Surrey in England. Hospitality programs can trace their roots back to 1946 when the first program was established in a college that later became part of the University of Strathclyde in the 1960s. Meanwhile, tourism programs had offered either higher diplomas in the colleges of higher education, or master or postgraduate diplomas at the University of Surrey or Strathclyde. In the late 1980s, that void was filled, and a number of tourism undergraduate programs emerged in a few short years. As in the United States, a number of the tourism programs emerged from university departments with no hospitality programming. Tourism programs were also in departments such as geography, business, and policy studies.

In terms of postgraduate work, universities in the United Kingdom offer postgraduate diplomas, master's by course work (MA, MSc, MBA), master's by research only (MPhil), and doctorates by research (known as PhD or DPhil), though some other titles (such as DBA) are now being used. Doctorates were formerly solely by research, though it is now becoming common for students to take one or two courses as part of their PhD studies (usually in research methodology). Taught master's degree programs are typically one year in length, whereas PhDs are three to five years in length.

The academic year starts in September or October, though various academic calendar years are now in use. Traditionally, universities were on a three-term system (each of approximately eleven weeks). The expansion of the university system saw a number of changes to this. Some universities decided to move to the U.S. semester system, others with closer links to Europe adopted a European semester system, others remained with the traditional three-term system, and one university has developed a four-term system.

The system of academic titles in the United Kingdom is not completely uniform. Because universities and polytechnics had different systems, when the polytechnics joined the university system many either kept their system, changed to the university system, or adapted the two. The typical titles in order are: assistant lecturer, lecturer, senior lecturer, principal lecturer (usually only found in the former polytechnics), reader (which indicates the person is primarily in a research position), and professor. Traditionally the title of professor was granted for life. Consequently, British universities offered very few of them—many departments might in fact never have a professor. That system is now changing, and the title of professor is being more commonly awarded. The review and reform of higher education by the previous Thatcher Conservative government also saw the demise of tenure. Today most academic staff are on open-ended employment contracts, though some are also on fixed-term contracts. During the contract period the academic is regularly given performance reviews.

The sample program shown below is taken from Oxford Brookes University. The School of Hotel and Restaurant Management is an independent school within the university, which offers a range of undergraduate and postgraduate programs. The school offers a three-year single honors program in conjunction with another field of study (similar to a U.S. double major), and a four-year joint honors program (which includes a one-year internship period). The school also offers a master's in international hotel management (on-campus/internal) and an MBA in hospitality (open learning/external). The school also cooperates in a multidisciplinary degree in tourism with other schools within the university, such as the School of Planning and the School of Business.

Sample U.K. Program: Oxford Brookes University

BA/BSc Hospitality Management Studies (joint honors)*

Program Structure

This is a modular program that normally takes four years of full-time study. There are three components:

Year 1: Basic level. Students will develop an understanding of industry and develop the skills, knowledge, and capability necessary both for successful learning in the workplace and for effective advanced-level study.

Year 2: Supervised work experience. Forty weeks of work experience form a central component of the program. Assistance is given in finding an appropriate placement. Placements are currently avail-

---

*Details provided by OBU.

able throughout the United Kingdom, Europe, America, and the Far East and are all paid. Academic credit is awarded for the learning achieved during the placements, which are supervised by tutors from the school.

Years 3 and 4: Advanced level. In the final two years of the program you will study a range of managerial subjects focusing in particular on finance, accountancy, marketing, human resource management, and operations management. Your complete program of study will depend on your own particular interests. All modules are written with a clear description of the learning outcomes to be achieved, the learning and teaching methods to be provided, and the assessment methods used.

Assessment

A variety of assessment methods are used, including assessment by mentors within the workplace, case studies, reports, essays, oral presentations, portfolios of learning, poster presentation, computer simulations, and written examinations. Assessment is designed as an opportunity for students to demonstrate their learning achievements.

Special Features

In addition to the supervised work experience, all students undertake independent research in a specific topic area. This research is undertaken in the final year and helps you to develop analytical and critical awareness of the industry, and provides sound evidence of your individual scholarship. The student body is international, with over 20 percent of students originating from outside the United Kingdom. Hence study and learning is within a multicultural environment similar to that often found in the hotel and restaurant industry. You will also have an opportunity to strengthen your international perspective through our exchange program, which enables students to study in one of five prestigious North American universities as part of advanced studies.

Employment Opportunities

More than 80 percent of graduates normally gain immediate permanent employment, and the vast majority of these are employed within the hotel and restaurant industry. Others will continue within higher education and some choose to travel.

Complete Module Requirement Listing

Stage 1—core units:

Understanding hospitality
Hospitality operations skills*
Hospitality operations principles and practices
Business law I
Introduction to accounting
Business economics
Information analysis
Introduction to work in hospitality organizations

Stage 2—second and third year modules: you will choose at least fourteen from the following list, and for the award of honors you will need to complete a dissertation or project. Supplementary to degree requirements, additional modules from any subject can be taken for personal interest or to enhance career opportunities.

- Restaurant operations management
- Hotel rooms management
- Gastronomy
- Strategic analysis of hospitality businesses
- Principles of hospitality marketing
- Hospitality operations management
- Marketing management in the hospitality business
- Understanding leisure
- Work organization in the hospitality industry
- Managing people in the hospitality industry
- Employee relations in the hospitality industry
- Management accounting for the hospitality industry
- Financial analysis and control in the hospitality industry
- Financial decision making in the hospitality industry
- Tourism and hospitality management information systems

---

*Triple weighted unit.

- Food service operations management
- Food issues
- Issues in hospitality management
- Supervised work experience
- One of either: French, German, Italian, Spanish, or English languages in a business context

UNDERSTANDING THE AUSTRALIAN SYSTEM

The Australian model of higher education has been historically based on the United Kingdom's, though recently there has been a significant U.S. influence. Since 1988, five major reports have influenced the way in which Australia has addressed its education and training needs. In turn, these have had specific implications for hospitality and tourism education. The first and probably most significant of these was the Dawkins report of 1988. It looked at the need for Australia to develop comprehensive skills training across the educational spectrum. One major outcome of this report was the upgrading of the former Colleges of Advanced Education (CAE), which was similar to the United Kingdom's change of polytechnics to university status. The system expanded from approximately twenty-one to thirty-nine universities. Today there are publicly funded universities and colleges, of which there are some thirty-seven; and private universities, two of which are Bond University on the Gold Coast and Notre Dame University in Perth. There are a number of subdegree private colleges in Australia, and an extensive state-based system of two-year colleges known as TAFE (Technical and Further Education).

Although all the public universities belong to a national scheme, high school students still apply through the various state-based admission schemes. As in the United States, most students study within their state of residence, although there are no extra fees for studying in another state or territory. For undergraduate programs, students pay subsidized fees for their program through HECS (the higher education contribution scheme). Through this scheme, the student can pay fees up front (and receive a discount), or pay the fees through the tax system after graduation, once earnings reach a certain level. Universities also offer full-fee programs, where the full cost of the program is passed on to the student. There are no requirements for students to live on campus as is common in the United States, and is traditional in the United Kingdom. Given the relatively high fees, many students choose universities that are close to home. Unlike the United States, and more like the United Kingdom, the majority of the public universities are located in the main urban areas. There are of course a number of smaller rural regional universities, many of them specializing in external study courses.

The development of university-level hospitality and tourism degrees in Australia has been a recent phenomenon in comparison with the United States and the United Kingdom. As has been noted, the Hotel School at Cornell University in the United States was established in 1922. In the United Kingdom, the Scottish Hotel School was established in 1944, and it formally became part of the University of Strathclyde in 1964 (Gee, 1994). But it was not until the mid-1970s, that the then-Foostcray Institute of Technology in Melbourne (which is now part of Victoria University of Technology) and the Gatton Agricultural College (now part of the University of Queensland) introduced their programs in hospitality management. It should be noted that the origins of current university-level hospitality and tourism education in Australia predated the first courses being offered within institutions designated as universities. The tertiary-level institutions focusing on diploma and degree-level vocational education were known as CAEs and were similar in their mission to the former polytechnics in the United Kingdom. By 1990, the recommendation of mergers that came out of the Dawkins report saw the CAEs either joining with established universities, or together with one other and upgrading their status to that of a university. Coupled with the expansion of the university sector, and the undersupply of graduates for a growing tourism industry, the number of courses in hospitality and tourism grew quickly. As in the United Kingdom and United States they often grew out of a number of related departments, such as business, natural resources, leisure and recreation studies, and geography as well as hospitality.

In the United States and United Kingdom, hospitality management programs were well established before those in tourism. However, in Australia, unlike the United States and the United Kingdom, the rapid development and growth of hospitality management and tourism programs occurred almost simultaneously. This happened for a number of reasons relating to the development of the industries in Australia (Hobson, 1995). Furthermore, in Australia the term "tourism" became more prominently used, as it was seen to be more inclusive. Consequently, there has been considerable overlap in terms of course content and direction, as well as the naming of the various programs around the nation.

Back in 1987 Craig-Smith, Davidson, and French (1995) identified that there were only three institutions offering hospitality and tourism programs in Australia. Three years later, in 1990, there were sixteen; by 1995, twenty-one were listed. Of the programs offered by the universities, eight indicated they focused specifically on tourism, five specifically on hotel and hospitality management, and eight universities claim to have programming in both areas. However, such identification of actual programming is difficult at best. This is because in some cases the programs award an actual degree title of hotel management or tourism, whereas in other cases they are seen as a subset of a degree program in areas such as business or leisure. The growth and diversification of programs has continued and by 1997, some twenty-seven out of the thirty-seven universities in the country offered some type of hospitality and tourism programming. Despite its relatively small population size, there is now considerable diversity of programs within the system. Most hospitality and tourism programs include some internship period.

Australian degree programs are usually three years in duration for an ordinary degree. A honors-level degree normally involves an extra year of study, which is made up of some coursework but is largely independent research. The U.S. system of discrete courses (referred to as units) is now used, with students typically taking four or five units per semester. The academic year still starts in the traditional autumn/fall season, but being in the southern hemisphere means that the month is February or March. The academic calendar is divided into two semesters—February to June and July to November. Some universities are now offering a trimester academic year, with a third full semester offered over the summer (Christmas and New Year) holiday period. Students receive grades based on a number of different systems. Some universities use the A-F system, while others may use systems such as Higher Distinction, Distinction, Credit, Pass, and Fail. Showing how the Australian system has blended ideas from the United States and United Kingdom, universities may calculate a GPA, but then award an honors degree on classifications similar to the U.K. system.

At the graduate level, Australian universities offer graduate certificates, diplomas, and master's degrees by coursework. As in the United Kingdom, the degree awarded has been typically an MSc, MA, or MBA if by coursework, or an MPhil if by research. More recently though, a number of new names have been used such as master's in international tourism management, which is abbreviated MITM. Doctorate degrees (PhD) have traditionally followed the U.K. model of being by solely by research. But, as is happening in the United Kingdom, some doctorates now require some units of research methodology. American-style coursework DBAs also started to appear in the 1990s. In order to enroll in a PhD program, a student would normally complete an ordinary degree, complete an honors year, enter an MPhil program, and finally proceed in a PhD program.

For academic staff, the concept of tenure still exists in Australia. The percentage of staff in contract and tenure positions varies considerably among universities. Established research universities may have more than 65 percent of their staff on tenure, whereas newer universities often only have around 35 percent tenured. Most other full-time staff are employed on anything from one- to five-year contracts. Generally, a tenure review occurs after three years. The order of academic titles in Australia is also a mixture of the U.K. and U.S. styles. For most universities, it is tutor, assistant lecturer, lecturer, senior lecturer, associate professor, and professor.

An example is the School of Tourism and Hospitality Management at Southern Cross University (SCU). SCU operates on two campuses in Lismore and Coffs Harbour in New South Wales. At the Lismore campus the school offers a bachelor of business (BBus) in tourism (by both internal and external modes), and at the Coffs Harbour campus a BBus in hotel and catering management (internal/on-campus mode only). Through a partnership arrangement with the Sydney Inter-Continental Hotel, the separately established hotel school also offers a full-fee paying BBus in hotel management. In addition, the school offers exclusive partnership programs for various associations and companies in the industry by external study. For example, a flexible entry and exit certificate/advanced diploma/BBus Club Management is offered to employees of the Registered Club Association. The school also offers employees of Ansett Australian Airlines a diploma in business management. At the taught master's level, the school offers a discrete master's in international tourism management (MITM) and a master's in international hotel management (MIHM), as well as various combinations within the university's MBA program. By research students can take an honors program, an MPhil, and PhD.

Sample Australian Program: Southern Cross University

Bachelor of Business in Hotel and Catering Management

The twenty-four units that constitute the BBus in hotel and catering management* must include:

    a. Eighteen (18) units from Part A of the schedule (core units)
    b. A minimum of four (4) units from Part B of the schedule
    c. Two (2) free elective units offered by the university

Part A:

    MN411 Tourism and Hospitality Studies I
    MK127 Introduction to Tourism and Hospitality Marketing
    BS207 Personal Communications for the Tourism
      and Hospitality Industry
    MN428 Food and Beverage Service Delivery Systems
    MN429 Food Preparation and Production Systems
    MN431 Hotel Operations
    MN414 Introduction to Tourism and Hospitality Management
    MN413 Human Resource Management in the Tourism
      and Hospitality Industry
    AC206 Financial Analysis for Tourism and Hospitality
    MN430 Tourism and Hospitality Services Management
    LA205 Industrial Relations and Law for Tourism and Hospitality

*Details provided by SCU.

MN417 Strategic Management for Tourism and Hospitality
   Enterprises
MN419 Food and Beverage Management
MK128 Tourism and Hospitality Sales and Promotion
MN221 Internship Study I
MN222 Internship Study II
MN223 Internship Study III
MN224 Internship Study IV

Part B:

MN412 Tourism and Hospitality Studies II
AC 207 Hospitality and Tourism Financial Management
MN418 Accommodation and Information Technology Systems
MN424 Economic Analysis for Tourism and Hospitality
MN426 Gaming and Club Management
MN427 Entrepreneurship in Tourism and Hospitality
MN425 Pacific Asia Tourism Marketing and Development
MN420 Conventions, Meetings, and Exhibitions Management
MN415 Tourism and Hospitality Research and Analysis
MN416 Tourism and Hospitality Industry Project

The program is structured so that students spend five semesters on campus, with the last semester being the supervised internship placement. Students are placed domestically or internationally and are paid. As in the United Kingdom, it is usual for a tutor to visit the students during their internship. If that is not possible, extensive phone calls may be made to the student and employer to monitor progress. Students are also encouraged to go on an exchange program. Currently, the partners are the University of Lincolnshire & Humberside in the United Kingdom (for tourism students), and the University of Wisconsin–Stout (for hotel management students).

COMPARISON OF PROGRAMS

Despite differences in the education systems, there are remarkable similarities. One only has to look at the types and titles of courses/units offered with the various degree programs to see this.

Furthermore, programs in all three countries typically use a traditional lecture format as a central part of their on-campus delivery method, have a mixture of theoretical and practical courses, have work experience components for students, and draw on advice from industry through advisory boards.

Of course, many differences between the countries do exist. The use of the lecture-only format is prevalent in the United States, whereas in the United Kingdom and Australia lectures are accompanied by smaller seminar/tutorial sessions. In the United Kingdom many universities have very extensive kitchen and restaurant training facilities, which are often limited or totally absent from many U.S. and Australian universities. A pop quiz, as a method of assessment, would be unheard of in the United Kingdom or Australia, while it is common in the United States. In Australia, the students will often call their professor/lecturer by his or her first name from day one, whereas in the United States the term Doctor or Professor is usually used by students as a preface for all academic staff. As many students and academic staff on exchange have found, the closer one is to one particular system, the larger the differences in the other may appear. For example, when you look at determining a student's result, the U.S. system tends to use the very top of the percentage range, the United Kingdom is more toward the middle and Australia is often in between (see Table 10.1). This does not mean that an American working in the United Kingdom is going to give all the students A and B grades; rather the grading is done differently to get a different spread of marks. So while aspects of the system may appear quite different, the outcomes are often very similar.

Having said all that, one needs to consider whether there are fundamental differences in the hospitality education provided to students. The answer is equivocal. Although there are enormous differences, they tend to be in the myriad of details that make up a university education—how courses are taught, books used, expectations created by staff, standards used, exams set, and so forth. Such differences can be found within a national education system, as much as between different systems. However, given that the details are an important part of the education experience, it is true to say that there are a substantial number of differences between these countries.

TABLE 10.1. Comparison of Marking Percentages Used to Calculate Grades

United States	United Kingdom	Australia
A = 90%+	First class = 70%+	Higher Distinction = 85%+
B = 80-90%	Upper second class = 60-70%	Distinction = 75-85%
C = 70-80%	Lower second class = 50-60%	Credit = 65-74%
D = 60-70%	Third class = 40-50%	Pass = 50-64%

THE FUTURE

Looking to the future, the first question might be, will we see an international convergence of hospitality education? There are three points to support such a contention. One is that as the industries become increasingly global, companies will demand a "standard" hospitality graduate armed with defined set of knowledge. Second, the marketplace for students is becoming increasingly global, and potential students want reassuring that education in Country A is not going to be better or worse than in Country B. Third, sources of information are becoming global. Publishers are demanding textbooks that will have international appeal, and through the World Wide Web, students can now find information on the hotel industry in London and New York as easily as in Tashkent or Hanoi.

The opposing question might be asked, though—will we see a move away from the homogenization of hospitality education? Again, there are a number of points to support such a contention. First, the developing countries that have typically sent students overseas to study are now rapidly developing their own hospitality education. So, the number of these overseas students may eventually decline. Second, the growth of a larger pool of students in any one country means that it makes economic sense for publishers to commission texts that are more nationally focused. Third, as diverse sectors of the hospitality and tourism industries mature, there will be a demand for more specialized and niche courses—such as in airline management, club management, gaming, ecotourism, and so forth.

While some may see these as clearly opposing views of the future directions of education in this field, the diversity within the industries and the education systems may allow for both to occur simultaneously. The hospitality and tourism industry is still commonly referred to as if it were a singular industry, rather than a diverse group of industries. As the various industries/sectors that make up that umbrella term "hospitality and tourism" grow and mature (e.g., gaming, airline, etc.), they may each define a more specific set of knowledge. But of course, many students will want to hedge their bets, unsure of what the future holds for their careers.

So, on one hand it is likely there will still be a need for a generalist degree (such as a typical generalist bachelor of business degree currently offered students interested in business), yet on the other hand there will also be a need for much more specific niche courses focusing on the details of the various individual sectors.

CONCLUSION

The main objective of this chapter has been to give an overview of degree-level hospitality education in three countries. As stressed at the beginning, the diversity of the systems and the programs within them is such that broad-based comparisons are hard to make.

Nevertheless, it has been the intention of this chapter to help demystify three relatively similar systems. In a shrinking world, the discussions of how to internationalize hospitality programs (Doherty and Roper, 1997), best practice, and benchmarking of quality education are going to take an increasingly global perspective. Furthermore, the international nature of the hospitality and tourism industries means that students and companies are also going to be looking for international exposure and experience. Consequently, educators will be expected to provide for this (Hobson and Josiam, 1995), and having a fuller understanding of other systems is but the first step.

REFERENCES

Bloomquist, P. and Moreo, P. (1997). What's in a name? An exploration of program names in the field of hospitality education. *Journal of Hospitality & Tourism Education, 9,* 10-15.

Craig-Smith, S., Davidson, M., and French, C. (1995). Hospitality and tourism education in Australia: Challenges and opportunities. In Faulkner, B., Fagence,

M., Davidson, M., and Craig-Smith, S. (Eds.), *Proceedings of the 1994 Tourism Research and Education in Australia Conference*, Canberra, Australia: Bureau of Travel Research, 311-320.

Doherty, L. and Roper, A. (1997). Removing our culturally tinted glasses: An approach of teaching masters courses. *Journal of Hospitality & Tourism Education, 9*, 82-86.

Formica, S. (1997). The development of hospitality and tourism education in Italy. *Journal of Hospitality & Tourism Education, 9*, 48-54.

Gee, D. (1994). The Scottish Hotel School—The first fifty years. In Seaton, A.V., Jenkins, C.L., Wood, R.C., Dieke, P.U.C., Bennet, M.M., MacLellan, L.R., and Smith. R. (Eds.), *Tourism: The state of the art*. Chichester, UK: John Wiley and Sons, pp. xvi-xxiii.

Hobson, J.S.P. (1995, Fall). The development of hospitality and tourism education in Australia. *The Hospitality & Tourism Educator, 7*(4), 25-29.

Hobson, J.S.P. and Josiam, B. (1995). An integrated approach to internationalising the hospitality and tourism curriculum in the USA. *Journal of Transnational Management Development, 2*(1), pp. 13-34.

Hughes, H. (1991, July). Hotel and catering degree in the UK: The CNAA review. In Go, F. (Ed.), *New horizons in tourism and hospitality education training and research*. Conference proceedings, Calgary, Canada, 391-502.

Samefink, W. and Smetana-Novak, J. (1994). Internationalizing the hospitality curriculum: a new model. *The Hospitality & Tourism Educator, 6*, 51-54.

Stear, L. and Griffin, T. (1991, July). The relationship between tourism and hospitality: The myths, the reality, the causes and the consequences for tourism education. In Go, F. (Ed.), *New horizons in tourism and hospitality education training and research*. Conference proceedings, Calgary, Canada, 383-394.

Chapter 11

Graduate Programs in Hospitality Management Education

Robert H. Bosselman

Graduate education in the field of hospitality management is a recent entry. Although the number of students seeking master's and doctoral degrees appears to increase each year, the hospitality industry struggles to accept individuals with advanced degrees. Additional discussion surrounds the very nature of these programs, as hospitality management has long focused attention on undergraduate and other postsecondary curricula. Indeed, while much of hospitality management has practical application of knowledge, some would suggest that has not been the mission of graduate education. This chapter will explore graduate education in hospitality management, addressing the issues noted above, as well as providing a historical basis for such programs.

OVERVIEW OF GRADUATE EDUCATION

What Is Graduate Education?

Graduate education may be succinctly described as the capstone of the educational process, as well as the source of scholars and scholarship. Graduate education can be more properly defined by the Council of Graduate Schools (Dickey, Woolston, and LaPidus, 1991, p. 2):

> Graduate education is advanced, focused, and scholarly. It is advanced in the sense that it is based upon the assumption that graduate students have acquired fundamental knowledge, both

general and specific, in prior studies. It is focused in that its objective is to deal in depth with a specific discipline or field of study rather than to provide a broad educational experience. It is scholarly in that it is based on the premise of an evolving knowledge base, developed by those in the field and subject to challenge and validation by generally accepted procedures. All graduate students must understand and be able to use that knowledge base; doctoral students must contribute to its development.

In short, graduate education should provide intellectual leadership in society.

Graduate schools in the United States are over 100 years old, although their current composition has emerged in the post-World War II and Cold War era. Specifically, increased federal funding for research has led to expansion of graduate education. Over the past forty years graduate programs have evolved from traditional academic fields to include most professional fields. The distinction between these programs has grown less dramatic. Many graduate programs today are interdepartmental and interdisciplinary. Many programs allow part-time study, and even off-campus instruction. All graduate programs share a need for rigorous curriculum, a high-quality student body, and a faculty skilled in creativity (applied, intellectual, and/or practical). These needs lead to major objectives of graduate education. First, that graduate degrees awarded indicate a level of competence in the respective field of study. A second objective would be the development of graduates to carry on and extend the academic field of study. The third should be a research focus applied to the academic discipline, and practical to society's needs.

Graduate education can be characterized as a set of academic experiences that must be completed satisfactorily in order to receive the respective graduate degree. A master's degree would be awarded to a student who had completed (mastered) a planned program (a field of study) in a postbaccalaureate degree program. A doctoral degree has usually been defined as the highest academic degree given in an academic discipline. It also involves completion of a program, but more likely that program has been tailored for the individual by the institution. This approach best prepares the doctoral candidate for the academic life of instruction, scholarly activity, and professional leadership (as discussed in Chapter 6 of this text).

The Role of Research

In hospitality management education, programs often become confused by attempting to define themselves as either research or practical in orientation. While the general field has been practical in its orientation, graduate education has been dominated by a research orientation. A dichotomy need not exist between the two perspectives. If we were to trace the history of graduate education, we would find that graduate education originated due to a societal need for objective information. Approximately one hundred years ago, graduate programs in agriculture and science were created to meet the needs of the changing American population. At that time, the change was from agrarian to industrial. Today, the change is from industrial to informational. Graduate education has a place in this transition, as it serves as the training ground for information professionals.

But the question of practicality as an industry focus and the demand for intellectual creativity at the graduate level needs to be better understood by both parties. The hospitality industry is operation-oriented, and practical in its methods of operation. Although most hospitality operations would probably hesitate to identify the benefits of graduate education and research, most companies in business today utilize informational (environmental) scanning as a means of strategic planning. Much of the data utilized as a result of this environmental scanning has been generated by academic graduate programs. The American university has long been the site of experimentation and enlightenment. The Morrill Act of 1862 was created to make higher education available to the working class, and to extend knowledge to all phases of society. The search for knowledge and technological advancement in land-grant institutions influenced American life in many ways. To address individuals who suggest that graduate education in hospitality management, and particularly its research component, are not relevant to their real-world needs, hospitality educators need to provide evidence of scholarly efforts. For example, the industry always notes that operating costs need to be lowered, new consumer markets uncovered, new products or services developed, and new concepts created.

Since the late 1960s, actual spending on research and development activities by businesses has declined. In the face of increasing competitiveness, both domestic and international, hospitality firms need all the help they can get.

Research efforts need to be defined for hospitality management (see Chapter 8). Research quite often is misunderstood as not practical to real-world needs. As noted, the hospitality industry faces increasing competition, and can probably be characterized as in a mature industry cycle. In general, research is often referred to by one of three distinct classifications; basic, applied, or development. Basic research usually refers to original investigation that leads to the advancement of knowledge in the specific profession. Applied research also leads to advancement of knowledge in the specific profession, but usually has some commercial outcome with respect to process, service, or product. Development research refers to technical activities that convert research results (knowledge) into processes, services, or products. Clearly, applied and development research have implications for the hospitality industry, although basic research is more commonly associated with the academic arena.

So how can the academic programs and industry come together on the research issue? The answer is communication between graduate programs and industry groups and companies. The purpose of such communication should be to identify industry needs that academic programs can investigate; to foster an understanding of what research can accomplish for the industry; and to seek support for research efforts (including funding, facilities, and personnel). In the early 1980s, faculty at Virginia Tech's graduate program reported on research activities in the hospitality industry (Tse, Olsen, and Wyckoff, 1983; Olsen, Tse, and Bellas, 1984). The authors classified research into six broad categories, but found little effort in any by companies surveyed. Development research was receiving the most attention. A series of studies (Brymer and Rouselle, 1983; Brymer and Rouselle, 1986; Brymer, Rouselle, and Johns, 1990) identified research needs across a broad spectrum of hospitality firms. In general, the results suggested more research efforts into human resource areas. Of note was the finding that companies did utilize academic research, although the means of obtaining such information was not clear. A recent study of gaming resort properties (Chen et al., 1998) also found academic research to be of interest, and human resource issues of prime concern. The research also found that the best means of distributing research information was through trade journals.

Research has been identified as a key component of successful graduate programs. However, when hospitality management companies recruit on campuses, their aim is to find the best talent to help their specific company. Teaching more likely relates to this process than research. Excellent instruction in classrooms and laboratories produces better students, and coupled with work experiences, leads companies to the top schools. In fact, during the 1990s, companies have reduced campus visits markedly. Many companies now recruit only at top-tier schools such as Cornell University, UNLV, Florida International University, University of Houston, and Michigan State University. For years, U.S. schools have been lambasted over the emphasis on research. One critical point to remember is that faculty, particularly those at top-tier schools, came out of primarily research-oriented graduate programs. Of the five schools listed above (widely considered the top five in hospitality management), only UNLV offers courses in hospitality education methods. Based on the work of Bosselman (1996a), students in both the master's and doctoral programs at UNLV have the opportunity of gaining skills and techniques characterized as effective (best) practices in teaching. Doctoral students continue after completion of the class on teaching by mentoring under a faculty member (usually in their area of specialization) for a full semester. The student then is assigned a class section for a semester, under the direction of the mentor. By the time the doctoral student has completed the program, they have the experience of several semesters teaching under the supervision of established, effective teachers. Master's degree students who complete the course often go on to other hospitality programs for doctoral work, and report that the experience serves them well in class assignments during the doctoral program.

As more faculty positions call for doctoral degree candidates, the importance of graduate programs increases. Thus, the top programs will increase their level of prestige within the academic community. In addition, since all five of the top-tier schools have master's degree programs, and with Cornell and UNLV also having doctoral programs, hospitality industry companies are associating quality students with research-oriented programs. These programs then have the role of promoting research as a necessary component and communicating its importance to industry. All programs must balance effective instruction with meaningful research to produce top quality undergraduates and graduate students. Academic programs with weak or nonexistent research programs will get less funding from parent institutions. With funding becoming tighter, research offers an opportunity to generate additional funds. Because hospitality is a profession with an emphasis on practical operations, the problem of funding, educating, investigating, attracting, and retaining professionals is particularly noteworthy.

GRADUATE EDUCATION IN HOSPITALITY MANAGEMENT

There are several ways to characterize graduate programs in hospitality management. Some examples include type of degree offered, location of program in the academic structure, and academic characteristics of the degree. In a study of student selection practices (Bosselman, 1996b), it was found that of twenty-five programs surveyed, eleven (44 percent) were classified as a combination master's program (either a thesis track or a professional project/ paper track). Six programs (24 percent) were purely a professional master's degree. Seven respondents (28 percent) identified the graduate program as a combination master's and a research doctorate. Only one hospitality program claimed to be both a research master's and doctorate program. Most master's degrees in hospitality management are master of science (MS), although a few master of business administration (MBA) with emphasis in hospitality management are available. Professional master's degrees are usually a master of hospitality administration (MHA). Graduate degrees in hospitality management are primarily found associated with larger programs, separate schools or colleges, and in land grant institutions. Degree components can vary, although most utilize a core of hospitality-specific classes with the option of electives. The degree can focus on hospitality administration, hotel and restaurant administration (or management), institutional management (common in land grant programs), or be some combination of these degree components. There is no single common type of program or curriculum in the graduate segment of hospitality management education.

The Council on Hotel, Restaurant and Institutional Education lists over thirty-five institutions with master's and/or doctoral degrees worldwide. Approximately twenty-eight master's and twelve doctoral programs exist in the United States (CHRIE, 1995). There are approximately 2,900 graduate students in hospitality management worldwide, with close to two-thirds studying in the United States. According to Edelstein (1993), master's programs are available in just four percent of all U.S. institutions offering master's degrees; and doctoral degrees are available in just two percent of all U.S. institutions offering doctoral degrees. Hospitality management graduate enrollment represents less than one percent of institutional graduate enrollment in U.S. institutions (Rappole and McCain, 1996). While the ratio of undergraduate to graduate students enrolled in U.S. hospitality management programs was 18:1, the average U.S. institutional ratio stands at 7:1. This dramatic difference between hospitality management and more traditional academic disciplines reflects the more recent history of hospitality management education. Graduate enrollment exceeds 100 students in only three programs; Florida International University with 150, Cornell University with 110, and Johnson & Wales University with 100 students (numbers are approximate). The average number of master's students is closer to forty, with the number of doctoral students usually totaling fifteen. Many programs report significant international student presence in their graduate student populations. Although graduate hospitality programs are located in many nations, U.S. programs draw students from a worldwide market. Most programs seek students with some industry experience, usually at the management level.

Although the number of graduate programs in hospitality management has increased over the past twenty years, the location of the program within the institution influences its specific components. Independent, stand-alone colleges or schools (such as UNLV or FIU) have designed their own programs to fit the needs of their students. Many programs are housed in business or home economics colleges, which will have an influence on the philosophy and curriculum of the graduate program. However, graduate programs located in land grant universities (these are primarily located in home economics colleges) have certain advantages. Land grant institutions are centered around research, so such hospitality programs usually have strong research programs, and provide excellent training for future hospitality academics. Examples of such programs include Kansas State University, Pennsylvania State University, Purdue University, and Virginia Tech University.

Although rankings of the graduate hospitality programs have been released, none have followed a reliable or valid methodological approach, and thus should be interpreted as merely a guide. Factors such as quality of faculty and facilities, requirements for admittance and graduation, and employment opportunities for graduates should be factored into any study of graduate programs. Some might argue that selection criteria have a major impact on program quality. As noted previously (Bosselman, 1996b), few studies on admission practices exist. Using an instrument containing thirty-three items pertaining to graduate program admission (including standardized test scores, grade point averages, recommendations, etc.), it was revealed that undergraduate grade point average in the last two years was the top factor, with the Test of English as a Foreign Language (TOEFL) score a significant factor for international students. The majority of programs required either the Graduate Management Aptitude Test (GMAT) or the Graduate Record Examination (GRE). While there are no specific required performance levels on the standardized exams, scores of 600 or higher on TOEFL were suggested, and scores at or above the sixtieth percentile on either the GMAT or GRE verbal component. It should be noted that many U.S. institutions now require international graduate students with teaching assistantships to complete institution-specific testing of their English speaking and writing skills.

Any attempt to rank programs needs to employ a multidimensional approach (Bosselman et al., 1996). For example, citation analysis, or number of publications are often used to cite prestige of the hospitality program. However, one should consider that two graduate programs, Cornell and FIU, have their own journals. Since no study to date has controlled for this, these two schools may receive biased rankings. Size could be a factor, but what size would be referred to—number of graduate faculty, graduate faculty with doctoral degrees, graduate faculty in specific ranks, master's degree (and doctoral) students, or graduates from the program? Other possible measures might include how many research and/or teaching assistant-ships are available for graduate students, how much research funding the program produces annually, how long it takes an average master's (and doctoral) student to complete a degree, what percentage of master's students go on to doctoral work, and what percentage of master's graduates remain in the hospitality industry (three, five, and ten years after graduation).

With reference to placement of students upon graduation, Umbreit and Pederson (1989) reported that 26 percent of program graduates entered food service management, 15 percent entered lodging man-agement, 15 percent entered academia, 11 percent entered restaurant operations, 8 percent entered government, 3 percent entered club management, and 21 percent entered some other field. Five years after completion of degree, a full 29 percent were employed in teach-ing positions, with another 22 percent in corporate staff positions. Nearly half of the programs studied reported problems placing grad-uate students. It should be noted that hospitality management re-mains a relatively practice-oriented field, with most management lacking formal education. Graduate degrees in hospitality manage-ment are not yet well understood or appreciated by industry. How-ever, the burden of proof lies with the academic institutions. The schools must do a better job of promoting their programs, and com-municating to industry, particularly the merits of their graduate stu-dents. Students choosing to enter a doctoral program after a master's degree should recognize the importance of the network of faculty in hospitality management. Recommendation letters from well-known faculty, or from faculty known to the specific graduate program, were significant in admission to a hospitality graduate program (Bos-selman, 1996b).

THE MASTER'S DEGREE

Graduate Education Models

Just as there are numerous measures of program quality, and nu-merous types of programs, there are a number of proposals about what makes a good graduate program in hospitality management education. While graduate programs have existed for some time, the 1990s has seen a number of arguments presented for direction of program curriculum. Evans (1990) suggested a model based on three competency areas: industry, functional management, and research. Evans postulated that master's degree students in hospitality management should have an industry-specific focus, such as lodging, food service, convention, gaming, and so on. This premise was based on a perception that master's degree students entered graduate programs with significant management experience. The functional management competency refers to traditional business administration classes such as accounting, marketing, and human resources, among others. Ideally, Evans saw the graduate student taking a general business class and complementing it with a hospitality seminar, thus allowing the student to experience an in-depth approach to the field. Research needed to be incorporated into the entire curriculum, according to Evans. He noted that the hospitality field, while new to academia, nonetheless had the responsibility of seeking new knowledge to assist the industry in development. Evans also linked doctoral study to master's degrees.

Jones (1991) suggested that two separate master's models were needed—one for those seeking industry positions after graduation, and the other for those seeking to pursue doctoral studies. As Jones indicated, undergraduate programs produced a supply of entry-level managers, but it was mid-level management where industry faced shortages of qualified talent. In other words, undergraduate programs produced operational managers. However, the skills and competencies to succeed at upper levels of management were inadequate in the majority of entry-level staff. Jones's model differs from Evans's in the role of the functional competency. Jones suggests that functional specialization be left to programs that focus in such areas. The model includes a general management competency, coupled with two industry-specific courses and a research class. Jones assumes those without a background in hospitality or business education would take a full year of core requirement classes, and that his thirty-credit program could be completed in two semesters.

Cornell engaged in a major redesign of its professional master's degree program in 1992 (Enz, Renaghan, and Geller, 1993). The

Cornell study was the first where the graduate program sought the input of all major shareholders: alumni, faculty, entering students, and industry professionals. The redesigned Cornell M.P.S. program was introduced in the fall term of 1994. The program has centered on themes of strategic orientation, communications, management style, leadership, analytical ability, ethical awareness, and international scope. Students are selectively chosen, and individualized plans of study prepared based on their strengths and weaknesses. Students supplement classroom exercises with group projects and industry residency, thus exposing them to both interdisciplinary and experiential learning.

While debate continues over what type of graduate hospitality management program should exist, only one study to date has examined the actual competencies needed for graduate programs (Partlow, 1990). A survey of hospitality educators and managers differentiated competencies appropriate for development at a master's degree level, compared with a bachelor's degree level or through job experience. Five competencies were identified as requiring a master's degree: conduct/direct research, prepare funding proposals, manage all legal aspects of operation, apply research methodology and results to operations, and utilize appropriate investment management methods. A bachelor's degree was appropriate for the majority of competencies indicated, while seven competencies were deemed not related to level of education. Partlow suggested that graduate programs focus on the competencies identified as important, and leave the rest to undergraduate programs. It should be noted that they relate to research, law, and financial analysis.

A Look at Specific Master's Degree Programs

For comparative purposes, six programs will be examined: three land grant institutions, and three stand-alone programs. The land grant programs are Kansas State University, Pennsylvania State University, and Virginia Polytechnic Institute and State University. The three stand-alone programs are Florida International University, the University of Houston, and UNLV. The three land grant programs are based in colleges of home economics, now widely referred to as human ecology or human development. All three include institutional management in their program names, reflecting the link to nutrition and dietetics. All three offer a number of teaching/research assistantships, and all three have active research agendas. Faculty in these programs are a combination of hospitality professionals and dietetics/nutrition professionals. Virginia Tech requires forty-five hours for degree completion; Penn State requires thirty-six credit hours, and Kansas State has both a thirty-hour and a thirty-six-hour program. All three also have doctoral programs. Virginia Tech's program includes classes in finance, marketing, administration, human resources, statistics, methodology, a core of hospitality management classes, plus a thesis. If one recalls Evans' model (1990), that is not a surprise, since Virginia Tech was where Evans earned his doctorate and taught for a short period. Both Penn State and Kansas State are less involved, utilizing a curriculum that contains a brief core plus a concentration in hospitality-specific electives. Both have a thesis and nonthesis route to the degree. Both programs are well known for their research into food service areas. One might describe these two programs as more similar to Jones's (1991) model, in that there does not appear to be a focus in functional competencies.

The three stand-alone programs all represent newer institutions; FIU's School of Hospitality Management began in 1972; the Conrad N. Hilton College of Hotel and Restaurant Management started in 1968; and the William F. Harrah College of Hotel Administration began in 1967. UNLV's master's degree program has thirty-six required hours, FIU requires thirty-nine hours, and Houston stipulates a program of forty-three hours. All three programs assume a student enters with prerequisite classes such as accounting, statistics, computer literacy, economics, marketing, and finance. All three programs are similar in that there is a core of required classes, which are hospitality specific, as well as electives. Houston mandates a professional paper, while FIU students choose a professional project. UNLV students can choose between a thesis or a professional paper. Only UNLV offers a doctoral degree. A closer look at UNLV's master's degree program is presented in Exhibit 11.1.

As can be observed in UNLV's program, there are opportunities for students to focus in a particular area of hospitality management, as well as develop functional or industry-related competencies. For students pursuing further education through a doctoral degree, a first-level statistics class and a methods class are provided.

EXHIBIT 11.1. Master of Science Degree Requirements (UNLV)

Required Courses (all three credits each):

HOA 701 Operations Analysis in Hospitality Management
HOA 703 Human Resources and Behavior in the Hospitality Industry
HOA 705 Financial Analysis for the Service Industries
HOA 711 Laws of Innkeeping and Food Service
HOA 735 Research Methodology
HOA 740 Marketing Systems in Hospitality
CEP 721 Descriptive and Inferential Statistics

One of the following (all three credits each):

HOA 716 Principles and Practices in Hotel Management
HOA 718 Principles of Casino and Gaming Management
HOA 720 Principles and Practices of Food Service Management

One of the following (all three credits each):

HOA 760 Research Seminar in Hotel Administration
HOA 761 Research Seminar in Food Service Management
HOA 762 Research Seminar in Hospitality Education
HOA 763 Research Seminar in Casino and Gaming Management

Supporting Courses: Graduate-level courses approved by the student's chair (graduate advisor) (3-9 credits). Students are allowed to substitute a supporting course for HOA 760/1/2/3 if they are taking a concentration in a specific area and they have approval of their advisor.

HOA 791 Professional Paper (3 credits) or **HOA 799 Thesis** (6 credits)

Total Hours Required for Degree: 36

The master's degree, regardless of which institution was selected, can be observed to provide a strong background in hospitality management, and a basic level of research methodology and statistics. Programs are flexible to the degree that students with previous management experience in the hospitality industry will enhance their professional capabilities. Master's degree programs provide the foundation for further academic pursuit of a doctoral degree. One of the growing concerns of master's degree programs relates to the level of industry experience prior to enrollment. What seems to be occurring in hospitality management graduate education reflects the impact of education in society in general. Many undergraduate students seek a master's degree immediately upon completion of their undergraduate programs. Although this is common in traditional educational disciplines such as the liberal arts or sciences, the hospitality field is an operationally oriented industry. Students receive a more thorough academic experience if they enter the master's degree program with management experience already in hand. While most schools have lowered their work experience requirement to one year, an argument could be made for a minimum of three years of management-level experience. Where hospitality management education programs were founded by individuals without doctoral degrees, today in every major university program the doctoral degree is a basic requirement for an academic position. The number of years of industry work experience among faculty appears to be declining. University administrations embrace academic rather than practically oriented faculty. Hospitality management education has succeeded in the academic arena, but in doing so has it lost its very culture? This challenge now faces programs in the field.

THE DOCTORAL DEGREE

The doctoral degree (PhD, EdD, etc.) has long been recognized as the mark of highest achievement in academia. First awarded in the United States about the time of the Civil War by Yale University for a degree in philosophy, doctoral studies now cover numerous academic fields. Hospitality management doctoral studies are relatively new, with most programs being less than twenty years old. A doctoral program usually bears a design that prepares students for a lifetime career of intellectual inquiry (expressed through scholarship and research) in an academic environment. Programs are based on individual freedom of inquiry, and the development of the individual to make significant contributions to knowledge. Primary to this structure has been the ability to review critically the literature of the field, and to apply appropriate processes to examining critical issues in the chosen discipline. This program takes place under the direction of those experienced in research and teaching. Students choose a specific area of study, and a professor with whom to work. Ideally this faculty member has conducted research in the student's chosen area, and can guide the student's development. Students engage in a plan of study, which can vary in number of classes, and write a dissertation (a major research project). Doctoral students must pass a series of comprehensive examinations conducted by faculty supervising the degree plan of study. In addition, the dissertation work must be presented for an oral examination by graduate faculty and peers. If successful, the student demonstrates knowledge and skills expected of a scholar, and enhances the knowledge of the field.

Importance of Program Infrastructure

In most programs, particularly hospitality management, a graduate program is not created unless there exists a strong undergraduate program. Faculty likely teach both undergraduate and graduate-level classes. While undergraduate, and to an extent master's degree programs are set for all students, a doctoral program will be tailored for the individual student. The student and major advisor (and possibly members of the doctoral committee) design a plan of study that allows the student to become an expert in the chosen field. In hospitality management education, faculty likely have both a primary and a secondary focus. Depending on work history, faculty and students will consider lodging, food service, tourism, or gaming as their major area of expertise. Some faculty will then supplement this primary area with a functional specialization such as marketing, human resources, or finance. A doctoral candidate's background then will determine to some extent the type of curriculum engaged in for the degree.

Although the hospitality field is considered a relative newcomer to academia, most doctoral programs are located in strong schools with well-known faculty. This provides students with differing educational philosophies and enough faculty for supervision, evaluation, and examination. It is likely that academic interests of the faculty will complement one another. In some cases, a specific hospitality program may be oriented in a specific field of study, for example, food service operations. Students would be wise to choose an institution where faculty of similar interests are in residence, and are conducting research in the student's chosen area of study. Quality of the graduate faculty ranks as the most important factor in the doctoral program. These faculty must be active scholars and role models in instruction. They not only teach and supervise the research of the doctoral student, but they provide an example of how to perform as an academic. It is not uncommon for the doctoral student to mentor under the advising faculty member in a specific class (or classes), or to review manuscripts written by the faculty member. The faculty member can also impart knowledge of the academic culture to the doctoral student.

Graduate faculty supervising doctoral students may have one or several students under their supervision. There are no set criteria; it depends on the individual faculty member. However, institutional resources are critical to the process. First and foremost there must be organizational commitment to graduate study. This can be best exemplified through the degree of financial support provided for research and instructional programs. Other examples of support include salaries for faculty commensurate with experience and ability, office space sufficient to conduct necessary tasks, sufficient clerical and technical assistance, adequate supplies, and research/teaching assistantships for graduate students. A library with adequate resources is also a major requirement for any graduate program. In some cases, a particular school may be known for a specialized holding. For example, UNLV houses the world's largest collection of gaming-related documents and resources. Another consideration for the prospective doctoral student is the hospitality-related facilities available for research and instruction. Classroom and seminar rooms should be modern, well-kept facilities with adequate audiovisual features. In hospitality management education, it is understood that a doctoral program will provide access to food service labs, computer labs with up-to-date software, possibly a front office lab or a working lodging facility, and other appropriate facilities. For example, at UNLV there exists a working gaming lab, with all types of equipment available for students, as well as a gaming resource center. Many hospitality management programs operate their own facilities (such as Cornell's Statler Hotel, or Houston's University Hilton) or are located with immediate access to the local industry (such as FIU or UNLV).

Program Content

A doctoral program constitutes a major step for any hospitality management program. The expectations for faculty and doctoral students are considerable, with emphasis on achieving new levels of knowledge and understanding for the hospitality field. Students are expected to become experts in their chosen fields. Demand for faculty continues to be strong, and with the current "graying" of hospitality management faculty, such demand appears to be a long-term trend. The content of doctoral programs does not appear to be as controversial as that of master's degree programs. Many doctoral programs follow the traditional German model, commonly referred to as the epistemological model. This approach emphasizes the pursuit of knowledge for the sake of knowledge. In other words, there was little or no concern for practical value. The opposite approach was the utilitarian view, which suggests an application of knowledge to society.

Riegel (1987) has suggested that hospitality management doctoral programs should emphasize both scholarship and application. Riegel notes the difficulty facing hospitality education, as it lacks its own body of knowledge. He indicates that hospitality management can be described as a "multidisciplinary application area" (p. 31), which should follow to some extent a professional model of graduate education. In his model, Riegel includes core components of general industry knowledge and business administration as it applies to the hospitality industry (this latter area would be similar to the functional area identified by Jones). It would be possible that a student would enter doctoral work with this core already in place, through prior undergraduate and graduate study, as well as work history. A third component of the model would be an area of specialization. Research methodology skills make up a fourth component of the model, with a fifth segment composed of learning how to be effective in the classroom.

A doctoral program would likely consist of lectures, seminars, discussions, independent studies, and research projects. The first two years of study would be devoted to formal classes. Research work can then begin if the student entered the program prepared for such effort. At the conclusion of course work, a comprehensive examination would be taken to determine the extent of the student's working knowledge of the field. Once successfully completed, the student can devote full-time effort to the proposed research study (dissertation). It might be necessary to have the student defend the research proposal before the dissertation committee. The final oral defense takes place when the research has been completed. The guidelines for doctoral study are set by the institution, not the hospitality program. Standards of the program must meet the institutional guidelines, and can exceed them. Prospective students should review the degree guidelines when choosing a potential program for study. Most programs require the student to be in residence for at least one full year. Since the purpose of the doctorate focuses on the development of the individual, it makes sense that the student would want to work closely and often with their supervising faculty. A sample doctoral program is noted in Exhibit 11.2.

THE CHALLENGE OF GRADUATE EDUCATION

As noted earlier in this chapter, hospitality management has only recently entered the graduate education market. While the majority of hospitality faculty at four-year institutions have doctoral degrees, a greater percentage of faculty in hospitality management education do not have a doctoral degree compared with traditional academic fields. Nearly all position announcements for hospitality faculty at four-year programs list the doctorate as a minimum requirement, although ABD (all but dissertation) would likely merit attention as well. This scenario differs from the early days of hospitality education, when faculty were hired on the basis of their experiences. This situation also merits attention as it pertains to the current (and future) condition within universities. Despite growing numbers of college-age students, many academic areas are in a state of declining enrollments. Many institutions are cutting back staff, even tenured faculty, to save limited budgetary dollars. It also appears that the percentage of students seeking careers in academia has leveled off, and in many fields declined. The result has been an increase of part-time faculty hired to teach classes. The use of part-time faculty cuts budgetary expenditure significantly (Bowen and Schuster, 1986). Fortunately for hospitality management education, enroll-

EXHIBIT 11.2. Doctoral Degree Requirements
(UNLV College of Hotel Administration)

Required Courses in Hotel Administration

HOA 779: Seminar on Issues and Trends in Hospitality Management
HOA 778: Readings in Hospitality Management
HOA 735: Doctoral Research Methods
HOA 762: Research Seminar in Hospitality Education

Required Courses in Methodology

Students must take one course in quantitative methodology, and one course in qualitative methodology. Courses are available from different departments on campus. Student chooses appropriate class with assistance from advisor.

Required Statistics Courses

Students are required to take a minimum of two courses in advanced statistics. The selection takes place with assistance from the advisor.

Major Area of Study

A minimum of nine credits in the major area. Courses are determined with assistance from the advisor.

Minor Area of Study

A minimum of six hours in the minor area. Courses are determined with assistance from the advisor.

Dissertation Credits: 12 credits

Electives: 9 credits

Total Credits Required: 60 credits (at least 24 credits must be in the Hotel College, excluding dissertation hours, and 12 credits must be outside the college; all credits must be at the 700 level or higher)

---

ments are stable at four-year schools (with a few exceptions), and increasing rapidly at two-year and vocational programs. This suggests that hospitality management education remains a growth field in education. However, the debate over doctoral degrees remains.

This conflict over degrees often centers on the question of whether we as faculty are in the business of education or the education business. The former philosophy focuses on the "publish or perish" approach (research the priority over teaching), while the latter focuses on the importance of teaching and learning. If a faculty member seeks employment at a particular school, the faculty member must be willing to commit to the institutional philosophy. The same is true for doctoral students. The school where they earn their doctoral degrees will have a profound long-term influence on their approach to higher education. As such, the current hospitality management education programs with doctoral studies will have the most significant influence over the future of hospitality education. These programs must maintain a strong working relationship with industry to keep hospitality management education viable for the long term. To not do so risks the future of the field in higher education. Such programs likely are considered strong at undergraduate, master's, and doctoral levels. These programs will continue to thrive, and will attract the best faculty and students. This scenario is not unlike any industry, where the power of the competitive market prevails.

The field of hospitality management education has come a long way since the early 1920s, when a committee of hoteliers decided that Cornell University should train hotel managers. Their initial concept had the training taking place in city hotels, with no degree awarded. Approximately eighty years later the field has grown to include 175 four-year schools, some 500 two-year/technical schools, around thirty master's programs, and a dozen doctoral programs (in the United States alone). Yet it remains an academic area still in a growth mode, although some would argue the field has reached maturity, much like the industry. Graduate education thus has its most critical challenge in the determination of the identity of hospitality management education. This discussion will likely continue for some time.

REFERENCES

Bosselman, R.H. (1996a). The missing element in graduate program curriculum: Teaching our future teachers. *Proceedings of the Conference on Graduate Education and Graduate Studies Research*. Houston, TX: University of Houston, pp. 219-226.

Bosselman, R.H. (1996b). Student selection: North American practices for hospitality and tourism graduate programmes. *International Journal of Contemporary Hospitality Management, 8*(4), 34-36.

Bosselman, R.H., Chon, K.S., Teare, R., and Costa, J. (1996). A review of graduate education and research in hospitality and tourism management. *International Journal of Contemporary Hospitality Management, 8*(4), 37-40.

Bowen, H.R. and Schuster, J.H. (1986). *American professors: A national resource imperiled.* New York: Oxford University Press.

Brymer, R.A. and Rouselle, J.R. (1983). The research needs of the hospitality industry: A survey. *Proceedings of the Council on Hotel, Restaurant and Institutional Education Annual Conference,* Orlando, FL, pp. 169-180.

Brymer, R.A. and Rouselle, J.R. (1986). Research demand in the hospitality industry. *Proceedings of the Council on Hotel, Restaurant, and Institutional Education Annual Conference,* Boston, MA.

Brymer, R.A., Rouselle, J.R., and Johns, T.R. (1990). Academic research interests of hospitality corporations. *Hospitality Research Journal, 14,* 1-10.

Chen, C., Jones, T., Kincaid, C., Ramdeen, C., Raymakers, S., and Bosselman, R.H. (1998). Academic research interests of casino resort properties. Paper submitted for Annual CHRIE Conference. Miami, Florida.

CHRIE (1995). *A guide to college programs in hospitality and tourism,* Fourth edition. New York: John Wiley and Sons, Inc.

Dickey, K., Woolston, V., and LaPidus, J.B. (1991). *Graduate study in the United States.* Washington, DC: Council of Graduate Schools.

Edelstein, S. (1993). The chronological development of four year and post baccalaureate degree programs of hospitality management in the United States. Unpublished master's thesis, University of Houston, Houston, TX.

Enz, C.A., Renaghan, L.M., and Geller, A.N. (1993). Graduate-level education: A survey of stakeholders. *The Cornell H.R.A. Quarterly, 34,* 90-95.

Evans, M.R. (1990). Graduate education: The next frontier. *The Cornell H.R.A. Quarterly, 31,* 92-94.

Jones, W.P. (1991). Another graduate-education model. *The Cornell H.R.A. Quarterly, 32,* 70-72.

Olsen, M.D., Tse, E.C., and Bellas, C.D. (1984). A proposed classification system for research and development activities with the hospitality industries. *Hospitality Education and Research Journal, 8,* 55-62.

Partlow, C.G. (1990). Identification of graduate level competencies in hospitality management. *Hospitality Research Journal, 14,* 223-229.

Rappole, C. and McCain, A.M. (1996). The chronological development, enrollment patterns, and education models of four year and post baccalaureate degree programs of hospitality management in the United States. *Proceedings of the Conference on Graduate Education and Graduate Students Research.* Houston, TX: University of Houston, pp. 300-306.

Riegel, C.D. (1987). Defining the doctorate: A body of knowledge for the hospitality educator. *The Cornell H.R.A. Quarterly, 28,* 29-33.

Tse, E.C., Olsen, M.D., and Wyckoff, D.D. (1983). The state of the art in research and development activities in the hospitality service industries. *Hospitality Education and Research Journal, 8*, 91-96.

Umbreit, W.T. and Pederson, D. (1989). A survey of hospitality education graduate schools. *Hospitality and Tourism Educator, 2*, 14-15, 45.

Chapter 12

The Current State
of Hospitality Education

Clayton W. Barrows

As is evident, the field of hospitality management education has undergone many changes over the past seventy-five years and even more drastic changes over the past ten years. Although this book has focused exclusively upon the field of hospitality management education, it is important to remember that no single academic area, including ours, operates in a vacuum. The entire field of higher education has changed dramatically over the past decade and continues to adapt to the changing social, political, and economic landscape. Some of these changes are worth noting for the simple fact that they already do, or threaten to, affect the field of hospitality education.

This chapter will first explore some of the major changes affecting higher education in general. Next, it will review some specific changes in hospitality management education programs, emphasizing some trends that have been explored in earlier chapters and identifying some that have not. Finally, the chapter will summarize some of the critical thoughts that have been expressed in this book.

INSTITUTIONAL TRENDS IN HIGHER EDUCATION

Some of the changes that affect our programs, or will at some point in the future, are identified here.

Tuition Costs

One of the more significant developments affecting higher education is the increased cost of attending college. This particular issue has not been confined to discussions among academics but has spread to the popular press, as it affects such a large segment of the general population. It seems that all of higher education's constituents have a vested interest in the cost of obtaining a college degree. Several private colleges and universities (most notably Harvard) have reached or surpassed the $30,000 per-year level for tuition, room, and board. When this is multiplied by four (or more), it represents a very large investment, indeed. And like any investment, investors want assurances that it is sound and they are getting adequate returns. It seems that the major increases are occurring at private colleges around the country. While it is doubtful that Harvard is either going to see enrollments drop or experience financial exigency, other less-endowed private colleges may face some financial hardships in the not-too-distant future. Further, it is not just the private colleges that have experienced tuition increases. Although not to the same degree, the same situation has occurred in public universities where students tend to be even more price sensitive. As a result, public university budgets are coming under greater scrutiny by state governments. Some states are attempting to hold the line on tuition increases while at least one state (Massachusetts) has actually lowered tuition at its public universities.

Budgetary Concerns

One reaction to the increased costs has been for governing boards to focus more on internal budgetary matters. As a result, colleges and universities are being viewed more and more as businesses. While it does not seem that they will ever be able to be run purely as for-profit businesses (for the simple reason that they are not), they will continue to be more cost driven, as are private businesses. This new level of cost consciousness has, and will surely continue, to trickle down to hospitality programs, most of which are at publicly funded state universities. Such an emphasis on costs will surely affect the way that all academic units go about their business. Universities and their smaller academic units will have to continue to "work smarter" and make more efficient use of the resources available to them or suffer the consequences.

Faculty Workloads

Another relatively recent development in higher education, which is not entirely unrelated to the cost issue discussed above, is the greater attention being paid to faculty workloads and individual accountability. Essentially, many states are focusing on what it is that faculty actually do (see Chapter 6). Unfortunately, those not familiar with how universities work may presume that a faculty member who teaches two courses a semester works a grand total of six hours a week. Obviously, this could not be further from the truth. This view completely discounts (or ignores) the role of research (Chapter 8) and service (Chapter 9) and the amount of time that all of these activities combined require of the individual faculty member. On the other hand, it has been true for a very long time that teaching loads can be, and are, unevenly distributed among faculty members within a department. Departments generally start with a standard teaching load for faculty (often established by their respective colleges), which is subsequently reduced should a faculty member receive a grant, take on significant administrative duties, teach graduate-level classes, or spend a significant portion of their time conducting research. What can and does happen (although perhaps less frequently in hospitality than in the sciences and some other fields) is that in any one department, one individual may teach three or even four courses each semester while another faculty member may not teach any. Hopefully, the latter case can be justified. However, to the outside observer, it may be viewed as an abomination for a college professor to be teaching less than his or her fair share or not to be teaching any courses at all! But once one understands the various responsibilities of faculty members and how the system works, it begins to make sense.

This arrangement has led to some of the increased scrutiny, however, and two likely scenarios may result: (1) that teaching loads will increase across colleges and departments even for those with significant other duties, and/or (2) different tracks may be established whereby a faculty member can choose to be a teacher or a researcher. Each of these have occurred in some universities, in part, as a result of a renewed emphasis upon teaching and the attempt to strike a healthier institutional balance between teaching and research. Both of these scenarios are being played out in different systems around the country. Like any other change, there are likely to be both positive and negative repercussions.

Some legislators and college administrators are going even further and questioning the merit of the entire tenure system. Some believe that the tenure system is ineffective and that certain faculty members take advantage of it. While some institutions and/or systems are moving toward abolishing tenure altogether, the real movement seems to be toward developing more structured processes for tenure and promotion. At the very least, this trend will continue and has already trickled down to hospitality programs.

Reorganization and Downsizing

A third trend affecting every type of institution is reorganization and downsizing. No area of the university has gone unaffected by these actions. Universities and state governing boards across the country seem to be employing some of the same strategies in trying to create more efficient institutions.

One strategy has been to eliminate duplicate programs in states that have more than one program offered at different universities. Every university is expected to offer mainstream programs (in the sciences and liberal arts, for example). However, certain special and unique programs of study in education and other professional fields have recently come under scrutiny and in many instances have been eliminated. States that have taken such action are expected to continue to track enrollments in the remaining programs and to do periodic reviews. Although several hospitality programs have been eliminated in recent years, this author is not aware of any that have been closed due specifically to these efforts.

Reorganization has also affected the makeup of individual colleges. In some cases, entire colleges have been eliminated, with the individual academic units being moved to other colleges within the university. When one considers the administrative and support positions that are eliminated when a college is dissolved, the cost savings can be substantial, although sometimes the cost savings are not apparent for several years. In other cases, colleges are not so much eliminated as they are realigned. Recently, such changes have resulted in several mergers of hospitality and leisure/tourism programs such as at Pennsylvania State University. In others, hospitality programs have been moved to colleges of business, as in the cases of Georgia State University and the University of Massachusetts. Other moves are pending.

Finally, downsizing may simply result in the loss of faculty positions as long-time faculty members retire. Often, when openings are frozen, they may be moved to a program that demonstrates a greater need for a faculty line. In other cases, the opening may be frozen indefinitely.

Summary of Trends in Higher Education

Each of the trends identified above signify the turbulent times that higher education is currently in. As such changes continue, they cannot help but affect hospitality programs. The next section will take a closer look at some of the changes occurring within hospitality management programs.

TRENDS IN HOSPITALITY MANAGEMENT EDUCATION

Many of the changes taking place have been documented in the preceding chapters. They range from numerous programs reevaluating their missions to undergoing accreditation to the ways in which faculty are evaluated. All of these changes affect the way that hospitality programs set objectives and go about achieving them. This section will review some of the major changes taking place.

Emphasis on Research and Scholarship

The increased emphasis on research and scholarship should not come as any surprise to those who have been involved in hospitality education for even a few years. The change has been a rapid one. While research has long been supported and even encouraged, it was not until relatively recently that it played such a significant role in hospitality programs. Much has changed in the past ten to twenty years that has contributed to this. First, it was not that long ago that most faculty teaching in hospitality programs had master's degrees only—few had doctorates. Many faculty members (if not most) were former practitioners who had made the switch to academia in the latter stages of their careers. Their primary roles tended to be teaching and extension work. Much of the research they conducted came under the auspices of grants or consulting. Many faculty members who had earned doctorates and adequate research preparation published in their "home" fields. Few faculty had doctorates for the simple reason that few programs offered doctoral degrees in hospitality. For instance, when this author was studying for his undergraduate degree, the faculty with doctorates had them in engineering, food science, accounting, and education. Even up until about five years ago, it was still possible to get a tenure-track position at a major state university without the doctorate.

All of this is changing and changing quickly. Now most of the prominent programs boast of the percentage of full-time faculty members who have their terminal degrees. Many of those have degrees in hospitality management or closely related fields. The field, as a whole, has many more terminally qualified faculty than ever before.

In addition to greater academic preparation, many programs are merging into more mainstream colleges that have higher expectations for research and scholarship. For instance, more and more programs seem to be moving out of professional colleges into colleges of business or management (e.g., University of Massachusetts, Georgia State University).

With the increase in terminal qualifications and movement to new academic units have come increased research expectations. This seems to be happening at the same time that doctoral graduates are entering the professoriate with a greater level of preparedness. In other words, the research and publication expectation is there and new, younger faculty are fully aware of it. This is due in large part to the research orientation of such doctoral programs as Virginia Tech and Cornell.

Scholarly Publications

At the same time that the research capabilities of new faculty members are increasing, so too are the potential outlets for scholarly activities. It would probably not be an exaggeration to suggest that the number of academically oriented, refereed journals has more than quadrupled in the last ten years. Examples of new journals that have been introduced during this decade include those by The Haworth Press (*Journal of Restaurant and Foodservice Marketing; Journal of International Hospitality, Leisure & Tourism Management*); Wiley (*Progress in Tourism and Hospitality Research*); and those published independently, such as *Praxis: The Journal of Applied Hospitality Management* by the School of Hospitality Administration at Georgia State University.

Along with the proliferation of journals, there has also been an increase in opportunities to present research at conferences around the country and around the world. For many years the annual conference sponsored by CHRIE was the primary outlet for hospitality-related research presentations. There are now numerous other hospitality research conferences. One of the newer conferences is the Graduate Education and Graduate Students Research Conference, now in its third year. Along with hospitality-specific conferences, other groups, such as the Southern Management Association, have established hospitality tracks within a broader conference program. Again, the opportunities for research presentations have increased tremendously and is just another indication of the changes occurring in the area of hospitality research and scholarship.

Funding

Finally, the opportunity for funded research seems to be increasing. As was discussed in Chapter 8, groups such as the Statler Foundation and the American Hotel Foundation offer funding for applied research projects on a competitive basis. Further, many colleges and universities, among others, support research projects. For instance, in recent years the University of New Orleans started a Faculty Development Award that funds research projects across the university. Further, separate colleges within the university offer Summer Research Grants on a competitive basis. Funding sources such as these have arisen from the desire to encourage a higher level of research on college campuses.

Hospitality Faculty

Changes are occurring with hospitality faculty as well. Because of the specialized nature of the field, it has always been relatively small, with relatively few faculty. Judging by the accounts of the early CHRIE meetings, some of the annual meetings were able to draw the majority of hospitality faculty under one roof! As a result, a certain level of camaraderie existed, which continues to this day. The field has been growing gradually, though, and many of the faculty that were responsible for starting programs in the 1960s and 1970s are beginning to approach retirement age. At the same time, new leaders are emerging who will steer programs into the next decade.

Also as a new wave of faculty enters the field, newer faculty are becoming much more specialized than were their predecessors. Many faculty, until very recently, were by necessity "jacks-of-all-trades." That is to say that faculty in smaller programs generally taught a wide range of courses. Now, as existing programs grow and develop, as faculty enter with a greater level of preparedness, and as the area becomes more specialized, faculty are in turn becoming more specialized and presiding over specialized niches in their academic programs. In this way, hospitality education is becoming more like other, more established, academic areas with ever increasing areas of specialization.

Finally, with the increase in academic rigor comes a new breed of faculty who typically have less industry experience. Again, this would seem to be a direct result of the continued development of hospitality education and the greater need for academically prepared faculty. On the other hand, some industry experience is essential in properly preparing future faculty for jobs in academia. The ability to draw from personal experience in both the classroom and research context is critical. It also helps to bridge the gap between academia and industry—a gap that continues to persist and is discussed elsewhere in this text.

In sum, the demands on new faculty members are changing—focusing more on research and scholarship. The times when one could be hired for a tenure-track position without the doctorate are all but gone. In fact, the time when the hospitality doctorate is the required degree may not be far away. Faculty are entering the profession with more and greater research skills and developing specialized niches of research and teaching. As this happens, so too is the field attracting a different type of student.

Hospitality Students

While the emphases of hospitality programs and the makeup of hospitality faculty changes, so too are the students that we teach. Even without delving below the surface, changes are apparent. The increased emphasis on internationalization and forging international agreements is drawing more students from abroad to programs in the United States. A recent report in *The Chronicle of Higher Education* (Desruisseaux, 1997) indicates that the United States continues to attract more foreign students than any other country. Despite this, over the past ten years, more and more students are being drawn to Australia and England, indicating increasing competition for these students. Similarly, hospitality programs are seeing increasing numbers of international students, particularly at the graduate levels (Hsu, 1996). This of course has a bearing on how programs recruit students as well as how programs are structured to accommodate students of different nationalities. Hsu identifies some of the concerns of international students studying in U.S. hospitality programs. She suggests that programs need to be understanding of students' needs and flexible in their accommodations of international students. Clearly, international students bring with them different needs and expectations that have a direct bearing on the ability of programs to deliver.

The increase in nontraditional students across college campuses as well as in hospitality programs has also been well documented. Older students, students pursuing second careers, and part-time students are entering colleges and universities increasingly. The needs and demands of these groups of students affect the range of services provided, as well as the delivery of those services.

Program and Curriculum Issues

One final change that will be mentioned is that of program and curriculum matters. The many program issues that have surfaced in recent years can really be reduced to a single basic question: How specialized should hospitality education be? A second question might be: What should the curriculum look like? As usual, there is no right answer to this question, which has resulted in the healthy mix of programs that exist today. The role of the mission was discussed early on in Chapter 1. Different programs embrace different missions, which will result in different course offerings, and so on. The argument surrounding how specialized (or how general) programs should be has been bandied about for some time (recently by Lewis, 1993).

Suffice it to say that programs continue to debate course content, which degree programs should be offered, and entire curriculums. The debate will not subside anytime soon. Almost every issue of the *Journal of Hospitality & Tourism Education* includes at least one article focusing on curriculum issues. The topic is on the minds of educators, perhaps now more than ever. At the very least, it can be stated that today's hospitality educators are concerned with the relevance of what they are teaching. The field will continue to prosper as long as this is true.

International Exchanges and the Internationalization of Programs

Chapter 10 reviewed and compared hospitality programs in three different countries on three different continents. There are many additional aspects of the internationalizing of hospitality education, however. Many programs, of their own accord or under pressure from their colleges and universities, have taken measures to expose their students to the international arena. In some cases, this has meant simply adding some international examples to their classes. Other programs have added courses on the international hospitality industry (such as at the University of New Orleans). Still others have taken the trends toward globalization to heart and developed true internationally focused programs (such as at Oxford Brookes University; Doherty and Roper, 1997). Others allow students to study abroad for a semester, or a full year, in an effort to introduce an international element. But the single biggest trend in this area seems to be the programs that are aggressively pursuing international partnerships between two countries. The number of programs that have entered into such agreements over the last ten years are too numerous to recount. The trend continues, however, and has served to make the world of hospitality management education seem smaller, while at the same time opening up new opportunities for both students and faculty. Of all of the changes affecting the field, this has perhaps had the biggest impact and should continue to do so for many years to come.

Interaction with Industry

Finally, the field of hospitality education has always had close ties with the greater hospitality industry. This relationship has been discussed and explored in a variety of chapters. In this author's opinion, both parties seem to be making even more of an effort to work together toward a common goal. In recent years, new programs have been generously endowed, companies have sponsored faculty internships, recruiters are appearing on college campuses in greater numbers, and programs and companies are joining together to work on common projects. Together, these actions indicate how intertwined the industry and education continue to be.

Now, more than ever, hospitality education programs are looking for companies to become more involved in the education side of the business. The extent of this relationship can take a variety of forms: numerous examples of this were cited in earlier chapters from industry being represented on advisory councils to getting more involved in the classroom. Two things are clear, however: (1) a higher degree of interaction is occurring, and (2) such interaction benefits both groups in the long run.

Summary of Trends in Hospitality Management Education

The changes taking place in the field are many, and the few that have been identified here just scratch the surface. Certainly, however, the changes relating to faculty, faculty responsibilities, the students they serve, program issues, internationalization, and interaction with industry cover a broad spectrum that affects every hospitality program in existence. Add these to the issues surrounding all colleges and universities with respect to rising tuition, budgetary concerns, faculty accountability, questions regarding tenure, and university reorganization and it becomes clear that nothing is sacred and everything is subject to scrutiny in today's educational environment. While these are just a few of the issues facing hospitality management programs, others are bound to surface during these dynamic times.

CONCLUSION

This book has identified, examined, analyzed, and deconstructed some of the critical elements that, together, contribute to make hospitality management education what it is. At the heart of the 175 some odd four-year programs (in the United States) are the faculty who teach, participate in scholarly activities, and provide valued services to their respective institutions and the industry at large. The intent of the book was to provide a glimpse into the workings of universities, hospitality programs, and of the individual faculty member. Faculty members have many responsibilities that are everchanging. But it is important to remember that those individuals chose academic careers and most are entirely dedicated to what they are doing.

The book began by taking a look at the origins of hospitality education and some of the underlying beliefs associated with today's programs. Successive chapters highlighted the factors that make hospitality management different from other academic areas and the importance of the relationship between academia and industry. The ways in which hospitality programs achieve quality were then examined. Recommendations were then made regarding professional preparation for those wishing to enter academia. Four chapters then examined the role of faculty members and what their jobs entail. Finally, the growing areas of international programs and graduate studies were discussed.

At the very least, the reader will have ascertained that the field of hospitality management has evolved, yet has still been able to remember its beginnings and preserve some of its traditionally held beliefs and practices. The short term should find the field continuing to struggle with such age-old arguments as whether programs should be "training" or "educating" their students; how "pure" or "applied" our research should be; and how much input the industry should have in overseeing individual programs. The long term should find the field continuing to evolve and finding its place in the ivory tower secure.

REFERENCES

Desruisseaux, P. (1997). Foreign enrollment rises slightly at college in the United States. *The Chronicle of Higher Education* (December 12), p. A42.

Doherty, L. and Roper, A. (1997). Removing our culturally tinted glasses: An approach to teaching international masters courses. *Journal of Hospitality & Tourism Education, 9,* 82-86.

Hsu, C.H.C. (1996). Needs and concerns of international students: What can educators do? *Hospitality & Tourism Educator, 8,* 68-75.

Lewis, R.C. (1993). Hospitality management education: Here today, gone tomorrow? *Hospitality Research Journal, 17,* 273-283.

Index

Page numbers followed by the letter "e" indicate exhibits; those followed by the letter "t" indicate tables.

Order Your Own Copy of
This Important Book for Your Personal Library!

HOSPITALITY MANAGEMENT EDUCATION

_____ in hardbound at $49.95 (ISBN: 0-7890-0441-0)

COST OF BOOKS_____

OUTSIDE USA/CANADA/
MEXICO: ADD 20%_____

POSTAGE & HANDLING_____
*(US: $3.00 for first book & $1.25
for each additional book)*
*Outside US: $4.75 for first book
& $1.75 for each additional book)*

SUBTOTAL_____

IN CANADA: ADD 7% GST_____

STATE TAX_____
*(NY, OH & MN residents, please
add appropriate local sales tax)*

FINAL TOTAL_____
*(If paying in Canadian funds,
convert using the current
exchange rate. UNESCO
coupons welcome.)*

☐ **BILL ME LATER:** (\$5 service charge will be added)
(Bill-me option is good on US/Canada/Mexico orders only;
not good to jobbers, wholesalers, or subscription agencies.)

☐ Check here if billing address is different from
shipping address and attach purchase order and
billing address information.

Signature_____

☐ **PAYMENT ENCLOSED: $**_____

☐ **PLEASE CHARGE TO MY CREDIT CARD.**

☐ Visa ☐ MasterCard ☐ AmEx ☐ Discover
☐ Diner's Club

Account #_____

Exp. Date_____

Signature_____

Prices in US dollars and subject to change without notice.

NAME _____

INSTITUTION _____

ADDRESS _____

CITY _____

STATE/ZIP _____

COUNTRY _____ COUNTY (NY residents only) _____

TEL _____ FAX _____

E-MAIL_____
May we use your e-mail address for confirmations and other types of information? ☐ Yes ☐ No

Order From Your Local Bookstore or Directly From
The Haworth Press, Inc.
10 Alice Street, Binghamton, New York 13904-1580 • USA
TELEPHONE: 1-800-HAWORTH (1-800-429-6784) / Outside US/Canada: (607) 722-5857
FAX: 1-800-895-0582 / Outside US/Canada: (607) 772-6362
E-mail: getinfo@haworthpressinc.com
PLEASE PHOTOCOPY THIS FORM FOR YOUR PERSONAL USE.

BOF96

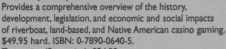

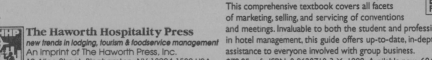